The *Parzival* of Wolfram von Eschenbach

UNC | COLLEGE OF ARTS AND SCIENCES
Germanic and Slavic Languages and Literatures

From 1949 to 2004, UNC Press and the UNC Department of Germanic & Slavic Languages and Literatures published the UNC Studies in the Germanic Languages and Literatures series. Monographs, anthologies, and critical editions in the series covered an array of topics including medieval and modern literature, theater, linguistics, philology, onomastics, and the history of ideas. Through the generous support of the National Endowment for the Humanities and the Andrew W. Mellon Foundation, books in the series have been reissued in new paperback and open access digital editions. For a complete list of books visit www.uncpress.org.

The *Parzival* of Wolfram von Eschenbach

TRANSLATED INTO ENGLISH VERSE WITH

INTRODUCTION, NOTES, CONNECTING SUMMARIES

BY EDWIN H. ZEYDEL AND BAYARD QUINCY MORGAN

UNC Studies in the Germanic Languages and Literatures
Number 5

Copyright © 1951

This work is licensed under a Creative Commons CC BY-NC-ND license. To view a copy of the license, visit http://creativecommons.org/licenses.

Suggested citation: Zeydel, Edwin H., and Bayard Quincy Morgan. *The Parzival of Wolfram von Eschenbach: Translated into English Verse with Introduction, Notes, Connecting Summaries.* Chapel Hill: University of North Carolina Press, 1951. DOI: https://doi.org/10.5149/9781469658735_Zeydel

Library of Congress Cataloging-in-Publication Data
Names: Zeydel, Edwin H.
Title: The *Parzival* of Wolfram von Eschenbach : Translated into English verse with introduction, notes, connecting summaries / by Edwin H. Zeydel.
Other titles: University of North Carolina Studies in the Germanic Languages and Literatures ; no. 5.
Description: Chapel Hill : University of North Carolina Press, [1951] Series: University of North Carolina Studies in the Germanic Languages and Literatures.
Identifiers: LCCN 51006040 | ISBN 978-1-4696-5872-8 (pbk: alk. paper) | ISBN 978-1-4696-5873-5 (ebook)
Subjects: Perceval (Legendary character) — Romances.
Classification: LCC PD25 .N6 NO. 5 | DCC 831/ .24

ACKNOWLEDGEMENT

Appreciation and thanks are due to the Charles Phelps Taft Memorial Fund at the University of Cincinnati for a grant to subsidize this publication

PREFACE

The main purpose of this work is to furnish English-speaking readers an adequate introduction to a poem which critics of many lands have agreed in calling one of the noblest literary creations of the Middle Ages. The only English translation of Wolfram's *Parzival*, by Jessie L. Weston, appeared as long ago as 1894 and, while reproducing the thought of Wolfram with some fidelity, missed his spirit and metrical flavor entirely by the unfortunate choice of long lines in place of the rhyming couplets.

The present rendering is in a sense a companion to the English edition of another German masterpiece of the same period, the *Tristan and Isolde* of Gottfried von Strassburg (Princeton, 1948), by one of the present collaborators.

We have made a line-for-line rendering of the passages translated, in as close an approximation to the rhythm, rhyme, and style as we could achieve. Although realizing that there is a school of critics that objects to this treatment of the medieval *vers de romance* and prefers a prose rendering, we are of the opinion that to divorce form from content, where the two are inseparable, would mean the destruction of the peculiar charm of this great poem. An approximation to the original form, even at the risk of being forced into occasional harshness in style—it must be borne in mind that Wolfram himself became famous for his stylistic pecularities—seems a far lesser evil than the complete sacrifice of that form. The genius of Wolfram's many-sided art cannot be caught in prose.

The entire 25,000 lines have, however, not been translated here, for we felt that completeness might lessen the chance of winning new friends for Wolfram and his poem. Even some of the editions and translations intended for modern *German* readers who are not specialists follow a similar method. Nearly one-half of the work is offered here in translation, the rest being retold in prose summaries, so that no part of the story as a whole in its many phases is lost. The Lachmann system of numbering manuscript pages of thirty lines each has been adhered to because Parzival scholarship has adopted this plan.

The diversity of Wolfram's metre can hardly be approached

in our language, and must be experienced to be fully appreciated. For the most part, his lines have either four beats with masculine rhyme, or three beats with feminine rhyme, the former being much more common. The rhythm is basically iambic, but lines with a trochaic first foot are not infrequent; and Wolfram is also prone to substitute a dactylic foot for iamb or trochee. On the other hand, he may choose to set two stresses side by side, and in one case the name Condwiramurs makes up an entire line, so that each syllable must have been stressed. Obviously no such variety of metrical form can be achieved in English, but we have been at pains to avoid the monotony of straight iambic tetrameter. In reading our translation, care should be taken to give the trochaic lines (e.g. 110,15 and 26; 118,4; 119,10 and 22) their true value, and as a rule to give the lines with feminine rhyme only three beats.

Generally the translation is based upon Lachmann's excellent text (Hartl revision), which usually follows manuscript D, but when what seemed better readings were found (in G or in conjectures of more recent critics) they have been adopted sparingly. The better modern German renderings, especially those of Hertz, Pannier, and Stapel, have been consulted. Since we have a medieval world before us in this poem, a certain archaic flavor in our translation seemed to us defensible, the more so that the shortness of many lines and the exigencies of rhyming sometimes pushed our backs to the wall.

A special problem is presented by the second personal pronoun, which Wolfram makes a part of his social picture. Thus, in the conversation between Sigunë and Parzival (250 ff.), the shift on Sigunë's part from the formal *ir* of her first speech to the familiar *du* when she recognizes him as her cousin, and then back to the (now hostile) *ir* of her last speeches, is not only expressive but highly dramatic. English has been impoverished by the loss of a similar distinction. Unwilling to sacrifice this color completely, we have used English *thou* and *thee* where Wolfram uses *du*, elsewhere perforce *you*, with a sparing use of *ye* as a plural pronoun.

Throughout we have endeavored to present what seemed to us the best fruit of the vast body of *Parzival* research, and we have not hesitated to add the results of our own researches on the subject, the product of many years of preoccupation with it. The Introduction aims to present the significance of Wolfram's poem both as a work of art and as a document in the history of western civilization, as well as the development of the various legends involved. The contribution of Richard Wagner and other recent writers have not been neglected. The Notes are supplied to point out possible source material and to explain details of Wolfram's art, as well as medieval allusions and other matters pertaining to the history of the Parzival story. They will, it is hoped, show the results of our own research. We are grateful to the Editor of these Studies, Professor Richard Jente, for his interest in our work and for many useful suggestions and improvements. As for other acknowledgements, we have made them at the points where they are pertinent. Our deep gratitude is extended to the Charles Phelps Taft Memorial Fund of the University of Cincinnati for financing our undertaking.

The first-mentioned collaborator is responsible for final decisions.

EDWIN H. ZEYDEL
BAYARD QUINCY MORGAN

Contents

	Page
Introduction	
1. The Place of Wolfram's *Parzival* in Literature	1
2. Themes and Leitmotifs in *Parzival*	3
3. Parzival, King Arthur, and the Holy Grail	5
4. Questions relating to Source and Composition of Wolfram's Work	9
5. Other Problems raised by Wolfram's Work	16
6. The Manuscripts, Editions, and Translations	20
7. The Influence of Wolfram's *Parzival*	22
8. Wolfram, the Man, and His Works	25
9. Additional Bibliography	27
Text	
Book One: Gahmuret and Belakanë	35
Book Two: Gahmuret and Herzeloydë	43
Book Three: Parzival's Youth	57
Book Four: Parzival and Condwiramur	93
Book Five: Parzival at the Grail Castle	113
Book Six: Parzival at King Arthur's Court	141
Book Seven: Gawan and Obilot	171
Book Eight: Gawan and Antikonie	183
Book Nine: Parzival Visits Trevrizent	191
Book Ten: Gawan and Orgeluse	235
Book Eleven: Gawan and the Marvelous Bed	245
Book Twelve: Gawan and Gramoflanz	251
Book Thirteen: Clinschor	263
Book Fourteen: Parzival and Gawan	273
Book Fifteen: Parzival and Feirefiz	297
Book Sixteen: Parzival becomes King of the Grail	321
Notes	343

INTRODUCTION

1. The Place of Wolfram's *Parzival* in Literature

The *Parzival* of Wolfram von Eschenbach, written probably between 1195 and 1210, takes its well-merited place beside the romances of Crestien de Troyes, Gottfried von Strassburg's *Tristan and Isolde*, Dante's *Divine Comedy*, Petrarch's sonnets, and Chaucer's *Canterbury Tales* as one of the finest literary achievements of the Middle Ages. Ever since the early years of the nineteenth century, when Karl Lachmann published the first critical edition of *Parzival* and Jacob Grimm called attention to Wolfram as the medieval German poet who is "richest in thought and feeling"[1], Wolfram's reputation has been high throughout Western Europe, although in non-German countries knowledge of him is still regrettably limited to scholars.

Karl Bartsch, an early German critic and editor, called Wolfram the most powerful and most profound of all the courtly romancers and assigned him a place beside Dante.[2] The noted British scholar, Jessie L. Weston, who made the only hitherto available English translation of *Parzival* about three generations ago (1894), spoke of him as "the most important and most individual poet of medieval Germany" in her article in the *Encyclopedia Britannica*.[3] More recently another learned British authority, Margaret F. Richey, wrote of him as "the chief interpreter of the life of medieval chivalry ... indisputably greatest among the poets of medieval Germany", and found him as fresh and real as he was seven hundred years ago, "nearer to us than Dante, nearer even than Chaucer."[4] More recently still, in an Italian work by G. V. Amoretti and in a French edition of selections from *Parzival* by André Moret, equally high praise is accorded Wolfram and his masterpiece.[5]

The greatness of *Parzival* may be considered from several points of view. They are 1. its position among medieval romances of chivalry, 2. its underlying ideas, 3. its place among the Grail romances, and 4. its style and language.

The picture of chivalry that *Parzival* presents is uncommonly rich and full. We are introduced not only to the traditional phases, such as jousting for a damsel in distress, playing at the game of love, or battling with a mortal enemy. We see knighthood in all its ramifications and activities, depicted not in an allegorically bookish or clerky manner, but with reference to life and first-hand experience. The effect is that of a drama of human characters and destinies in all its facets. But the work goes further and deeper than that. It deals with the transfiguration of a knight to something higher and more perfect, more pleasing to God, for Parzival ultimately becomes the spiritual leader of Christendom. This spiritual element, however, is not to be confused with asceticism, monasticism, or mysticism, but is so skilfully linked with liberal humanism and with a sympathy for the world's joys and sorows that it blends with them. Wolfram presents the knightly and the religious elements not in juxtaposition, still less in conflict; although the latter wins predominance, the two combine into a unit.

Basically the plot of this long verse-narrative is simple enough. It is the story of the gradual maturing of a naive young lad who becomes a doughty knight but, falling prey to thoughtlessness and selfishness, thinks that he has been wronged by God, and acts blasphemously. He is shown the error of his ways and, after doubt (*zwîvel,* as described in the early sections) and pangs of conscience, is led to a true understanding of and love for God. In unfolding this story Wolfram introduces a wealth of characters and a maze of subordinate action, so deftly worked into the main plot that the unity of the poem is not destroyed. Throughout his masterpiece Wolfram reveals his high regard for women of character and advocates conjugal fidelity— a note but rarely struck in his day. Not celibacy and "holiness" but full-blooded living in the forms of decency, loyalty, and warmheartedness are the keynotes.

In all the literature of the Holy Grail we find no treatment so novel, so complete, and so satisfying as Wolfram's, and none so reverent and yet so secular. The hero's pursuit of the Grail is not a transcendental striving, not even a struggle for ethical perfection. It is merely a search to find his Redeemer and thereby peace and earthly happiness. To Wolfram the Grail is not a sacramental church relic, perhaps not even descending from heaven (see Note 20 to Book IX), but a stone of wonderful virtue, a sort of philosopher's stone. Itself a symbol, it may go back to pagan symbolism infiltrated with Christian elements. It represents the goal for which Parzival strives, at first falsely and hence in vain, but at last with supreme success—that human purification, atonement, and sacrifice which symbolize man's love of the Redeemer and thus renew his faith in Him. This symbol, the Grail, is kept purposely non-orthodox, embracing subordinate elements of a worldly nature.

Wolfram's language and style have often been censured for obscurity and crabbedness. Objections began during his lifetime, and his contemporary, Gottfried von Strassburg, is believed to have been his earliest critic. It must be admitted that profundity and obscurity frequently go hand in hand, and Wolfram is a profound writer with a vocabulary range that reminds one of Shakespeare. Often his thought does not yield its full meaning at once. Some of this difficulty, no doubt, is due to the lapse of seven hundred fifty years between Wolfram's day and ours; after all we do not read Chaucer today with any ease. But as a poet, when approached with intelligence and proper preparation, Wolfram will prove highly rewarding. His regally careless manner of exercising his great powers, his refusal to be restricted to stylistic conventions, his obscurity and extravagance will be seen not as defects or wilful eccentricities, but as marks of individuality, depth of thinking, and true greatness.

Wolfram has a rare ability to suit his style to the varying moods of his matter. He can write nature poetry in the sweetest romantic vein, he can also wax lyrical, didactic, personal, facetious, argumentative, even wrathful—for he is one of the most personal of medieval poets. He can unfold an intricately ramified narrative with suspense and clarity. He is a master of dramatic dialog and of character portrayal. And a heart-to-heart discussion of the deepest philosophical and religious truths ever broached by men becomes, in his hands, an unforgettable experience.

2. Themes and Leitmotifs in *Parzival*

The variety of themes comprising the main action of Wolfram's *Parzival* is remarkable. The most important are the life story of Young Parzival; King Arthur and the Round Table; the worldly advice of Gurnemanz; Parzival's rescue and marriage of Condwiramur, the lady in distress; the hero's frustrated approach to the Grail; the curse of Cundry; the purification of Parzival by Trevrizent; the punishment by God of the Grail king for his lust; Clinschor and the enchanted castle; the heathen Feirefiz *versus* his Christian half-brother; the winning of the Grail by virtue of pureness of heart and true active compassion. In addition there is a wealth of subordinate themes, skilfully woven into the main narrative.

It would be a mistake to believe that Wolfram invented all these themes, although the beginning and end of his poem are not found in any known source. Many of his themes occur readymade in that work which most critics agree was his principal source, the Perceval romance *Li Contes del Graal* of the great French story-teller Crestien de Troyes, written about 1180 in Paris at the behest of Philip of Flanders but cut short by the death of the author.[6] None the less Wolfram himself discredits Crestien as a source in Book XVI. On some of the themes, to be sure, Wolfram improved, unless the Kyot he mentions in 416,20 and elsewhere is a real source, or unless he used another source of which we do not know. To others again he failed to do full justice. Some are completely missing in, and even alien in spirit to, Crestien's poem. How many Wolfram himself contributed may never be known. Some of them are solely traditional or folkloristic. Others combine folk lore and ritual elements, many again are apparently historical reminiscences, while some may be grounded altogether in religion.

It should be noted, however, that as Wolfram handles his many-patterned material it becomes a well-planned design of intricate leitmotifs. Once such a leitmotif has been introduced, it is not often abandoned. Be it that of maternal love (Belakanë and Herzeloydë), conjugal love (Titurel, Frimutel, Herzeloydë, Schoysianë, Parzival), vainglorious love (Anfortas, Clamidê, Kingrun), base suspicion (Orilus), be it Cunnewarë's laughter, Antanor's speech, or Sigunë's tears—almost every motif is pursued to its logical conclusion.

Moreover, the treatment of these themes is delicately varied, contrasted, and paralleled. Each of the examples of conjugal love or fidelity is a variation of the others: Parzival is faithful to his love through life, Sigunë to hers into death. Parzival, the Christian, honors Feirefiz, while the heathen humbles himself before his Christian brother. The ugly sorceress (who curses and later blesses the hero) has a counterpart in her equally hideous brother Malcreatiurë. Gawan, the philandering butterfly-like adventurer, surrenders to the vampire-beauty Orgelusë, to whom he is unswervingly loyal, and both discover what appears to be abiding love. Gurnemanz is the bereaved husband and father, Herzeloydë and Belakanë the bereaved wives and mothers. Parzival is poor, Feirefiz rich. The former wins the Grail, the latter the Grail-bearer, Repanse. Gawan is earth-bound, Parzival becomes heaven-bound. Parzival asks a question, rediscovers his wife, and wins the Grail; Lohengrin is asked a question, loses his wife, and must return to the Grail. Lohengrin inherits the Grail kingdom, Kardeis a worldly realm. The steward Keyë is colorful and strict, King Arthur colorless and lenient. Crestien, a real source, lived in northern France, "Kyot," in a sense a fictitious one, is described as a Provençal. The Grail requires the exercise of the strictest chastity (235,28), yet under its very roof there are Grail maidens guilty of lasciviousness (244,2ff.). Munsalvaesche and Chastel Marveile contrast like day and night. Anfortas and Clinschor are both punished for physical excesses yet react quite differently. The theme of unseasonable snow is introduced three times (281,12; 446,6; 489,27), but each time for a different purpose.

Names, too, tend to appear in duplicate, and sometimes one contrasts with the other. There are two Cundrys, an ugly and a lovely one; two Kyots, a man of God and a lay necromancer; a cowardly Liddamus and one who is a worthy opponent of Feirefiz; Clauditte, a heathen mistress of Feirefiz, and Clauditte, an innocent little lass; two occurrences of Kahenise, of Kardeis, of Astor, of Affinamus, of Amphlisë, of Florie. Frequently, too, the names of persons to be associated have identical first syllables, as Am (i.e. n) phlise and Annore; Gahmuret, Gandin and Galoës; Obie and Obilot; Iblis and Ibert, Kingrisin and Kingrimursel; Gurnemanz and his son Gurzgri.

3. Parzival, King Arthur, and the Holy Grail

By the time Wolfram took over the subject of his romance, and indeed already when Crestien wrote his *Li Contes del Graal*, some ten or more years earlier, the three themes of Perceval, the Round Table of King Arthur, and the Grail had been closely linked.[7] However, this had not always been the case, and we are safe in assuming that originally these three strands existed separately. Which is the oldest, no one knows. The Perceval theme, or the motif of the pure-hearted but utterly inexperienced lad who goes out into the world, gains experience and wisdom by hard knocks, and ends as a famed and powerful ruler of men, is found in the tradition of all the Aryan people as a folk tale. The hero is usually the son of a widow of high rank, whose husband, of somewhat lower station, has fallen in battle. It has come down to us in the purest form of preservation in the fifteenth-century English *Syr Percyvelle of Galles*, which lacks the Grail motif and seems to be based upon the Celtic version of the formula.

Very early in its history the Celtic variant appears to have become tied in with the story of King Arthur. He, if he ever lived at all (as Nennius in the eighth century claims he did), was probably not a king but a chieftain or general of mixed Roman and British parentage who fought against the Saxon invaders, was betrayed by his wife, and died in battle. Soon he became legendary, or was grafted onto an already existing myth, appeared as a slayer of monsters and dragons, and then as a fairy king. He was surrounded by a court of knights but did not participate in their adventures. This Arthurian legend grew ever richer and left its traces in folk lore, travelling as far south as Italy. By the second half of the twelfth century, after the death of Geoffrey of Monmouth, it had passed into literature as a full-length legend and seems to have been linked almost immediately with the tale of Perceval. The legend of the Grail had apparently already become an integral part of the legend of King Arthur.

An analysis of the theme of the Holy Grail raises some of the most complicated and perplexing problems in all literature, partly because of the many variant treatments and partly because we lack some of the earlier versions. When we first meet the Grail, it is already a famous talisman and the object of a quest by the knights of King Arthur's Round Table. The word "Grail" itself is most acceptably explained as being derived from the Latin *gradalis*, *gradale*, a dish or vessel in which food is borne in layers (*gradatim*).

Years ago Jessie Weston assigned to the Grail a ritual origin, partly Christian and partly pagan, while Konrad Burdach, in his last work, *Der Gral* (1938), associated the legend with the lance of Longinus, the Last Supper and Crucifixion, as well as the liturgy of the Eastern Catholic Church. Others again have pointed to the Mohammedan *Kaaba,* others to an Arabian-alchemistic philosopher's stone, others to the Baphomet of the Templars, while still others[8] have seen the source for the Grail in the *Tabot* of the Abyssinian church.

After weighing all these theories and, indeed, adhering to some of them for a while, the present writers now incline to the views recently expressed by A. C. L. Brown[9] and William A. Nitze[10]—views somewhat similar to Weston's. Nitze has offered the clearest and most succinct explanation. According to him the Grail had its origin in the *coire* of the great Celtic god Dagda, a marvellous cauldron which satisfied all. This is identical with the Welsh *dysgl* and with the Grail, which passed on deviously to Crestien and Wolfram through Welsh or Irish storytellers (Bleheris?), perhaps by way of Breton or Latin versions which formed the source for a French version (the so-called *Livre*) used by Crestien. Meanwhile, by a process of syncretism, this originally pagan legend was more and more Christianized—by Crestien's source and by Crestien himself, but most thoroughly of all by Robert de Boron (soon after 1200), who probably used the same source, and in the French *Perlesvaus* (about 1220).

Thus gradually a pagan dish of plenty became, in specific Grail versions, such as Robert de Boron's *Joseph,* as well as in the Good Friday scene of the composite Perceval-Arthur-Grail corpus, the receptacle of the host reminiscent of the Mass (e.g. in *Diu Crône*); the cup used at the Last Supper or the dish in which the Paschal lamb was served (Robert de Boron); a crystal vase filled with blood (*Diu Crône*); a cup into which the lance bleeds (*Perlesvaus*); a dish containing a bleeding head (the Welsh *Peredur*); a gleaming jewel-studded vessel containing the host (Crestien); or a marvellous stone and food-providing talisman preventing death (Wolfram). Thus, once transferred to a Christian milieu, the legend readily lent itself to Christian embellishment and also afforded easy admission to such concepts as the angels who left the Grail behind on earth and the heaven-sent dove (the Holy Ghost), which renews its power. Indeed, all the Christian characteristics of the Grail can be explained by syncretism. If Mohammedan and Abyssinian elements, stressed by some critics, are admissible, it seems plausible to explain them in an analogous manner or by coincidence.

The non-Christian origin of the Grail seems all the more

plausible since no known version of the legend as such is accepted by any religious creed or organized faith, either Western or Eastern, and since the Grail is not an acknowledged Holy Relic of the Church. It never became more than a semi-religious legend.

Crestien's fragment *Li Contes del Graal* is the earliest version of each one of the three strands—Perceval, Arthur, Grail—that we possess. He had three continuators, 1. a pseudonymous Wauchier de Denain (about 1190), who incorporated the early, or even the earliest version of Bleheris, an importer of Welsh tales to France, 2. Gerbert de Montreuil (before 1225), and 3. Manessier (between 1214 and 1220). While the earliest extant treatment of the Grail theme by itself is in Robert de Boron's *Joseph* (soon after 1200), he also dealt with Perceval in a separate section of his comprehensive *Estoire du Saint Graal*, of which *Joseph*, too, is a part. Several works are based upon Robert de Boron's account of the Grail, a *Histoire del Saint Graal* from the early thirteenth century, a Dutch prose version by Jacob van Maerlant (about 1260), and a Middle English poem on Joseph of Arimathæa, as well as a rhymed English translation of Henry Lonelich from the middle of the fifteenth century.

In Wolfram the three strands are again closely linked. The English *Syr Percyvelle of Galles*, already mentioned, resembles the so-called *Lai de Tyolet* (late twelfth century) in some details but is probably to be linked with Crestien. The French prose novel of *Perlesvaus* (early thirteenth century) was soon translated into Welsh and, in the sixteenth century, into Spanish. The Welsh prose tale, *Peredur*, also of the thirteenth century, goes back to Crestien or a similar source, as does also a Norse prose version of the fourteenth century. The Middle Dutch *Moriaen* depends on Wolfram. The curious German poem *Diu Crône* (about 1220) by the Austrian Heinrich von dem Türlin describes the Grail first as a vase containing blood and later as a relic containing the host. Two of Crestien's continuators, Wauchier and Manessier, were translated into German by Wisse and Colin in the fourteenth century.

Besides all these versions there are the so-called Didot *Perceval*, some Dutch *Lancelot* and Flemish *Percheval* fragments, the *Small Quete*, and the *Great Quete* (by Walter Map?) of the thirteenth century, the latter translated into Welsh, Icelandic, and Dutch. The English text passed over into the prose novel of Malory's *Morte d'Arthur* (about 1470). There is also a Portuguese version. Provençal literature, significantly enough, seems to be familiar only with Crestien. The number of texts dealing with King Arthur and his knights is very large. In German alone over forty exist.

4. Questions relating to Source and Composition of Wolfram's Work

The origin of the Grail legend has been discussed as a famous literary crux. The study of Wolfram's *Parzival* leads to another crux, which has been the subject of heated argument and violent disagreement for over a century. Some have maintained that Crestien (and perhaps the first continuation, together with the Bliocadran Prolog) was Wolfram's only source, used for Book III through the first half of XIII, others have claimed that he did not draw upon Crestien directly at all but upon some other unknown source. Still others have taken Wolfram at his word (416,20 ff.; 431,2; 453,5 ff.; 455,2 ff.; 776,10; 805,10; 827,3 ff.) and have been ransacking French and Provençal literatures and chronicles for evidence of the existence of a suitable "Kyot" or "Kiot" who might have served him as his principal source, with Crestien in a secondary position (or *vice versa*). Others question if Kyot could have been a Provençal. Others, who deny a Kyot, have marshalled an array of other literary sources which Wolfram might have used instead. Still others conjecture that he depended upon oral traditions or reports, while an American scholar[11] has seen in Kyot a widely travelled minstrel whom Wolfram had an opportunity to hear (perhaps at the court of Herman of Thuringia or Count Rupprecht von Durne?).[12]

This controversy has involved some of the most noted names in German literary scholarship since Lachmann and Wackernagel, down to such recent writers as Schwietering, Mergell, Panzer, and Hermann Schneider. In England Weston, Richey, and Hatto, in France Wilmotte and Fourquet, and in Switzerland Singer have also been prolific in this field.

In the light of the present status of things it is unfortunately just as difficult to believe in a Kyot as it is to reject him. If we accept him we are confronted by the fact that not a single satisfactory reference to him has been found outside of Wolfram literature. The Kyot of Provins, the author of a *Bible,* long ago advocated by Wackernagel,[13] has been eliminated; the Guios "qui maint bel miracle traita", more recently favored by Wilmotte,[14] seems no more satisfactory, nor are the requirements met by the writer of the Cangé manuscript, who at the end of Crestien's Yvain says: "Cil qui l'escrist, Guioz ot non. . ." It is easily conceivable that Kyot's work has been lost, but it seems curious that his name at least is not mentioned by some source.

On the other hand, if Kyot is a fiction of Wolfram, who also seems to misinform us about the source of his poem *Willehalm* (125,20), we must explain how Wolfram came by a host of references, allusions, and influences which point to French and Eastern European sources. Why does he introduce the House of Anjou, the templars, and (seemingly) Richard I of England? Is the so-called Bliocadran prolog, attached to two Crestien manuscripts, the fragment of a source used by Wolfram? The present writers, like Weston, Panzer (see Note 19 below), and Sister Fuehrer[15], believe Wolfram was familiar with it (Bliocadran>Belakane?). And was the poem *Partenopois de Blois* (about 1188) a source, direct or indirect, for Wolfram's Gahmuret section (Books I and II)? Why is it that Wolfram agrees here and there with later versions when he deviates from Crestien?

There is certainly enough material in Wolfram which differs so sharply from Crestien (or is missing there altogether) that an assumption of another foreign source, or of many such sources, is not out of place, especially since some of this material is not of the kind that would have been readily accessible in Germany. On the other hand, it seems that Marta Marti[16] in her fourth revision of Bartsch goes too far in assuming that Wolfram might have been influenced even stylistically by a French source and derived even purely German references from it.

Among probable *German* references the following should be noted. Wolfram's idea (300,16; 752,12) that father and son are more than mere kinsmen, and have identical blood, is also in the *Sachsenspiegel* (about 1220). The astrology of 789,6, as well as the legend of Adam's daughters (518,1) and many other details may well be derived from the German *Lucidarius*[17] (indeed the Adam incident is omitted from the Latin *Elucidarium* of Honorius); the headdress customs of women (e.g. 202,25;

515,2; 807,28) are German; the story of Priest John (822,25) is found in Otto von Freising.[18] The frequent references to contemporaneous German literature (Heinrich von Veldeke, Hartman von Aue, *Nibelungenlied,* and Walther) must certainly stem from Wolfram himself. The story of St. Sylvester (795,30) seems to come from the *Kaiserchronik,* 8200 ff.

Other *non-German* sources which Wolfram may have used are writers basing upon Virgil, Ovid, Pliny the Elder, Solinus, Isidorus, Honorius, the *Physiologus,* Marbode, and Saxo Grammaticus, as well as the History of the Crusades of William of Tyre, the *Joufrois,* Hues de Rotelande's *Ipomedon,* and the French *Roman de Thèbes,* the last four especially for Books I-II and the Feirefiz episode. Moreover, it is quite possible that Wolfram relied upon oral sources—authorities whom he knew.

It is interesting to follow the gropings of scholars through the course of the last five generations, in their search for a solution to the Kyot problem. This search has been penetrating and patient, has weighed the external and internal evidence again and again, but has also revealed a regrettable subjective tendency toward riding preconceived notions, neglecting inconvenient evidence, and overstressing that which was needed for building up a hypothetical case. While most scholars have remained true to their original conviction for or against Kyot, so reputable a scholar as Wolfgang Golther made a complete *volte face* from his original position as a Kyot adherent.

During the last fifteen years or so there has developed a marked tendency among Wolfram scholars to deny a Kyot or a single second source categorically. Perhaps this is a natural reaction to the impression conveyed by Marta Marti in her edition of Bartsch, that hardly any originality attaches to Wolfram's work. These scholars, among them Friedrich Panzer, Bodo Mergell, Hermann Schneider, and the Hollander W. Snelleman[19], support the theory, for the most part independently of each other, that Crestien was Wolfram's only main source and that Kyot is merely a fiction. Panzer's argument in general terms is that by inventing Kyot, Wolfram wanted to make his bold, radical fabrications more exotic and more palatable to the public. Was he not to his contemporary Gottfried a "vindaere wilder maere," an inventor of improbable tales (*Tristan,* 4663)? This Kyot fiction, which Mergell believes even plays an integral part in the structure of Wolfram's work, was of course buttressed by other sources, literary and oral. Possibly Wolfram met and heard one or more French minstrels, for occasionally one came to Germany from France, as witness the presence of Wackernagel's Guiot de Provins at the Whitsuntide feast of Emperor Frederick I in 1184. Crestien himself in his *Erec* (19 ff., 2036 ff.) complains about the careless treatment of stories by many a *menestrel*.

The Dutch scholar J. H. Scholte in *Neophilologus* (XXXIII, 23 ff.; see also Zeydel, *ibid.* XXXIV, 11 ff.) presents a new theory. He believes that Kyot, the writer, is actually identical with the other Kyot—presumed to be a historical character—who plays a fairly important part in Wolfram's work as the father of Sigunë and kinsman of Parzival himself, the guardian of his wife Condwiramur, the tutor of his son Kardeis, and a knight who had taken holy orders. His name is Kyot of Katelangen, supposedly a Provençal and part of the Angevin background adopted by Wolfram. According to Scholte, Wolfram may have derived parts of his plot, especially that connected with the Angevin line and the Middle East, from this crusader-knight who had been in the retinue of Richard I and had been left behind on the continent by the English king as one of some two hundred hostages. To honor him, conjectures Scholte, Wolfram assigns him a twofold role. He is described as the venerable knight turned recluse (Wolfram's favorite Trevrizent-type) and in addition as a respected authority, more competent than Crestien. But his identity is kept secret under the pseudonym of Kyot.

Snelleman argues that the Angevin heritage of Parzival's father Gahmuret derives from Wolfram's conscious desire to glorify the House of Anjou in general[20] and the English king Richard I in particular as a living example of Arthurian knighthood. Shortly before Snelleman, Panzer had reached similar conclusions. Richard was considered by many the very prototype of knighthood: valorous, affable, and generous. He was the son of Eleonore of Aquitaine, was engaged to Alice (*cf.* Gahmuret's French queen Amphlise), the sister of the French king Philip II, but broke off the engagement to marry Berengaria (*cf.* Belakanë), the daughter of the king of Navarre. With the help of the duke of Burgundy he defeated the Sultan in battle and crowned his own nephew king of Jerusalem. On returning west from the Third Crusade, he was forced to land near Aquileja, entered the plain by way of Cilli at Mt. Rohitsch near Candine (present-day Haidin), also not far from Pettau, where the Grajena empties into the Drau. All these places are mentioned by Wolfram in Book IX as having been visited by Trevrizent, who like Gahmuret and Parzival bears traits of Richard. Falling into the hands of Duke Leopold VI of Austria, whom he had once insulted, Richard was imprisoned in Dürenstein on the Danube, turned over to Emperor Henry VI, and held for ransom.

The marriage of Feirefiz and Repanse reminds one of the relations of Joanna, sister of Richard, to Malek el Adel, the noble brother of the Sultan; the latter was said to lean toward Christianity. The House of Plantagenet, which Richard represented, was descended from the House of Anjou.

Another novel approach to the question of Wolfram's second source has recently been attempted by Hermann Schneider,[21] who, after detecting the impress of Hartman's *Gregorius* in the opening lines of Book I, conjectures that in Books XIV-XVI, where Crestien forsook Wolfram, the latter turned to *Iwein* for his chief guidance. The new sources for I-II and XV-XVI claimed by Panzer are given in Note 19.

This much, however, is certain, that Wolfram's work is not a cleverly pieced-together patchwork of "sources" and "influences", but a work of art, inspired and deriving its unity from the personality of the poet himself, whose originality in his *Lieder* has long been recognized. These veiled allusions, however far they may go, are merely backgrounds and raw materials for the poet, who used them to suit his special purposes and who moulded history into a new pattern to conform to his own ideals, as Goethe did in *Egmont* and Schiller in *Die Jungfrau von Orleans*.

Panzer also points out that Wolfram purposely erases actuality of locale, especially in Eastern place-names, so as to create an atmosphere of exoticism, and is intrigued by the strange names and sounds of the French and other languages he encounters, plays with them, varies them, and constructs new names arbitrarily, sometimes even out of mere successions of syllables (e.g. the anagram Sigune<co-si-ne), to produce kaleidoscopic results. As for the name Kyot-Kiot, one theory explains it as suggested by some such clause at *ki ot reprise oevre* —a scribe's entry in a manuscript. We venture a new conjecture,

viz. that it may have been suggested by a word in the very first line of Crestien's poem:

Qui petit seme petit quiaut (*or* quialt) . . .

The dates for the composition of Wolfram's *Parzival* can be fixed only on the basis of such evidence as the work itself affords. We assume but cannot prove that it was written between 1195 and 1210. At any rate it seems certain that by 1217, the date of the death of Herman of Thuringia, it had been completed. Schreiber's theory (see Note 12 above) that it was not written before 1236 is not plausible. Book III mentions Hartman's *Erec*, which would place it after 1190. Book V in its present form seems to have been composed after Hartman's *Iwein*, or about 1202-03. Book VI as we now have it was written apparently after the summer of 1204, when Wolfram sojourned at Herman's, and the present Book VII is to be assigned to a time after the siege of Erfurt (1203). In Book IX the conquest of Constantinople (1204) is referred to.

Marti believes that Wolfram improved as he progressed. Richey (p. 25) denies this and sees a deterioration. A searching examination of Wolfram's style has been made by Elisabeth Karg-Gasterstädt,[22] who points to four (or even five) types of writing in his book. Books III-VI, for example, belong to type 1, while all the Belakanë-Feirefiz-Flegetanis material is of type 2. References to Kyot, she thinks, were introduced later in order to give the Grail, originally assigned a heathen origin, a Christian background.

From what has been said, it should be clear that in spite of 120 years of research any attempt to trace the genesis and composition of Wolfram's poem must still be based largely upon conjecture. We shall make such a conjectural endeavor, based upon the research of many recent scholars.[23] Early in the nineties of the twelfth century, probably, Wolfram came into possession of a manuscript of Crestien's fragment *Li Contes del Graal* and subsequently, according to some, into possession of a second manuscript, after the first had been lost. The Landgrave of Thuringia, the Count of Wertheim, or a member of the Durne family may have given them to him. Perhaps one of these contained an early spurious continuation (Gauvain?) which he was in no position to distinguish from the work of Crestien himself. At any rate, he decided to base a German romance of his own upon the work. Desultorily he wrote a first draft of the present Books III-V (perhaps also most of VI), in which he followed Crestien rather closely and in which the hero was presented as a Waleis, i.e. Galois, just as he is described by Crestien. Perhaps Wolfram in his early draft even mentioned Crestien as his source.

Gradually, while he proceeded in the same vein with the first draft of Books VII-XIII, dissatisfaction with this source and the absence of any ending to it brought home to him the necessity of supplying an ending of his own. In this predicament it occurred or was suggested to him around 1196 or soon after, at the court of the Thuringian landgraves (Herman's predecessor Ludwig and Herman himself had crusaded), to weave the world-shaking events of the day, vivified by the ambitious dreams of Emperor Henry VI, into his work. His decision to do so was prompted by the English king's capture and detention for ransom in Austria and then in Germany. It is well known that these happenings stirred up a wave of warm sympathy for Richard among many of the nobles and prelates of the Empire, not to mention the Pope himself. Perhaps Wolfram met and secured more detailed information on the Holy Land, on Richard's part in the Third Crusade, and especially on his flight through Styria, from someone who had been in the king's retinue. He may have met Richard's trusted and much travelled *clericus*, Philip of Poitou (like Richard's mother a Provençal), who had accompanied his ruler to the Holy Land and was with him for a while even in his German captivity. Later, in 1197, Philip, already elected to the bishopric of Durham in 1195 and consecrated a priest in 1196, became bishop of Durham and in 1198 returned to Germany for the royal election of Otto. Philip clearly reflects Wolfram's favorite type, the fighter who becomes a man of God (Parzival, Trevrizent, Kyot of Katelangen). Philip could have given Wolfram rich material on the Crusade, as well as such English names as that of the tenth-century chancellor Turketal (128,8).

Experiences like these then prompted Wolfram to make Parzival an Angevin on his father's side, to stress the House of Anjou and generally to superimpose an Angevin element. With this new purpose he now wrote what is at present Books I and II, making full use of the new Angevin and Near Eastern sources, as well as many others, and thoroughly re-wrote the portion of his work, first III-VI and then VII-XIII, which he had already composed, weaving in the German *Lucidarius* and additional German and French material, improving upon Crestien wherever he could, but relying chiefly upon his own inventive genius.

To conceal from posterity the full extent of his originality and to give the work a more exotic stamp, he decided to minimize Crestien and to glorify his new authority in the fictitious Kyot motif as early as Book VIII, making it an integral part of the Anjou account, and to pit Kyot of Provence (the beloved homeland of Richard's mother) against Crestien. In doing so he eliminated possible earlier references to the latter. The closing books followed more rapidly, but not until the final book did he insert some disparaging remarks about Crestien's work.

In this way Wolfram's *German* poem, though far from being a *roman à clef*, became the only medieval romance to suggest a *French* family and an *English* king and to emphasize the fusion of Eastern and Western culture made possible by the Crusaders. East (Feirefiz) meets West (Parzival) in Book XV and almost conquers it. But in the end the West wins out, and Feirefiz becomes the progenitor of a line of Eastern Christian priests.

5. Other Problems Raised by Wolfram's Work

The central problem in Wolfram's poem, and the pivot around which the entire work turns, is the guilt of Parzival, the nature of that guilt, and the manner in which it is atoned for. If Parzival's sin—and he tells the hermit Trevrizent clearly enough that he is a man of sin (456,30)—is not properly understood, the deeper import of the work is missed, and it becomes just another romance of adventure. It is therefore surprising that the significance of the hero's sin has been so often missed, even by recent expounders of the work. As late as 1929 Hans Naumann[24] could speak of Wolfram's imparting ethical significance to the conventions of his time, as though this were the heart of the problem. And more recently (1941) Mockenhaupt, although applying the criteria of medieval theology to *Parzival*, stresses the hero's failure to ask the question of pity, as though *that* alone were the sin, and contends that Wolfram reluctantly took this over merely as part of the tradition. Others again, like

Misch and Keferstein,[25] make the mistake of underestimating the importance of religious matters as treated in medieval literature, and of slighting the religious and mystical elements in Wolfram's ethics.

Parzival's sin has several facets. For selfish gain, to satisfy personal ambition, and in sudden rage he kills Ither, his kinsman, then unrecognized by him. He deserts his bereft mother lightheartedly for the sake of adventure, and, although loving her, gives only lip-service to her memory after his departure, despite 173,9. His ostensible desire to search for her, which he uses at the end of Book IV as an excuse for leaving his wife, is soon submerged by other things. There is a difference between the desertion of his mother and that of his wife, to whom he remains true in body and in spirit. The argument that his abandonment of his mother was merely part of his chivalric duty, and not a sin, is refuted by the fact that Wolfram's goal for Parzival is something higher than chivalry, namely kingship of the Grail. He rides under arms on Good Friday, not merely in ignorance of the day, but in expressed hatred of God. He fails to show any pity to poor suffering Anfortas by word or action (*cf.* 170,25ff.), although being a close observer of everything that goes on about him. Here again, the allegation that Anfortas did not deserve the pity of a knight of chivalry because suffering is un-courteous, misses the point in view of Parzival's transcending goal. Worst of all, he blasphemes God by doubting Him, shutting his heart to Him, and defiantly believing that God bears a chivalrous obligation toward him, even though he has turned away from God. This is a violation of *triuwe*, a failure to recognize God's love for man (for God is love), a sin which can be atoned for only by a humble will for purification, by suffering, and sacrifice, and by acknowledgment of the love of the Redeemer. Such acknowledgment alone restores faith and a humble consciousness of man's dependence upon God.

The important thing, then, as Hermann Schneider has pointed out (p. 69), is not that the prodigal son finds his family or that a chosen knight discovers the Grail, but that a man destined for a lofty mission finds his way to God. In his ignorant striving Parzival had sincerely tried to do the right thing. But he had failed. He is no longer clean and pure even when he meets Anfortas the first time in Book V. It is worth noting, however, that his sins do not prejudice him in the worldly eyes of King Arthur and his court, and that he is not banished after Cundry's curse, but leaves of his own accord. But at the second meeting with Anfortas he is once more stainless and unblemished (*kiusch*), and as such, and such alone, a fit instrument for Grail kingship and thus for the redemption of his fellow-man. So he becomes king of the Grail, but even now his prime duty will be to serve for the good of others.

The steps by which Trevrizent leads Parzival to true atonement in Book IX show Wolfram's artistry at its best. We will avoid the term "psychology" purposely. Trevrizent prepares him by speaking of the introduction of sin into the world, of the fallen angels, of the sin of man's progenitors, of the sins of the Grail folk and of his own, Trevrizent's, sin, and of the sin of Parzival's kin in general. Sin thus becomes more than an act of commission or omission: an agent, a force, a power with which man must reckon. It cannot be abolished, and therefore ethical perfection is impossible on earth. The Grail and its kingdom, however, the symbol of peace in God, of practical piety and devoutness in everyday life, can indeed be attained and can become a lay ideal of life.

It has been pointed out before in this Introduction that Wolfram's Parzival is destined for higher things than the intermediate station of perfect worldly chivalry. This brings us to the suggestive studies of Gottfried Weber, especially *Der Gottesbegriff des Parzival* (Frankfurt, 1935) and *Parzival, Ringen und Vollendung* (Oberursel, 1948). In the progression of the hero from courtly knighthood to Grail knighthood and kingship, as Wolfram sees it, Weber, in his latest book, detects the transition, occurring in the thirteenth century, from the philosophy of St. Augustine to that of St. Thomas Aquinas. Weber believes that Wolfram had already advanced from the Augustinian notion that the highest ends (*sc.* the Grail) could be attained *passively* by the grace of God alone to the inchoate Thomistic idea that *active* individual striving on man's part is necessary if by God's grace he is to attain those highest ends. According to Weber, this new Thomistic God-man relationship alone makes possible Wolfram's unique harmonization of high chivalry and highest Christendom. On this basis Weber believes he has discovered a new concept of God in Book IX. Instead of the old feudal God of help, we now have the incomparable God, unto whom man is both like and unlike, a God of love in the concept of St. John, as Parzival is a knight of (brotherly) love.

It is essential to emphasize the fact that Wolfram never forgets that he is composing a poem, and not a religious disputation or colloquy. The Church is not directly involved at all, nor does a representative of the Church participate in the action of Book IX. Trevrizent is a hermit, not a priest, and his talk with Parzival is in the nature of a heart-to-heart talk, not of confession and absolution. In this respect Wolfram is wiser than Schiller was in the first version of Act V of *Maria Stuart*.

The question that is the expression of compassion, which Parzival must ask and which he finally does put, not without the kind of prodding which was tabu, is, like the Grail, a mere outward manifestation of something far deeper. It is not the few syllables, "oheim, waz wirret dir?"—what afflicts thee, uncle dear? (795,29)—that Parzival says to Anfortas, but his tears, his heartfelt pity, his *riuwe*, that redeem the suffering king and make Parzival, now an exemplar of *kiusche*, eligible for the kingship. The Grail, in a sense God's mouthpiece, already proclaims him king *before* he actually asks the question.

In Wolfram's *Parzival*, written seven hundred years after the conversion of the Franks, the full import of the Christian faith was thus finally revealed to the Germans.

One major question remains. What is the meaning of the role of Anfortas as Fisher King? The significance of the Fisher King has now, it would seem, been satisfactorily explained by Nitze in the article referred to in note 10 above. In Robert de Boron this figure is called Bron, a contamination and confusion of the Celtic god Bran and the biblical Hebron of Numbers 3, 19. In Crestien he is merely *roi pescheor*. Those who make the usual attempt to assign a purely Christian origin to the Fisher King point to the association of the Greek word for fish, Ἰχθύς, with Christ as Ἰησοῦς Χριστὸς Θεοῦ Υἱὸς Σωτήρ — Jesus Christ, God's Son, Saviour, an idea which probably derives from Mark 1, 17: "I will make you to become fishers of men." But this derivation has been refuted by A. C. L. Brown and Nitze, chiefly because the sacramental fish is omitted from the table in the story as told by Crestien and Wolfram. King Arthur, too, has been rejected as the original Fisher King. Nitze now postulates a Celtic, or Celtic-Welsh, origin, calling attention to the identity of the seating and arrangement in the Grail hall with that of the Old Irish banqueting hall at Tara. He points out that in Irish legend the god Nuadu is the ancestor-god and that in Welsh he becomes Nudd (Nodens) and Llud. Nuadu-Nudd-Nodens = Pescheor-Fisher. And the Fisher King, as one of the terrestrial gods upon whom the fertility of the land depends, had a physical disability, like Adonis or Attis in the Mediterranean cults. This explanation leaves only one point to be cleared up. Why in Wolfram does the Fisher King become a victim of his affliction because of a sin once committed? Such a sin seems to be implied neither in the original Celtic tradition nor in the Welsh version. This may be an invention of Wolfram, and if so, it is one of his finest. Could it have been suggested by a confusion, somewhere along the line of development, between Latin *piscator* (fisher) and *peccator* (sinner) ?

Other problems raised by Wolfram's poem are discussed in the Notes.

6. The Manuscripts, Editions, and Translations

We are fortunate in possessing at least one very good complete manuscript of *Parzival* and more than a dozen others of estimable value, in addition to about sixty fragmentary ones. Some of the latter, too, possess unique value for the scholar interested in textual criticism. The value of the better manuscripts is enhanced by the fact that they date from as early as the thirteenth century. Manuscript D, written on parchment about 1250 by three scribes and now in the Swiss city of St. Gall, is generally considered the best because it was executed in a conservative manner and usually retains the obviously more original forms. Of less value as a rule is G, written, also on parchment, between 1228 and 1236 by five scribes, and now located in Munich. It is illustrated. Often it alters and normalizes the text arbitrarily so as to be more widely understood and to conform to the rules of good writing that had been established by Hartman von Aue in the preceding generation. Occasionally, though, it offers a reading preferable to that of D. The other complete, or fairly complete, codices are now to be found in Heidelberg, Vienna, Munich, Hamburg, and other continental cities. Fragments are scattered in libraries throughout five European countries from Liverpool and London to Rome, but over two dozen of them are to be found in Berlin[26] and Munich. Unfortunately no complete collation of all the extant manuscripts has ever been achieved, although it is established that with two or three exceptions they all belong either to class D or class G. Those of type G are more numerous. For the most painstaking study of the entire subject of the manuscript tradition of *Parzival* we are still indebted to Karl Lachmann. It was he who prepared the first critical edition in 1833.

The continued popularity of *Parzival* after Wolfram's death is attested by the fact that it was one of the first German books to be printed in the latter half of the fifteenth century. In 1477 it appeared in a folio volume in Strassburg (Mentelin). There are at least five copies of this incunabulum in the United States, one in the Chapin Library in Williamstown, Mass., one in the Huntington Library in California, and another in the Pierpont Morgan Library in New York.[27] It offers a good text, based in part upon D, in part upon G.

During the later Middle Ages, however, Wolfram was better known for a work erroneously ascribed to him—the so-called *Younger Titurel* by a certain Albrecht, a continuation of the genuine *Titurel*, written in a mystifying, obscure style.

For over three hundred years no further editions of *Parzival* appeared. In 1784 Christoph Heinrich Myller, a Swiss who lived in Berlin, edited the work with the help of the Swiss poet and critic Bodmer. His text is far inferior to that of the 1477 edition. The superior Lachmann text of 1833 has been mentioned. It has remained popular ever since, the sixth edition, revised by Eduard Hartl, appearing in 1926. In 1870-71 the very popular redaction of Karl Bartsch came out. The fourth redaction by the Swiss scholar Marta Marti, assisted by Samuel Singer (1927-32), is practically a new work. The undated edition of Paul Piper in Kürschner's *Deutsche National-Literatur* (probably 1889 ff.), originally offered Books VII-XIII, the Gawan episode, only in excerpts, but in 1892 an additional volume appeared with the complete text of these seven books. The edition of Ernst Martin (1900-03) is still valuable because of its helpful 600-page commentary. Another redaction, by Albert Leitzmann, began appearing in 1902; although marred by arbitrary and confusing punctuation, it achieved popularity, going into the second printing in 1926 and appearing again in 1942 and 1947 ff. In the *Sammlung Göschen* selections from Wolfram were edited by Karl Marold (1892). Other editions or selections are those of Moret, published in France and referred to in note 5 above, and of H. H. Schmidt-Voigt (Frankfurt, 1942).

German translations or paraphrases, mostly dating from the nineteenth century, have been very numerous. Those of San Marte (pseudonym for Albert Schulz, 1833), Karl Simrock (1842), and Gotthold Bötticher (1885) are now little read, but the renderings of G. Bornhak (Teubner, 1891), Karl Pannier (Reclam, 1897), and Wilhelm Hertz (1898) are still widely used. The Hertz translation, revised by G. Rosenhagen and also reissued by F. H. von der Leyen, has usually been considered the best one in verse (last edition, 1943). Most editions of it contain a body of very learned notes. More recently two new attempts, one in prose by Wilhelm Stapel (Hamburg, 1938—revised in 1943) and another by Friedrich Knorr and Reinhard Fink (Jena, 1941) have reapproached the many difficult problems of interpretation.

The only hitherto available English translation, by Jessie L. Weston (London, 1894), now almost sixty years old, is fairly faithful in meaning but completely destroys the spirit of Wolfram and beclouds his style because of the unhappy choice of an alien meter. The story was retold in English by M. B. Sterling (New York, 1911), and there are a few excerpts in English translation in Bayard Taylor's *Studies* (1879) and in anthologies of Hawthorne and Winkworth. Recently the Trevrizent episode was translated by Charles W. Jones in *Medieval Literature in Translation* (New York, 1950). French translations by Maurice Wilmotte (Paris, 1933) and Ernest Tonnelat (Paris, 1934) have appeared.

7. The Influence of Wolfram's *Parzival*

It would be difficult to measure the influence of Wolfram upon later generations and upon European thought. Only details can be pointed out here[28] He was considered so great, even by his contemporaries, that they inevitably reacted to him, some imitating him, others calling him barbarian. Many German writers in the next generations and centuries, among them Wirnt von Grafenberg, Der Stricker, and Ulrich von Eschenbach, also reveal the impact of Wolfram. His participation in the legendary contest of minstrels in the Wartburg early in the thirteenth century, is told as though it was a fact. The nineteenth-century artist Moritz von Schwind used this contest as the theme for his frescoes in the Wartburg. In the *Wartburgkrieg*, a poem of the late thirteenth century, Wolfram appears in the second part as the defender of Christianity against the heathen sorcerer Klingsor (Clinschor).

More recently Richard Wagner has paid his respects to Wolfram in two operas, *Tannhäuser* (1845) and *Parsifal* (1882), especially in the latter. But as usual Wagner employs his sources very freely. It is a far cry from Wolfram's *Parzival* to Wagner's *Bühnenweihfestspiel*,[29] although not everyone will agree with Margaret Richey that Wagner's opera represents a complete obscuration of the source and an unreal romanticism.[30] To be sure, Wagner's plan, 650 years later, was inevitably different from Wolfram's, but it should not be overlooked that in essential points he understood Wolfram's purpose and motivation very well. Although he makes many changes in the legend to suit his purpose, he shows respect for its deeper meaning. Like Wolfram's Parzival, Wagner's Parsifal acquires experience and knowledge through suffering, and wisdom and kingship through the power of pity and renunciation. The atmosphere of Wagner is frankly much more religious and orthodox than is that of Wolfram. The Grail in Wagner becomes unequivocally the Cup of the Last Supper, and the spear, which plays a much more important part, is the one with which the side of the Saviour had been pierced. Klingsor assumes the role of rival and foe of Amfortas and the Grail knights. As part of his punishment Amfortas has been robbed of the Holy Spear. The symbolic shooting of the swan over the lake by young Parsifal is an invention of Wagner, as is the role played by Gurnemanz, who reminds us more of Wolfram's Trevrizent. Moreover, in place of Wolfram's long period of trial for Parzival, Wagner invents Klingsor's and Kundry's plot against the hero and the latter's complete victory over these forces of evil, as well as his conquest of the Spear in the garden. Among other inventions of Wagner are the temporary demoralization of the Grail knights (but *cf.* Wolfram 788,1 ff.) the death of Titurel (here Amfortas' father), Parsifal's baptism of Kundry, a character radically changed from

Wolfram, and her subsequent death, and Amfortas' renunciation of his kingship before the final arrival of Parsifal. Lastly Amfortas is healed not by virtue of a question but by the power of the Spear.

When we consider the mass of details and characters which Wolfram presents and compare them with the economy of Wagner, we are surprised how many of the original motifs Wagner succeeded in retaining nevertheless. Parsifal's childhood and youth are cleverly brought home to us, as is the sin of Amfortas. Although Feirefiz is completely missing, the heart of the Feirefiz action is hinted at in Kundry's baptism. Gawan, too, is absent, yet certain phases of the Klingsor plot suggest him. Although there is no Trevrizent, yet his function is completely fulfilled. Finally, even without the vital question, which would not have served Wagner's dramatic purpose well, he achieves a solution not out of harmony with the spirit of Wolfram's poem. In Wagner Parsifal's fault lies in his lack of spiritual perception, and his redemption is the result of compassion as well as self-renunciation, in keeping with Schopenhauer's philosophy.

The French sonnet "Parsifal" by Paul Verlaine seems to have been inspired by Wagner's opera. In the ailing Fisher King and his degenerate realm, as described by T. S. Eliot's poem "The Waste Land," the ills of modern civilization are strikingly symbolized.

Another influence of the Grail, as conceived by Wolfram, is the *Gralsfeier* periodically observed by the Catholics of the city of Basel. In a different way the anthroposophists have adopted the Grail as a lofty symbol, envisaging in its knowledge the highest attainable level of cognition.[31] In Ettal in southern Bavaria a Grail temple was established. A Wolfram von Eschenbach-Bund, founded at Amorbach in the Odenwald in 1935, publishes *Mitteilungen*.

Several works of a more popular type, explaining Wolfram's poem to the general public, retelling his story, or basing fictional material on him, have appeared in recent years. To the first category belongs Gertrud Bäumer's *Wolfram von Eschenbach* (1940), to the second, works of Will Vesper (1911), Albrecht Schaeffer (1922), Theodor Matthias (1925), Robert Janecke (1936), and Gottfried Baumecker (1941), and to the third Lily Hohenstein's *Wolfram von Eschenbach*, a novel (1944).

The seven hundredth anniversary of his death was widely observed in Germany, Austria, and Switzerland in 1920.

8. Wolfram, the Man, and His Works[32]

Neither the date nor the place of Wolfram's birth is known with certainty, and indeed we can be sure of very little else about him, except perhaps what he himself tells us in his writings. The year of his birth is usually set around 1165. After much painstaking research and consideration of the claims of various towns, it is now fairly certain that he hailed from Eschenbach near Ansbach in Bavaria (i.e. Central Franconia), a town which erected a statue to him in 1861 and since 1917 bears the name of Wolframs-Eschenbach. It is claimed that his grave was recently rediscovered there. Though not strictly a Bavarian, he was entitled to call himself one (121,7). The Eschenbach family belonged to the lower nobility and later came under the jurisdiction of the lords of Wertheim, one of whom Wolfram mentions in Parzival (184,4). The Eschenbachs were linked with a von Pleinfelden family but had their own coat-of-arms, a can or jug with a spout and an arched handle, on a shield, duplicated on the helmet with a projecting bush-design of tulip-like flowers. The coat-of-arms assigned to them in the Manesse (Heidelberg) Codex and often copied in that of the neighboring Mur family, sometimes used by the Eschenbachs as a seal. Wolfram was a born knight and proud of it, deeming his activities as such more important than his poetry (115,11 ff.).

Wolfram mentions several places near Eschenbach, among them Abenberg (i.e. Amberg), Trüdingen (i.e. Wasser-Trüdingen), Dollenstein, and the Lechfeld. He travelled in Bavaria and Thuringia and, according to those who see his own experiences, and not those of Richard I, reflected in Trevrizent's words (496,15 ff.), he may have gone as far as Italy and present-day Jugoslavia. Several times he was a guest at the court of Landgrave Herman of Thuringia in the Wartburg; it was Herman, deeply interested in French literature, who gave him the manuscript of the now lost chanson de geste, *Bataille d'Aliscans*, upon which he based the poem *Willehalm*, which some scholars call finished, others fragmentary. At the Wartburg he met Walther von der Vogelweide, the great lyric poet, and perhaps other contemporary German poets and even French minstrels. He may also have been a friend of the far-travelled Count Rupprecht von Durne, who had estates near Wertheim, and perhaps Wildenberg, to which he refers (230,13), was a castle of that count.[33] It is possible, too, that Wolfram was present at the siege of Erfurt in 1203, which he mentions (379,18).

Wolfram seems to have performed chivalrous service to two ladies, with the first of whom he broke because she treated him ill (114,8 ff.); he apparently dedicates *Parzival* to a second woman (827,29 f.). There is also reason to believe that Wolfram was married and had a daughter.

Wolfram, the proud knight, was also a man of great tolerance —the Feirefiz episode (XV f.) proves this abundantly—and deep religious convictions. His personality was unusually strong, but he probably made many enemies with a bent for sarcasm of which he accuses himself (487,10 f.). He possessed a keen and whimsical sense of humor, which crops up at the most unexpected times, as when he tells his readers that a certain statement is true if they wish it to be (59,27), or when he assures them not on his, but on *their* oath, of the food-dispensing qualities of the Grail (238,9 ff.). More than once he jests grimly about his own poverty (e.g. 184,29 ff.).

Wolfram probably died soon after Landgrave Herman, whose death is chronicled in 1217. He was buried in the Frauenmünster in Eschenbach.

Wolfram was well acquainted with contemporaneous literature. He knew the *Rolandslied* of Kuonrat and the *Kaiserchronik*, as well as the *Nibelungenlied* and the heroic legends, the works of Herbort von Fritzlar, the *Lucidarius*, the romance of Tristan by Eilhart, the works of Heinrich von Veldeke, Hartman von Aue, and Gottfried von Strassburg. He seems to have had no direct knowledge of Latin but a better acquaintance with French than some critics would concede. Surprising in his remark, made twice (*Parzival* 115,27 ff. and *Willehalm* 2,19), that he was illiterate. This is indeed amazing and has been questioned by many, especially in recent years. These critics usually interpret it as a jesting dig at Hartman, who had expressed pride over his own book learning in *Der arme Heinrich*, and later, perhaps annoyed by Wolfram's remark, repeated the statement in *Iwein* (1202). Other critics tend to believe Wolfram, pointing out that knowledge of reading and writing was very rare in non-clerical circles at that time, and that Ulrich von Lichtenstein, too, was illiterate. If they were correct, we would have to assume that Wolfram was endowed with an astounding memory and a no less astounding ability to marshal what he had heard, and that he was blessed with excellent readers and copyists, as well as with very learned friends.

Wolfram seems to have begun his literary career as a singer of *Minnelieder*, of which nine have come down to us. Especially noteworthy are his so-called *Wächterlieder*, or *Tagelieder*, a type in which a watchman warns the lovers, who have spent the night together clandestinely, of the approach of daybreak.[34] Later writers in this genre, among them Reinmar von Zweter, Der Winsbecke, and Heinrich von Meissen, reveal the influence of Wolfram. The form bears the imprint of the Provençal *Alba* and is echoed faintly in the balcony scene of Shakespeare's *Romeo and Juliet*. His first major work was probably *Parzival*, undoubtedly his masterpiece. There followed, according to most scholars, the two fragments of *Titurel*,[35] dealing with the love of Sigunë and Schionatulander (remembered from *Parzival*) and written in peculiar four-line stanzas with exclusively feminine rhyme, each line divided by a cæsura. Wolfram tired of the task before concluding it. Finally he began his *Willehalm*, the source being the chanson de geste, already mentioned, which he obtained from the Thuringian landgrave. It is possible that he undertook the work at the behest of Herman, for the subject does not seem as congenial to him as that of *Parzival*. It recounts the deeds of a vassal of Ludwig the Pious, William of Orange, in contest against the Saracens and depicts many lively battle scenes.

9. Additional Bibliography

In addition to the works already referred to in this Introduction, the following are of special interest to the student of *Parzival*. They are selected from the vast flood of books and articles, of which there appears to be no end. The older literature up to 1897 will be found in Friedrich Panzer's *Bibliographie zu Wolfram von Eschenbach*, München, 1897; only more recent literature is considered here. Further bibliography will be found in the Notes.

General

Ehrismann, Gustav, *Geschichte der deutschen Literatur bis zum Ausgang des Mittelalters*, 2. Teil, II, 1. Hälfte, München, 1927, pp. 225 ff.

——————, "Wolframprobleme," *Germanisch-Romanische Monatsschrift* I, pp. 657-674.

——————, "Ueber Wolframs Ethik," *Zeitschrift für deutsches Altertum* XLIX, pp. 405-465.

Neumann, Friedrich, "Wolframs von Eschenbach Ritterideal," *Deutsche Vierteljahrschrift für Literaturwissenschaft und Geistesgeschichte* V, pp. 9-24.

Richey, Margaret F., *Gahmuret Anschevin. A Contribution to the Study of Wolfram von Eschenbach*, Oxford, 1923.

Buttell, Sister M. P., *Religious Ideology and Christian Humanism in Cluniac Verse*, Washington, 1948.

Style

Singer, Samuel, "Wolframs Stil und der Stoff des Parzival," *Sitzungsberichte der Wiener Akademie der Wissenschaften* 180 (1916).

Textual Criticism, Exegesis, Sources

Singer, Samuel, "Bemerkungen zu Wolframs Parzival," *Abhandlungen zur germanischen Philologie. Festgabe für R. Heinzel*, Halle, 1898.

Hagen, Paul, "Wolfram und Kiot," *Zeitschrift für deutsche Philologie* XXXVIII, pp. 1-38, 198-237.

Lichtenstein, Julius, "Zur Parzivalfrage," *Beiträge zur Geschichte der deutschen Sprache* XXII, pp. 1-93.

Palgen, Rudolf, *Der Stein der Weisen. Quellenstudien zum Parzival*, Breslau, 1922.

Singer, Samuel, "Ueber die Quelle von Wolframs Parzival," *Zeitschrift für deutsches Altertum* XLIV, pp. 321-342.

Bruce, J. D., *The Evolution of the Arthurian Romance from the Beginnings down to the Year 1300*. Hesperia, Erg.-Reihe 8-9. 2nd ed., Göttingen, 1928.

Golther, Wolfgang, *Parzival und der Gral in der Dichtung des Mittelalters und der Neuzeit*, Stuttgart, 1925.

Iselin, L. E., *Der morgenländische Ursprung der Grallegende*, Halle, 1909.
Junk, Victor, "Gralsage und Graldichtung des Mittelalters," *Sitzungsberichte der Wiener Akademie der Wissenschaften* 168,4.
Rohr, F., *Parzival und der heilige Gral. Eine neue Deutung der Symbolik der Graldichtungen*, Hildesheim, 1923.
Wechssler, Eduard, *Die Sage vom heiligen Gral in ihrer Entwicklung bis auf Wagners Parsifal*, Halle, 1898.
Hecker, Hermann, *Das ethische Wortfeld in Wolframs Parzival*, Würzburg, 1940.
Halbach, K. H., "Wolfram von Eschenbach und Goethe als Sprachschöpfer," *Von deutscher Art in Sprache und Dichtung* I, herausgegeben von G. Fricke, Fr. Koch und Kl. Lugowski, Stuttgart and Berlin, 1941.
Schwietering, J., "Parzivals Schuld; zur Religiosität Wolframs in ihrer Beziehung zur Mystik," in *Zeitschrift für deutsches Altertum* LXXXI, pp. 44 ff.
Keferstein, Georg, "Die Gawanhandlung in Wolframs Parzival," in *Germanisch-Romanische Monatsschrift* XXV, pp. 256-274.
Three of the manuscripts of the G class (K, Sigma, and Tau) have recently been studied in the Ottendorfer Memorial Series (1935-1940) by the Americans F. J. Nock, A. van Eerden, and G. Kreye, respectively.
Work now in progress by American scholars in fields related to the present study can best be surveyed in the News Letters of the Arthurian Group (Comparative Literature III) of the Modern Language Association of America and in the same Association's annual *Research in Progress*.

---

[1] Jacob Grimm in "Rede auf Lachmann" (*Kleinere Schriften* I, 2. Auflage, Berlin, 1879, p. 157); "den an Gedanken und Gemüt reichsten Dichter unserer Vorzeit."

[2] *Wolframs von Eschenbach Parzival und Titurel*. Herausgegeben von Karl Bartsch. 1. Teil, 2. Auflage, Leipzig, 1875, p. v.

[3] Vol. 23, 1948, p. 698. See also the same author's *The Legend of Sir Perceval*, I, London, 1906, and *From Ritual to Romance*, Cambridge, 1920.

[4] *The Story of Parzival and the Graal as related by Wolfram von Eschenbach*. Interpreted and discussed by Margaret F. Richey. Oxford, 1935, pp. 1, 3.

[5] G. V. Amoretti, *Parzival. Wolfram von Eschenbach, K. L. Immermann*,

R. Wagner. Pisa, 1931, and André Moret, *Wolfram d'Eschenbach, Parzival. Morceaux choisis, avec introduction, notes et glossaire.* Paris, 1943.

[6] Cf. Sister Mary A. Rachbauer, *Wolfram von Eschenbach: A Study of the Relation of the Content of Books 3-6 and 9 of the Parzival to the Crestien Manuscripts.* Catholic University Studies in German, 4, Washington, 1934. Cf. also note 11 below. With many changes in detail, some more or less unimportant, others vital (*e.g.* the deeper significance of Parzival's question to the King of the Grail) Wolfram's tale generally corresponds to Crestien's from the time of young Parzival's meeting with the knights in Book III to Book XIII.

[7] It should be noted, though, that in some versions not Perceval but Gawain is the Grail-seeker. This is true of the first continuation of Crestien, written before Wolfram, and of Heinrich von dem Türlin, who came later. Still later Sir Galahad also figured as a Grail-seeker.

[8] Helen Adolf, "Oriental Sources for Grail Romances," In *PMLA* LXII, 2, pp. 306 ff. Cf. also Max Semper in *Deutsche Vierteljahrschrift* XII, p. 92 ff.

[9] *The Origin of the Grail Legend*, Cambridge, Mass., 1943.

[10] *Medieval Studies in Honor of J. D. M. Ford*, Cambridge, Mass., 1948, pp. 177 ff.

[11] E. K. Heller, "Studies on the Story of Gawain in Crestien and Wolfram," in *Journal of English and Germanic Philology* XXIV, 4, pp. 502 f.

[12] Albert Schreiber, *Neue Bausteine zu einer Lebensgeschichte Wolframs von Eschenbach*, Frankfurt, 1922, and the same author's "Die Herkunft der Edelherren von Durne," in *Zeitschrift für die Geschichte des Oberrheins*, N. F. 48, 1934.

[13] Wilhelm Wackernagel, *Altfranzösische Lieder und Leiche aus Handschriften zu Bern und Neuenburg*, Basel, 1846, p. 191.

[14] Maurice Wilmotte, *Le poème du Gral et ses auteurs*, Paris, 1930, pp. 16 ff.

[15] Sister Mary Rosina Fuehrer, *A Study of the Relation of the Dutch Lancelot and the Flemish Perchevael Fragments to the Manuscripts of Chrétien's Conte del Graal.* Catholic University Studies in German, 14, Washington, 1939.

[16] *Wolframs von Eschenbach Parzivâl und Titurel*, herausgegeben von Karl Bartsch. 4. Auflage bearbeitet von Marta Marti. 3 Teile. Leipzig, 1927, 1929, 1932 (introduction to I, *passim*). However, if J. L. Riordan's new theory of three periods of German Arthurian romances (soon to be published)—*viz.* 1. The Period of Dependence, *ca.* 1190-1220, 2. The Period of Imitation, *ca.* 1220-1325, and 3. The Period of Absorption, 14th and 15th centuries—is applied to Wolfram, his work would fall entirely into the Period of Dependence and the contention of the more recent German critics that Wolfram is a quite self-reliant poet would tend to be weakened.

[17] *Lucidarius* aus der Berliner Handschrift herausgegeben von Felix Heidlauf. Berlin, 1915. *Deutsche Texte des Mittelalters* XXVIII. For *Parzival* 789,6, see *Lucidarius*, p. 22; for 581,1, see p. 12. The *Lucidarius* (late twelfth century) has striking general similarity to the dialog of Parzival and Trevrizent in Book IX; it, too, is a dialog between a master and his

disciple, and it deals with similar subjects, such as the planets, the meaning and symbolism of the Catholic ritual, sin, atonement, sacrifice, damnation, holy days, the passion of Christ. The devils come "mit michelme grimme" (pp. 30, 61—*cf. Parzival* 120,19); the uncovering of the altar on Good Friday is referred to (p. 52—*Parzival* 459,23 f.); the victims of hell "wunschent daz si sterbin, unde mugent doch nicht ersterben" (p. 62— *Parzival* 501,30, 787,1 ff.). *Cf.* also our Notes Nos. 35, 47, 70, and 76 to Book IX, especially the last-named, Note 24 to Book XII, and Note 14 to Book XIII. We are confident that Wolfram knew and used the *Lucidarius*— a rather inconvenient fact for all Kyot adherents. *Cf.* Singer, *Wolfram und der Gral. Neue Parzivâl-Studien*, Bern, 1939, p. 43. Besides the correspondences between *Lucidarius* and *Parzival* noted, Professor Hermann Weigand of Yale University has called our attention to several others: With *Lucidarius*, pp 6, 19-24 (evil demons inhabit the region between the earth and the moon) *cf. Parzival* 658,26 ff. With *Lucidarius*, pp. 11, 27 f. (monster men in India have their heads set hindside afore) *cf. Parzivâl* 519,2 ff. With *Lucidarius*, pp. 28-29 (the point of gestation at which the human foetus is endowed with life) *cf. Parzival* 109,5 f., where Wolfram deviates but agrees with a passage in the *Wartburgkrieg*. With *Lucidarius*, pp. 5-6 (the peculiar motion of the planets brakes the firmament and keeps it from bursting) *cf. Parzival* 782, 14 ff. (also *Willehalm* 2, 2 f.).

[18] *Wolframs von Eschenbach Parzival und Titurel* herausgegeben und erklärt von Ernst Martin, Halle. I, Text, 1900; II, Kommentar, 1903 (*cf.* II, 532).

[19] W. Snelleman, *Das Haus Anjou und der Orient in Wolframs Parzival*. Nijkerk, 1941 (Amsterdam dissertation).

Friedrich Panzer, "Gahmuret. Quellenstudien zu Wolframs Parzival," in *Sitzungsberichte der Heidelberger Akademie der Wissenschaften*. Philosophisch-Historische Klasse. No. 1, Heidelberg, 1940. According to Panzer's stimulating study, the non-Crestien portions of Wolfram, especially I-II and XV-XVI, depend upon several French sources, *viz.* the *Roman de Thebes*, the *Ipomedon* of Huet de Rotelande (the source for the duel between Parzival and Feirefiz), and the *Joufrois* (suggesting the tournament of Kanvoleis). Panzer also finds new connections between *Parzival* and the *Kaiserchronik*, as well as Veldeke's *Enit*.

Bodo Mergell, *Wolfram von Eschenbach und seine französischen Quellen*, II: *Wolframs Parzival. Münster*, 1943. The first volume, on *Willehalm*, had come out in 1936.

Hermann Schneider, "Parzival-Studien", in *Sitzungsberichte der Bayrischen Akademie der Wissenschaften*, 1944-46. Heft 4, München, 1947.

[20] But *cf.* Golther's view in our Note 15 to Book I. This radical disagreement illustrates drastically the quandary of Parzivâl research in many moot points and the sharp disagreements still prevailing as to source and genesis. A much better case, it seems, has been made out for the claim that Wolfram refers to the House of Anjou. Could it be that Wolfram purposely mystifies his readers and slyly has both explanations in mind?

[21] *Cf.* the reference to Schneider's article in Note 19 above. The present allusion is to pp. 32 ff., especially p. 38.

²² Elisabeth Karg-Gasterstädt, *Zur Entstehungsgeschichte des Parzival*, Halle, 1925.

²³ These conjectures are based upon: 1. Paul Hagen's article in *Zeitschrift für deutsche Philologie* XXXVIII, pp. 1 ff., 198 ff.; 2. J. J. A. Frantzen's *Over de bron van den Parzival van W. von Eschenbach* (*Handlingen v. h. Zesde Ned. Philologencongres*, Groningen, 1910); 3. H. J. Weigand's article in *PMLA* LIII, 4, pp. 917 ff.; 4. J. Fourquet's *Wolfram d'Eschenbach et le Conte del Graal*, Paris, 1938; 5., 6., 7. writings of F. Panzer, W. Snelleman, and B. Mergell (see note 19); and 8. the articles of A. T. Hatto in *Modern Language Review* (London, vols. XLI ff.).

²⁴ Hans Naumann, "The Significance of Form in Courtly Culture about the Year 1200," in *Journal of English and Germanic Philology* XXVIII, pp. 329 ff. See also the same writer's *Deutsches Dichten und Denken*, Berlin, 1938, pp. 115 ff.

²⁵ Georg Misch, "Wolframs Parzival, eine Studie zur Geschichte der Autobiographie," in *Deutsche Vierteljahrschrift für Literaturwissenschaft* V, 213-315. Misch studies the work not only as a courtly romance but as a unique work of peculiarly German stamp, a story of development of soul, of will, of character, not merely of the intellect, striking the very core of life. Also: Georg Keferstein, *Parzivals ethischer Weg; ritterlicher Lebensstil im Hochmittelalter*, Weimar, 1937. Keferstein emphasizes the actions of the characters but slights the thought behind them. The work of Benedikt Mockenhaupt referred to in the previous sentence is *Die Frömmigkeit im Parzival Wolframs von Eschenbach*, Bonn, 1942.

²⁶ Hans-Friedrich Rosenfeld, "Die Berliner Parzival-Fragmente," in *Festgabe zum 60. Geburtstag von Hermann Degering*, Leipzig, 1926, pp. 192 ff.

²⁷ Margaret B. Stilwell, *Incunabula in American Libraries*. A second census of fifteenth-century books owned in the United States, Mexico, and Canada. New York, 1940.

²⁸ Wolfgang Golther, *op. cit.*, devotes much space to the subject.

²⁹ Wagner changed the name of the hero to Parsifal because he deemed it Arabic: *Parsi*, unsullied, *fal*, fool. He also changed other names, *e.g.* Amfortas. In 1932 the Graz professor von Suhtscheck claimed that many of Wolfram's principal place names in Parzival were of Iranian derivation

³⁰ *Op. cit.*, p. 194.

³¹ Ernst Uehli, *Eine neue Gralsuche* (Goetheanum-Bücherei), Stuttgart, 1921. Also. L. J. Frohnmeyer, *Die theosophische Bewegung*, 2nd. ed., Stuttgart, 1923, p. 66. Wolfgang Golther, *op. cit.*, pp. 266 ff., mentions various recent English, American, and German writers who have dealt with the Grail theme, among them Hawker, Westwood, Lowell, Morris, Tennyson, Uhland, Fouqué, Immermann, Widmann, Vollmöller, and Lienhard.

³² For facts pertaining to the life of Wolfram see C. Heidingsfelder, "Die Heimat Wolframs von Eschenbach," in *Historisch-politische Blätter* 162; J. B. Kurz, "Heimat und Geschlecht Wolframs von Eschenbach," in *Beilage zum 61. Jahresbericht des Historischen Vereins für Mittelfranken*, Ansbach, 1916 (Erlangen dissertation, 1917); Friedrich von Klocke, "Zur Familiengeschichte Wolframs von Eschenbach und seines Geschlechts,"

in *Zentralstelle für deutsche Personen- und Familiengeschichte* XV (1930); and the works of Albert Schreiber referred to in Note 12 above.

[33] See the works referred to in Note 12 above.

[34] See W. Mohr, "Wolframs Tagelieder," in the Kluckhohn-Schneider *Festschrift*, Tübingen, 1948, pp. 148-165.

[35] Margaret Richey, *op. cit.*, pp. 8-9, believes that this was Wolfram's *last* work.

Book One
Gahmuret and Belakanë

Book One

GAHMURET AND BELAKANË

When indecision's in the heart　　　　　1
The soul is bound to grieve and smart.[1]*
For scorned alike and fêted
Is he who bold is rated
But vacillates twixt dark and light[2]
Like magpies in their black and white.
Yet such a one may well be glad,
For both in him their part have had,[3]
Twixt heaven and hell he's drifting.
The man whose faith is shifting　　　　10
Is wholly black as darkest night
Inside and out, devoid of light.
But fate on him's conferring
Pure white, whose faith's unerring.
This winged lesson[4] will elude
All folk of simple mind and mood:
They're powerless to grasp it,
'Twill flee before they clasp it,
Just like a hare that leaps for fear.
The metal placed against the rear　　　20
Of mirrors, and a blind man's dream[5]
Reflect things merely as they seem.
Yet they afford the countenance
A dim and transient, fleeting glance:
The joy it gives is all too weak.
Who will attempt my hair to tweak
Where none grows, here inside my hand?
He has a grip I don't command.[6]
If I cry out against such fears,
Intelligence in me appears.[7]
Should I for faith be peering　　　　　2
Just where it's disappearing,
Like fire inside a water-well
Or dew where long the sunlight fell?
So wise a man I've never known

---

* The superior figures refer to the Notes, pp. 343 ff. below.

As would not willingly be shown
The conduct that my tale requires
And what good lessons it inspires.
And this to do 'twill never fail:
'Twill boldly chase and shrewdly quail,   10
Retreating first, then turning,
Both honoring and spurning.[8]
Whoso can manage that aright
Has proved himself a cunning wight;
He'll shun excess, won't hesitate,
His grasp on matters is first-rate.
Aye, falseness in a fellow-man
Must lead to hell, as well it can,
And spoils a name, like wheat in hail.
His faith is given so short a tail   20
That in a fly-infested wood
Not e'en three bites would find it good.[9]

  These diverse kinds of definition
Describe not only men's condition:
For women too this rule I make.
The one who would my counsel take
Should know the man to whom she'll yield
Her good name and her honor's shield,
On whom she then might shower
Her love and virtue's flower,
That she need not be rueing   3
Her chaste and loyal doing.
I pray to God, to ward off scath,
That women keep the middle path.
Their modesty is their moral crown:
I cannot wish them more renown.
The worthless woman's low in price.
How lasting is a crust of ice
On which the August sunbeams shine?
Thus swiftly doth her fame decline.   10
Some women fair are rated:
But if hearts are falsely freighted,
Their value I no higher hold
Than blue glass in a ring of gold.
I think it not a little thing

If one should take a mean brass ring
And put in it a ruby fine
With all its properties divine[10]
(That's like a rightful woman's way).
If proper rules she will obey, 20
I'll not explore her outward mien
Nor what outside her heart is seen.[11]
If *in* her breast she's fortified,
A good name she may bear with pride.
   Were I to test both wife and man[12]
As full and justly as I can,
This tale would never have an end.
Now listen to this story's trend.
'Twill tell in equal measure
Of sorrow and of pleasure.
Concern and joy your lot will be. 4
And were I not *one* man, but three,
And each of them had just the same
Ability as I can claim,
'Twould really be a tour de force
For them to tell this story's course,
Which I alone will now relate.
Their toil and effort would be great.
A tale I would for you renew
Of loyalty both tried and true, 10
Of woman as she ought to be,
And a manly man's simplicity,
Which hardship could not bend or break.
In fear his heart would never quake:
All steel, whenas to strife he came,
His hand, in triumph and in fame,
Won for him many a noble prize.
A bold one he, and later wise
(Such was the hero of my lay),
To women's eyes a radiant ray; 20
To women's hearts he brought distress
But always fled unrighteousness.
The one whose deeds to tell I've sworn[13]
Is—in my story—not yet born,

But he's the hero of my song
And all that thereto doth belong.

The hero's father, Gahmuret, called Anshevin because his father, Gandin, had been king of Anjou, is left without heritage at home because he is a younger son. Well armed and equipped, though, he fares forth on knightly adventure. He serves the Caliph of Bagdad in war and arrives in Zazamanc, where Belakanë, Moorish queen, is being besieged by the kinsmen of Isenhart, a suitor of hers who, they charge, has lost his life on her account. Belakanë implores Gahmuret for help, which he promises. He takes shelter with her burgrave and under his guidance inspects the fortifications. At mealtime the queen seeks him out and waits upon him. He spends a sleepless night yearning for her and for chivalrous adventure. The next morning he rides into battle and vanquishes the hostile chieftains. He returns, cohabits with Belakanë, who becomes his wife, and through her wins her kingdom. Then he releases the prisoners he had made, receives a costly tent which had belonged to Isenhart, and is promised the latter's arms, as well as a diamond-studded helmet, which are to be returned to him from Scotland. Now Isenhart is buried. But Gahmuret's happiness is short-lived. He soon yearns to desert Belakanë and engage in further knightly adventures. Leaving her a letter which reveals the reason for his sudden departure as well as his lineage (he is related to King Arthur and descended from a fairy), he secretly boards a ship and takes Isenhart's tent along. (4, 27—57, 14)

>The woman[14] bore, when time was due,   57
>A son who had a twofold hue.
>In him a miracle was seen:
>Both white and swarthy was his sheen.
>The queen then kissed the child on sight;
>She kissed him often where he was white.   20
>The mother named her infant fine
>Feirefiz Anshevine.[15]
>In time whole forests he'd destroy.[16]
>His hands, since jousting gave him joy,
>The spears full many shattered
>While holes in shields they battered.
>Like magpies he was black and white
>Of hair and skin, a curious sight.

GAHMURET AND BELAKANË

A year it was and longer yet
That praise was sung of Gahmuret
Throughout the land of Zazamanc:[17]   58
His hand achieved victorious rank.
As yet he floated on the sea,
The strong winds hurt him wondrously.
A sail of red silk he espied
Borne by a ship, and men inside
From Scotland sent by Fridebrand[18]
To Lady Belakanë's land.
He[19] hoped her pardon he'd incur
(Though he had lost his kin through her)   10
When she in strife by him was sought.
The diamond helmet they had brought,
A sword, a corselet, greaves a pair.
(Now wasn't that a wonder rare
That he[20] this vessel should espy?
The story tells it so, not I.)
They gave the helmet; then swore he
That he their messenger would be
When he should reach the lady's ear.
They parted then, and this I hear: 20
The ocean bore him to a bay
And to Seville he took his way.
With gold the valiant man repaid
His mariner for all his aid,
The toil and trouble he had had.
Their parting made the sailor sad.

Book Two
Gahmuret and Herzeloydë

Book Two

GAHMURET AND HERZELOYDë

In Spain, the country he had found,
He knew the monarch far renowned.
His kinsman 'twas, Sir Kaÿlet:
To him he went in Dolet.[1]
But he on knightly quest had fared,
Where foemen's shields might not be spared.
He[2] too prepared for chivalry
(The story so reports to me).
Well-painted lances there were seen
Adorned with velvet pennants green.
Upon each pennant one could see
Such costly ermine anchors three,
Their richness was by none denied.
For they were long and they were wide,
The fighter's fingers they would touch
When to the spear-tip tied, not much
Beyond a span in measure.
The doughty man with pleasure
A hundred lances saw prepared,
And after him in state they fared
With Kaÿlet's own retinue.
Both love and honor were his due,
And this they gave with worthiness,
The which their lord did not distress.
He rode, I wot, for many a day,
Till strange tents loomed upon the way.
That was the land of Waleis.[3]
For pitched in front of Kanvoleis[4]
Were many tents o'er all the lea.
I say this not uncertainly:
'Tis true, if so ye do command.[5]
He bade his men to halt and stand.
And now his prudent master-squire
Was sent ahead before his sire.
He did the things his master said:
He scoured the town for roof and bed.

The squire went at his task with speed,
By laden beasts accompanied.
No single house he there espied
But it had shields[6] on every side,
And on the walls suspended
Were spears in rows extended.
The lovely queen of Waleis,
She had proclaimed for Kanvoleis   10
A tournament of such a kind
That still it haunts the fearful mind
When timid souls such frays behold:
Their hand would never be so bold.
She was a maiden, not a wife.
Two lands,[7] her person too for life,
Were his, whoso to victory rode.
But many a knight in vain bestrode
His steed and found himself unhorsed.
Now they that thus to earth were forced,   20
Found loss for prowess vaunted.
There many a knight undaunted
No kind of knightly valor lacked.
They forward charged and then attacked
With horses onward bounding
And flashing swords resounding.

Gahmuret has his tent pitched in a meadow in plain view of the young queen's castle. She and her ladies watch the work with interest. With a show of pomp Gahmuret enters the tent. (60, 27—61, 28).

The queen's court soon was hearing
That now a guest was nearing.
'Twas from a distant land he came,   62
But no one knew the stranger's name.
"His folk are versed in chivalrous way,[8]
Both French and heathenish are they.
Their language shows that some, O Queen,
May possibly be Anshevîn.
Their spirit's proud, their garb is neat
And tailored well from head to feet.
Their squires were easy to approach
And they are free of all reproach.   10

They say: Whoever wealth would seek,
If to their lord he will but speak,
That lord will offer largess free.
I asked of them who he might be:
Their answer was both prompt and frank:
He is the king of Zazamanc."
A page it was who told her this.
"Ah, what a gorgeous tent is his!
Your crown and all your spacious land
Outweigh not half its value grand." 20
"Thou needst not praise his tent so high.
My lips to thee give this reply:
It may be owned by such a man
As brooks no poverty, nor can."
These words were added by the queen:
"O dear, when will himself be seen?"

The knights have set up two camps, one inside, the other outside the town. In the preliminary tournament Gahmuret captures four kings, but two of his own men, Kaylet and Killirjakac, are also made prisoners. Meanwhile envoys come from Queen Amphlise of France, whom Gahmuret had once loved, offering him her hand and her kingdom. In the evening Queen Herzeloydë visits Gahmuret in his tent to discuss an exchange of prisoners. All agree that he deserves the grand prize—Herzeloydë's hand in marriage. Amphlise's messengers protest, but to no avail. However, Gahmuret, yearning for his wife Belakanë, is still more saddened by news of the death of his older brother, Galoës. (62, 27—93, 10).

Now when the sun to shine began, 93
They all agreed, as man to man,
The inner and the outer host,
Whoever held a fighter's post,
If young he was or old in years,
If valorous or lamed with fears,
Should not engage in jousting fray.
The sun revealed its forenoon ray.
From strife the knights were all so worn,
The steeds with spurs so pricked and torn, 20
That e'en the stoutest knights lay numb,
By sheer fatigue still overcome.

The queen herself went riding
To them on the plain abiding
And took them with her back to town.
She bade the lords of best renown
To ride forthwith to Leoplane.⁹
Her bidding they would not disdain.
They came where mass the men did sing
For Zazamanc's unhappy king.
Now when they'd spoke the blessing,   94
Came Herzeloydë pressing.
To Gahmuret a claim she stated,
To her was he adjudicated.
He told her, "Queen, I have a wife
Who's dearer to me than my life.
But even if I had her not,
Another reason yet I wot
Whereby I must avoid your sight,
Should one concede me what is right."   10
   "The Mooress you should be leaving
And to my love be cleaving.
In the Christian cross more power lies.
Now rid yourself of heathen ties
And love me as good Christians do,
For I am sick for love of you.
Or shall my claim be weaker seen
Than that of her, the Frenchmen's queen?¹⁰
Her envoys spoke with honeyed word,
They said so much, it was absurd."   20
"Yes, she's in truth my lady fair.
To her in Anjou did I bear
Good service, born of courtly ways.
Her help still brightens all my days,
Since I was taught by her so well,
Whom woman's frailty ne'er befell.
Although we were but youngsters yet,
We were delighted when we met.
The noble lady, queen Amphlise,
Has all that men in women prize.
With me she fell to sharing   95
The tithes her land was bearing;

Since poorer then I used to be
I took her bounty willingly.
Still poverty's my fashion.
So, lady, have compassion.
For my beloved brother's dead.
To press me now would be ill-bred.
Seek love of those who joy profess:
My lot is naught but sheer distress."   10
"Let me no longer waste and pine:
Give answer, why won't you be mine?"
"Your question I will not ignore:
A tourney was proclaimed before,
But so far this has not occurred,
And witnesses support my word."
"The vesper games did interfere:
The best knights grew so weary here
That jousting then was ended."
"Your city I defended   20
With others who were stout and brave.
Of me no further answer crave:
Some men fought better far than I.
Your claim to me I must deny.
Your greeting, nothing more, I want,
If this you are inclined to grant."

   Now as I've heard the tale aright,
The maiden and the noble knight
Went to a judge, her plea to hear.
By then the noon of day was near.
The judge right soon his verdict conned: 96
"The knight who here his helmet donned
And who has joined in knightly fray,
If he's deserved the prize today,
Shall be the queen's to have and hold."
These words the jurymen extolled.
The queen said, "Lord, now you are mine.
I'll serve you well, as I incline,
And make your life with joy so bright
That after grief will come delight."   10
But in his soul the grief lived on.
Now April's shimmering[11] was gone,

And on its heels there soon were seen
The tiny blades of grass all green.
The meadow, green appearing,
All timid hearts was cheering
And every soul elated.
The trees, with blossoms freighted,
Were sweet in Maytime's breezes mild.
Now since he was a fairy's child, 20
He had to love and love must want.
The queen was eager this to grant.
To Herzeloyd he turned his eyes,
His sweet lips spoke in decorous wise:
"If with you happy I'm to be,
I beg you, leave me always free.
If e'er my grief has taken flight
I'd fain go faring like a knight.
If jousting be to me refused,
I still can play the trick I used
What time I fled and left my wife: 97
Her too I'd won in chivalrous strife.
When joust and tournament she banned
I let her have both folk and land."
Said she, "Lord, your own heart obey,
I'll always let you have your way."
"Still many a spear I'd like to rend,
Each month a joust I'd fain attend;
Let this be my condition,
For this I crave permission." 10
She promised that, I've heard it said:
He got the lands and eke the maid.

 And now these three young squires were seen,
Dispatched by fair Amphlise, the queen;
Her chaplain, too, was there at need.
When judge and jury had agreed,
He heard and saw it with regret,
Then spoke by stealth to Gahmuret:
"My mistress has the tidings heard
What at Patelamunt occurred, 20
How you the highest prize there gained
And thus a twofold crown obtained.

She too has lands and lofty mood,
Gives you herself and riches good."
"Since knighthood she bestowed on me,
I must, by knighthood's own decree,
By virtue of my station,
Stand fast, shun perturbation.
If shield from her I had not won,
All this of course had stayed undone.
Though I may sorrow or rejoice, 98
The verdict holds, I have no choice."[12]
Go back and give her homage due
And say I'll be her champion too.
Though every crown on earth I'd earn,
'Tis chiefly she for whom I'd yearn."[13]
To them he riches proffered:
They took not what he offered.
And homeward then the envoys fared;
The queen's good name at least was spared. 10
But to no one they bade adieu:
With angry folk that's nothing new.
Her envoys three, of noble kind,
For weeping they were almost blind.
   To those who bore their shields invert[14]
Some jousting friend[15] could now assert:
"It seems that Herzeloyd the queen
Has won her prize, the Anshevîn."
"What, was from Anjou someone here?
Our lord,[16] alas, did not appear: 20
Mid Saracens he's playing knight,
That's on our hearts the greatest blight."
"Well, he who earned the highest prize,
Unhorsed those knights before your eyes,
Who thrust and smote as ne'er before
And who the costly anchor wore
On jeweled helmet flaming,[17]
That's just the one you're naming.
I heard it from King Kaÿlet:
The Anshevîn was Gahmuret.
No doubt, he has succeeded." 99
To horse his men now speeded.

Their clothes were tearstained, eyes were dim,
When they at last had come to him.
They greeted him, them greeted he,
Both joy and grief were there to see.
His faithful liegemen kissing,
He said, "Do not be missing
In boundless grief my brother dead,
For I will glad you in his stead.   10
Turn up your shields in the proper way
And take the road of joy today.
My father's arms to wear were best:
His land my anchor hath possessed,
A sign of errant knighthood still,[18]
Let take and wear it whoso will.
My life must now show pleasure,
For I'm rich beyond all measure.
If I'm the people's lord to be,
My grief would cause them misery.   20
Dame Herzeloydë, help me try
To beg and urge them, you and I,
That all the kings and princes here
Should tarry, as they hold me dear,
Till thou'st bestowed on me the prize
For which requited *Minnë*[19] sighs."
Then both requested all to bide:
Straightway the noble guests complied.
Now each repaired to his own bed.
The queen to her beloved said,
"Entrust yourself now to my care."   100
Through secret ways she led him there.
The guests were treated well and cheered,
Although the host had disappeared.
Their retinues were now as one.
He left, accompanied by none,
Except two noble squires as aides.
The Queen escorted by her maids
Led him to where he found delight
And all his sorrows took to flight.   10
Subdued was now his sadness,
His soul restored to gladness:

Through love alone could this have been.
Herzeloyd, the lovely queen,
Was reft of her virginity.[20]
Their lips they spared not, he and she,
They kissed with mouths exerted,
And grief through joy diverted.

Gahmuret absents himself occasionally to attend tournaments, as he had said he would. Once he hears that his friend, the Caliph of Bagdad, called the Baruk, or Blessed One, is being hard pressed by his foes. He hastens to his aid and is treacherously slain. The Baruk has him interred with elaborate ceremony. Herzeloydë, who has been forewarned of her husband's death by terrifying dreams and who is expecting a child, is apprized. (100, 19— 110, 9)

    Now hear a different story,   **110**
How Herzeloydë was impelled.
Her unborn child she clasped and held
With arms and fingers tightly.
Said she, "Pray God may rightly
Send me the fruit of Gahmuret:
Upon this prayer my heart is set.
God, turn my mind from senseless pain,[21]
For Gahmuret would die again
If I myself should harry
While in my womb I carry   **20**
What I conceived of him alone
Who loved me as his very own."
    If any saw, she little cared:
Her shirt she snatched, her breast she bared.
The little breasts, soft and white,
Now engaged her care and sight
And to her crimson lips were pressed:
Her womanhood was manifest.[22]
Then said this woman wise and good,
"Thou dost contain an infant's food:
The child has sent it on ahead   **111**
Since its life in me was heralded."
For thus she saw her wish come true,
That o'er her heart its food now grew.
The lady with her fingers pressed

The infant's milk out of her breast.
Said she, "Thou'rt born of loyalty.
Had they not once baptizèd me,
I'd take thee for my christening.
Myself I'll oft be moistening 10
With thee and tear-drops flowing,
Concealing grief and showing:
For Gahmuret I wish to mourn."
To her she had a garment borne,
A shirt all red with spattered gore
That in the Baruk's host he wore
When he was doomed his life to lose,
As he a martial end to choose
Displayed a manful, true desire.
Then for the lance did she inquire 20
That slew her lord in yonder fray.
Ipomidon of Ninivê [23]
His fearful prowess thus had shown,
The proud high knight of Babylon:
The shirt was tattered, almost gone.
The lady fain had put it on
As formerly in love and trust
When he returned from knightly joust.
The others took it from her hand.
The noblest knights throughout the land
The spear and blood did then inter 112
In church, as though a corpse it were.
Gahmuret's whole nation
Was steeped in lamentation.

   And now, when fourteen days were done,
The woman bore an infant son:
So strong the infant was of limb,
She well-nigh died in bearing him.
From here this story takes its start,
And this is now its opening part. 10
For now his birth is stated
Whose tale shall be related.
The joy and grief his father had,
The father's life, his death so sad,
Of that ye've heard a goodly share.

GAHMURET AND HERZELOYDË 55

<blockquote>

Now learn too how his offspring rare,
This story's main endeavor,
Was kept, they hoped forever.
From knighthood he should be concealed
Until his wit should be revealed.   20
When the queen her mind regained
And to her heart the baby strained,
She and other women there
Surveyed his body everywhere
To see he really was a boy.
They fondled him with double joy
Because a little man was he.
With swords a smith he came to be,
And sparks from helmets oft he struck.
His heart showed manliness and pluck.
The queen was full of blisses: 113
She showered him with kisses
And said, as if she could not cease,
"Bon fiz, scher fiz, bea fiz."[24]
</blockquote>

After praising Herzeloydë as a mother, Wolfram comments as an afterthought upon a criticism raised against him for censuring a woman who has proved untrue to him. (113, 5—114, 4)

<blockquote>

Whoso of women speaketh praise,   114
Thereto I no objection raise:
I'd welcome joys that they can know.
To one, however, I would show
No service, no, nor loyalty:
My wrath must e'er undying be   10
Gainst her, who faithfulness doth lack.
I am Wolfram von Eschenbach,
And I know how to sing good songs,
And I am like a pair of tongs
That hold a deep resentment tight
Against her who put such despite
Upon both me and honor too
That hate from me must be her due.
For this the others wish me ill:
Alas that that's my portion still.   20
Yet though their hate is grief to me,
In them true womanhood I see,
</blockquote>

Since I indeed have spoke amiss
And thus endangered my own bliss;
Belike that won't occur again.
But let them not o'erhasty strain
To storm my home defences now:
For stout defence they must allow.
For I have not my skill forgot,
The measure now as then I wot
Of both their manner and their style.   115
She who is chaste and without guile,
Her champion I'll gladly be:
I much regret her grief to see.

   That man enjoys a spavin'd fame
Who gives all women a bad name
To please the one he would select.
The fair one who will but inspect
My case, and see and hear me,
Will find deceit not near me.   10
To me bold chivalry is dear,
And where my powers weak appear,
The one who loves me for my song,
Methinks her wits are going wrong.
If I for love of woman yearn,
Yet fail with lance and shield to earn
By rights of her true love reward,
Let her scant praise to me accord.
That knight doth play for highest stakes
Who knightly love his ambition makes.   20

   If the fair won't call it flattery,
I'd like to tell, if you agree,
More of this tale, unknown to you,
And these adventures brave and new.
But whoso my account will brook,
Let him not think I made a book.
I know no single book-stave,
Though plenty over letters slave.
And this adventure story
Takes not from books its glory.
Ere one should murmur 'book' to me,   116
I'd rather wholly naked be
While sitting in my bath at ease—
But with a fig-leaf, if you please.

Book Three
Parzival's Youth

Book Three

PARZIVAL'S YOUTH

Wolfram opens the book with observations on women and their loyalty and praises Herzeloydë for her fidelity and renunciation of wealth and position. (116, 5—117, 6)

<pre>
         She left her land in steadfast woe   117
      And to a forest chose to go;
      Soltanë's[1] desert land she sought,
      To fields and flowers not giving thought.   10
      Her grief of heart was so entire,
      For flower-wreaths she'd no desire,
      Were they of red or yellow hue.
      She took there, with his weal in view,
      Of Gahmuret the noble son.
      The folk that she as servants won
      Must farm each forest clearing.
      With skill she went on rearing
      Her son. Ere he became aware
      Of life, she trained the servants there   20
      And warned them all, both man and wife,
      That they should ne'er, on pain of life,
      Refer to knights or knighthood bold.
      "If my dear child were ever told
      Of knights and knightly station,
      'Twould be my ruination.
      I bid you now, be keen and shrewd
      And tell him naught of knightlihood."
         With care they did as bidden,
      Such things from him were hidden.
      In bleak Soltanë reared, he heard   118
      Of royal pomp no single word.
      One knightly art he came to know,
      Little arrows and a bow
      He cut with hands that well were skilled,
      And many birds he shot and killed.
      But when a little bird was slain,
      Whose song had rung so loud and plain,
      He wept aloud and tore his hair:
      It had the punishment to bear.   10
</pre>

He had a proud and stately look,
And on the meadows by the brook
He washed himself each morrow
And had no thought of sorrow,
But for the birdsong in the air,[2]
Whose sweetness filled his heart with care
And rent his little breast apart.
All weeping to the queen he'd dart,
And she would say, "Who injured thee?
Thou wast but out upon the lea."
But why it was he could not say:
Thus children act in our own day.
The cause she long was tracing.
One day she saw him facing
The treetops, whence the birdsong welled.
She saw his breast and how it swelled
With joy to hear the twittering song:
This to his nature must belong.
His mother turned a hate-filled eye
Upon all birds, she knew not why.
Their singing now she planned to still.
The herdsmen all and those who till,
She bade them hasten everywhere
And all the birds to catch and snare.
The birds were better mounted,
On death some never counted:
Full many kept on winging
And still made merry singing.
   The queen was questioned by her son:
"What is it the birds have done?"
He asked for their protection.
She kissed him with affection:
"What right to thwart His will have I,
Since He's the mighty God on high?
Should birds for my sake give up joy?"
Then said to her the little boy,
"O Mother, what is God, I pray?"
"My son, I'll tell thee straightaway.
The sun itself is not so bright
As He, who forfeited His might
To take the shape of humankind.

Son, this teaching bear in mind:
Pray to God in need and dearth:
His love helps all who dwell on earth.
There's one that's called the lord of hell:
He's black, and falseness knows him well.
Of him refrain from thinking,
From wavering doubt be shrinking."
His mother taught him well to mark
The difference twixt light and dark.³
The lad then sped the plain to win.   **120**
He learned to hurl the javelin,
And many a stag he thus destroyed,
Which queen and servants much enjoyed.
Regardless of the thaw or snow,
His shooting caused the game much woe.
By this be now astounded:
When so much game he'd grounded
As e'en a mule might hardly bear,
He'd bear it home undressed from there.   10
   One day upon a hunt he went
Along a slope of long extent
And plucked a twig, its leaf to blow,⁴
Near where a path was seen to go.
The sound of hoof-beats struck his ear
And he began to poise his spear:
"What noise have I been hearing?
What if the devil were nearing
In fury, doing evil?
I know I'd best the devil.   20
Mother speaks of him with fright,
I think her courage is but slight."
Thus did he stand inviting strife.
But look! here riding for dear life
Three knights approach, a handsome sight,
From head to foot in armor dight.
The lad conceived the notion odd
That each of them must be a god.
No longer then he stood at ease:
In the path he fell upon his knees
And loud he cried upon the Lord: **121**
"Help God! Thou canst help afford."

The foremost knight was moved to wrath
To see this stripling in the path:
"This fool of Waleis, praying,
Our journey is delaying."
There's a trait we Bayers claim,
And the Valois are just the same:
More stupid than Bavarians, they[5]
Show manliness in any fray.   10
Whoe'er is born in either place
Leads the world in skill and grace.
  Now came with rein loose-flowing
And dazzling armor showing
A knight who was in utmost haste,
For in full armor he had raced
To catch those who had fled from thence:
Those two had snatched with violence
A lady shielded by his name;
The hero thought this might shame,   20
He must bewail the maiden's woe
Who far from him was forced to go.
These three comprised his knightly force.
He rode a fine Castilian horse,
his shield was pierced by many a lance.
His name was Karnahkarnanz[6]
Li cons Ulterlac.[7]
Said he, "Who would our passage block?"
He then dashed forward o'er the sod.
The lad thought: surely here's a god.
He'd never seen so bright a glow.   122
The surcoat brushed the dew below.
With little gilded tinkling bells
Before each leg, where footroom swells,
Well lengthened stirrups twinkled
And as he moved they tinkled.
His right arm likewise sounded
When moved or when it rebounded.
These bells should ring at every blow.
At seeking fame he was not slow.   10
Thus rode this prince so sightly,
Geared handsomely and brightly.

PARZIVAL'S YOUTH

The flower and paragon of men
Was asked by Karnahkarnanz then:
"Young sir, and didst thou see pass by
Two knights whose conduct must deny
Adherence to the knightly code?
They've ta'en a maid along this road
And have abandoned knightliness.
A stolen maid goes in distress." 20
The stripling thought, whate'er was said,
That this was God, as he was led
To think by Herzeloyd the queen,
Who spoke of heaven's dazzling sheen.
And so the stripling cried aloud,
"Help me, God with help endowed!"
O'er and o'er he down would get
To pray, this son of Gahmuret.
The rider said, "No God am I,
But His commands I don't deny.
Four knights before thee thou mayst see, 123
If right thine eyesight seems to be."
The lad continued then to say,
"Thou namest knights. What's that, I pray?
If thou'st not godly fortitude,
Then tell me, who gives knightlihood?"
"By royal Arthur that is done.
Young sir, when his house thou'st won,
Then he will give thee knightly name,
The which will never cause thee shame. 10
Thou mayst well be of knightly state."
The heroes eyed the candidate
And saw in him God's artistry.
The story hath disclosed to me
And doth with truthfulness attest:
This youngster was the handsomest
That ever lived since Adam's days,
And widely women sang his praise.
   Now once more the stripling spoke,
A peal of laughter to evoke: 20
"Ah, thou Knight-God, what mayst thou be?
So many a finger-ring[8] I see

Upon thee fixed, with wonder,
Up yonder and here under."
At that the boy began to feel
Whate'er he saw of polished steel:
The armor he was eyeing.
"My mother's maids keep trying
To carry rings on little chains
Where each one separate remains."
The boy inquired in childish mood,   **124**
"For what is such apparel good
To make thy clothing be of use?
I cannot pry these rings here loose."
The knight then showed his mighty blade:
"Now see, if an attack is made,
I fight the foe with heavy blows,
But his I ward off with these clothes:
Lest I by shots and stabs be harmed
There's need for me to be well armed."   **10**
At once the eager lad replied:
"If stags were dressed in such a hide,
They could resist my javelin.
Full many a one has slaughtered been."
   This long delay they must resent
With one so much on folly bent.
The prince: "May God watch over thee!
Thy comeliness I'd crave for me.
By God with sheer perfection blessed
Thou'dst be if thou but wit possessed.   **20**
God's power keep from thee all woe."
The three and he away did go:
In haste they soon were nearing
A spacious forest clearing.
The hero,[9] never shirking,
Found plows and tillers working.
The queen's men ne'er had grieved as now.
He saw them till the soil and plow:
Some harrowed where before they'd sowed,
And powerful oxen did they goad.
"Good morning!" said Karnahkarnanz   **125**
And asked them if they'd seen by chance

A maiden who was suffering woe.
The answer they could not forego,
His question might not be gainsaid:
"Aye, sir, two knights, with them a maid
Passed here this morning riding,
The maid her grief not hiding.
They plied the steeds with whip and spur,
The knights that were abducting her." 10
The knight was Sir Meljakanz,[10]
O'ertaken by Karnahkarnanz,
Who won from him the maid in strife:
With sadness had her fate been rife.
Her name was Imanë
From the Beafontanë.

   The peasants were despairing
That knights were past them faring:
"O what unhappy fate!" they cried,
"For if our squire has now espied 20
Upon those knights the helmets rent,
We shall have proven negligent.
The queen will now be wroth, we fear,
And well-deserved rebuke we'll hear,
For out to join us here he leapt
This morning while his mother slept."
The lad now showed no zest at all
For hunting stags, or large or small:
He went back to his mother soon.
When told, she fell into a swoon:
His words gave her a shock so sore, **126**
She lay unconscious on the floor.
When now the queen, sore grieving,
Her senses was retrieving,
She craved to know, however grave
Her grief might be: "Son, who gave
Thee tidings of the knightly way?
Whence hast thou this knowledge, pray?"
"Four men, Mother, spoke to me,
God's radiance could not brighter be. 10
They told me how to be a knight.
King Arthur's royal power and might,

The knightly rites pursuing,
Shall grant me knightly doing."
With that, fresh anguish plagued her now:
The lady knew not rightly how
A stratagem she might invent
To foil her son in his intent.
  This simple youth of noble seed
Now teased his mother for a steed.
Though mourning in her heart, she thought:
" 'Tis better I refused him naught,
But worthless it must be, and mean."
And further pondered then the queen:
"For mockery many show a flair:
Fool's attire my son shall wear
Upon his body sound and trim.
If they should pound and pummel him
He may come back to me again."
Alas, what grief and heartfelt pain!
The lady took some sackcloth stout
And cut a shirt and breeches out,
One single piece—his legs below
Were bare. Now everyone might know
The fool by cloth and garb he wore.
A dunce-cap on his head he bore.
A fresh rough calfskin did she use
To cut him out a pair of shoes:
These to his legs were fitted.
Great grief was not omitted.
The queen was fain to do the right,
She begged her son to stay that night:
"From hence thou'lt not be starting
Till counsel I'm imparting.
On paths without a clearing
Shun fords opaque appearing,
But where the shallow stream is clear
Thou mayst cross without a fear.
Be mannerly and pleasant
And greet whoe'er is present,
And when a man who's wise and gray
Would teach decorum, as he may,
Show zeal in him obeying,

Rude anger not displaying.
Son, now heed another thing:
If thou a goodly woman's ring
Canst win from her with her consent,
Take it: that's cure for discontent.
To give her kisses make all haste,
Her body tightly be embraced:
That gives thee joy and gladsome mood,   128
Provided she is chaste and good.
And thou shouldst know, son of mine,
That proud and haughty Laeheline
Has wrested from thy lords two lands
Which ought to serve thy royal hands:
Waleis and Norgal.
Thy prince, the lord of Turkental,
Won death of him in mortal feud,
Who drove thy folk to servitude."   10
"I'll venge this, Mother, an God will:
My javelin will wound him still."
   When morning came and night declined
The lad had soon made up his mind:
With speed to Arthur was his plan.
She kissed him and after him she ran.
The world ne'er knew a greater blight.
When she had lost her son from sight
(Away he rode, who likes that well?),
This faithful, loving woman fell   20
To earth, where grief, a savage knife,
So cut her that it took her life.
Her death, in sweet devotion's name,
Will spare her soul the hellish flame.
She was a mother, praise the Lord,
And walked the way of rich reward,
A root of kind docility,
A tree of true humility.
Alas that to us are not lent
Her kinfolk in direct descent![11]
No wonder falseness now is rife.   129
Each woman true, each faithful wife,
Should bless this stripling bold and fair

Who now forsakes his mother's care.
  Now the youth of promise grand
The forest sought of Breceliand [12]
And reached a brook within a dell
So shoal, a cock might cross it well.
But since there flowers and grass grew low
And shaded thus the water's flow,   10
To ford it no desire he showed:
All day along the stream he rode,
Just as his poor wit deemed it good.
He spent the night as best he could
Until the bright sun brought the day,
And then again he made his way
Till a good crossing was revealed.
Beyond the stream within a field
A handsome tent[13] he could detect,
With richest trappings 'twas bedecked: 20
'Twas velvet and of threefold hue
And high and very spacious too.
Sewed to the seams were edgings good,
Near it hung a leathern hood
In case of rain pulled over
The tent to shield and cover.
  Duke Orilus de Lalander,[14]
His wife untouched by slander
He found there sweetly lying,
With any richness vieing:
She seemed a knightly beauty.   130
Her own name was Jeschutë.[15]
The lady now was napping,
Revealing *Minnë's* trapping:
Two glowing lips like fire,
A love-sick knight's desire.
While the lady soundly slept,
Her red lips from each other crept
And showed the heat of *Minnë's* stress.
Thus lay ideal happiness.   10
There, snow-white, all sweetly
Assembled e'er so neatly,
Her shining, dainty teeth were set.

No one's accustomed me as yet
To kissing lips so passing fair:
To me that's pleasure more than rare.
Low had her sable cover dropped,
It reached her hips and there it stopped:
Through warmth she had it from her thrown
When by her lord left all alone. 20
Well-sculptured and well-formed was she,
In her was spared no artistry:
God wrought her form, with beauty blest.
Likewise the lovely one possessed
Long arms and hands and fingers white.
The lad now of a ring caught sight
Which drew him to the lady's side,
With whom a struggle now he tried,[16]
Remembering his mother's word
That a lady's ring should be preferred.
What's more, the handsome stripling sped **131**
To quit the rug and seek the bed.

  The sweet, chaste one woke with alarm
To find this stripling in her arm:
She must perforce awaken.
With shame, not laughter, shaken,
The lady, gently bred and chaste,
Said, "Who has now my name disgraced?
Young sir, 'tis far too much for you,
You should have other goals in view." 10
With loud lament she pleaded.
Her words he never heeded
But kissed her mouth with pressure strong,
Whereafter 'twas not very long
Until he crushed her to his breast
A ring from off her hand to wrest.
A brooch that on her shirt she wore
He crudely from the garment tore.
She fought with but a woman's might:
As well with a whole army fight. 20
Yet long they struggled on and strained.
Of hunger then the youth complained.
The lady, fair of skin was she:

She said, "I pray you, eat not me!
If you were wise for your own good
You'd find yourself some other food.
I've over there some bread and wine;
On two small partridge you can dine
With which a maid here wended.
They weren't for you intended."
    The hostess now was quite ignored.   **132**
His crop with food he filled and stored
And then he drank great draughts and strong.
The lady thought that far too long
He tarried in the tent with her.
It was a lad, she must infer,
That from his wits had parted.
With shame she sweat and smarted.
Yet she spoke admonishing:
"Squire, do not take my finger-ring   10
From me, and leave my brooch behind.
Begone! If you my lord should find
You'd smart for what he must resent
And this you'd surely fain prevent."
The well-born lad exclaimed with cheer,
"What, I your husband's anger fear?
But if disgraced I make you,
Why then I'll now forsake you."
Forthwith he stepped to where she lay:
Another kiss was giv'n that day.   20
The duchess grieved at that anew.
He left her, bidding no adieu,
But said, "May God your shepherd be,
For thus my mother counselled me."

Parzival leaves Jeschutë, and soon thereafter her husband Orilus returns. He notices her excitement and, realizing that an intruder has been with her, suspects her of infidelity. Meanwhile Parzival proceeds on his journey and finds Sigunë, holding in her lap the body of her lover, Schionatulander, who has just been slain by Orilus. Sigunë, it develops, is the daughter of Herzeloydë's sister and therefore a close relative of Parzival. She tells him about his family. Parzival continues his journey. (132, 25—142, 10)

Parzival's Youth

The evening was descending,
Great tiredness toward him wending,
And now this lad, still far from wise,
Beheld a house of moderate size.
Here dwelt a stingy host and mean,
As mid the lowly oft are seen.[17]
He spent the days in fishing,
To men no goodness wishing.
The lad's great hunger taught him
This course, that there he sought him   20
To speak of hunger to this oaf.
The host replied, "Not half a loaf
I'd give to you in thirty years.
Whoever at my door appears
To beg of me, in vain's his quest:
I only heed my interest
And then my children's, nothing more.
Today you'll enter not my door.
If you had coin or other pay,
Why then I'd welcome you to stay."
Thereon some pay he offered: 143
Jeschuté's brooch he proffered.
When this sight on the peasant broke,
His lips first smiled and then he spoke:
"Sweet child, if thou with us wilt bide,
We'll honor thee, all we inside."
"If thou wilt feed me well today,
Tomorrow telling me the way
To Arthur (him I'm fain to see)
This golden brooch will stay with thee."   10
"That will I," said the peasant.
"Ne'er saw I form so pleasant.
I'll bring thee, sure thou wilt astound,
To stand before the Table Round."
That night the stripling tarried there,
The morrow saw him otherwhere.
The dawn he scarce awaited.
The peasant hesitated
No whit, the stripling to precede
Upon his horse: both craved for speed.   20

My Lord Hartman von Auë,[18] hear:
Unto your Lady Guinevere
And to your lord King Arthur's court
A guest of mine will now report.
I beg, shield him from mockery!
He is no rote, no fiddle he:
Some other dupe let them annoy
And show good breeding to this boy!
Or else your Dame Enitë[19]
And her mother Karsnafitë
Will through my mill be tumbled,   144
Their fame abased and humbled.
If I with scorn my mouth must rend,
My friend with scorn I will defend.

  His way the fisher wended,
With him the stripling splendid;
A chief town they were nighing,
'Twas Nantes they were espying.
Said he, "Child, God with thee abide.
Look yonder, thou must ride inside."   10
The squire remarked with lack of wit,
"O lead me closer still to it!"
"May that not come into my mind!
That retinue's of such a kind,
If e'er a peasant should encroach,
His presence would incur reproach."
Alone the squire now had to ride
Upon a meadow not too wide,
With flowers studded bright and gay.
No Curvenal[20] could guide the way.   20
Of *courtoisie* he had no thought:
Of this untravelled men know naught.
His reins were made of simple bast,
His horse was feeble and not fast:
It stumbled oft and took a fall.
His saddle also over all
Its surface was not new of leather.
Of satin, ermine soft as feather,
Not much of that on him was spied,
Nor need his mantle e'er be tied.

Surcoat and mantelet he spurned,   **145**
And to his javelin he turned.
His father, e'er a model knight,
Better far was he bedight
When he at Kanvoleiz[21] appeared.
No man alive by him was feared.
A knight rode forward him to meet
And heard, as he'd been taught to greet:
"God keep you! so my mother would do."
"Squire, God reward both her and you."   10
King Arthur's cousin's son thus said,
By Utepandragun[22] well bred.
He claimed that by heredity
He was the lord of Brittany,
Ither of Kahaviez named,
And as the Red Knight widely famed.
  So red his armor was in hue,
Eyes seeing it were reddened too.
His charger red had hoofs that sped,
Its headpiece was of flaming red.   20
Velvet red his blanket showed,
His shield more red than fire glowed;
Red his coat of mail was dyed,
Cut not too snugly, not too wide.
His shaft was red, his spear the same,
And so, to suit the hero's aim,
His goodly sword was reddened,
But the blade in color leadened.
This monarch of Kukumerland[23]
A red-gold beaker held in hand,
Its sides with rich engraving crowned,   **146**
Taken from the Table Round.
His skin was white, his hair was red.
Speaking like a friend, he said,
"I praise thy body sweet, thy worth:
A woman pure brought thee to earth.
God bless her who gave birth to thee:
Such goodliness I ne'er did see.
Of true love thou'rt the sight complete,
Her victory and her defeat.   10

Much joy in women wilt thou find,
Though later for them thou'lt have pined.
Dear friend, if thither[24] thou'dst repair,
For my sake do apprize them there
And tell the king, tell every knight
That I have taken not to flight.
I'll gladly wait here, trusting
To face some knight in jousting:
There's naught in this that should astound.
I rode before the Table Round   20
To take possession of my land.[25]
This goblet then my awkward hand
Snatched up, so that the wine by hap
Splashed Guinevere and wet her lap.
My ownership I'd thus assert.
Should I a torch of straw invert,[26]
My hand with soot would be unclean;
I spurned that," said the fighter keen.
"Nor have I stolen anything:
I need not steal, for I'm a king.
Friend, tell the queen no harm was meant, **147**
I spilled the wine by accident
Among the worthy knights who gazed
And not a hand in protest raised.
Kings they and princes, ranking first,
Why should they leave their host to thirst?
Why come they not the cup to claim?
They forfeit else their glorious fame."
  The squire replied, "I will report
Thy words, repeat them to the court."   10
He rode for Nantes to see the king
With many pages following;
In courtyard where the palace loomed
The air with din and bustle boomed.
A throng now gathered all around.
Iwanet[27] neared with many a bound:
This squire, free of falsity,
Offered his escort now to be.
The stripling said, "God keep thee aye:
My mother taught me thus to say   20

Before I bade her last good-bye.
Now many an Arthur here I spy.
Who'll make me knight, I wonder?"
Iwanet laughed at his blunder:
"Thou seest not the right one here,
But soon before him thou'lt appear."
He led him to the palace hall
And found there knights and vassals all.
Amid the din his voice he raised:
"God keep you all, may you be praised,
But most the king, his wife no less.   148
On me my mother did impress
They should be chiefly greeted,
And all those rightly seated
At Table Round through chivalry,
She bade me greet them heartily.
But one thing here impedes me most:
I know not which of you is host.
To him a message I would bear
From one, all crimson in his wear,   10
Who'd wait for him out yonder.
A joust he seemed to ponder,
And with regret the knight is filled
That wine upon the queen he spilled.
O my, could I his harness own,
Bestowed by the king upon his throne!
My joy would be unsparing,
Such knightly harness wearing."
  The carefree stripling zestful
Found little that was restful,   20
Was thrust and jostled to and fro:
They saw his handsome body glow.
By each one thus 'twas rated:
No lord nor dame created
Could match this lad in winsomeness.
God surely used his sweetest stress
In Parzival's creation,
Who knew no perturbation.
To Arthur thus the lad was brought
Whom God ideally had wrought.

No one but had to love the boy. **149**
The queen surveyed him too with joy
Before she left the palace floor
Where wine was spilled on her before.
Arthur eyed this squire uncouth
And greeted thus the simple youth:
"Squire, may your greeting please the Lord,
Which with my service I'll reward
In person and likewise in kind:
Such is the will I have in mind." 10
"Would God 'twere true what now I hear!
It seems as if I'd spend a year
In waiting to become a knight;
That casts on me a fearful blight.
No longer, prithee, hesitate:
Let me enjoy the knightly state."
"I'll do it gladly," said the host,
"Unless my worthiness I've lost.
Thou art so full of splendor
That with my gifts I'll render 20
Thee rich in every costliness.
For thee I'd fain do nothing less.
Now till the morrow thou must bide,
Then well for thee will I provide."
The well-born squire spoke up and said,
And like a bustard fidgeted,
"For nothing will I beg today.
A knight I met upon my way:
If I can't have his harness now
I'll heed no royal gift or vow.
Else from my mother gifts I'll gain: **150**
I'm certain she's of royal strain."
   King Arthur to reply began:
"This armor's carried by a man,
So that I dare not give it thee.
E'en so I suffer misery
Without my own defection,
Since lacking his affection.
'Tis Ither, he of Kahaviez,
Who's pierced with woe my joy and peace." 10

"Your generous name you would abuse
If such a gift you should refuse.
Grant him his wish!" said Keyë[28] free,
"Send him to Ither on the lea.
If someone should the goblet bring,
Well, there's the top and here's the string:
The child may do some spinning,[29]
High praise from women winning.
Full oft must he be jousting,
To chance his luck entrusting.   20
Their lives, if lost, I would not rue:
A boar's head's worth a dog or two."[30]
"I like not to gainsay him,
But fear the knight may slay him,
Whom I would help a knight to be,"
Said Arthur with benignity.
And yet the squire his boon received,
Wherefor a many later grieved.
He hastened now to leave the king,
And young and old went following.
Iwanet, leading, took his hand   151
And led him to a lowly stand
Where back and forward he could spy,
And since the place was far from high
He found that he could hear and see
What caused him heartfelt misery.
The queen herself would not delay
And toward a window made her way
With knights and ladies thronging:
They soon looked on with longing.   10
There sat Dame Cunnewarë,[31] too,
So proud and beautiful to view.
She would not laugh in any wise
Till him she'd see who the highest prize
Had won, or would some day deserve.
She'd die ere from this will she'd swerve.
No laughing mood came o'er her
Till this lad rode before her:
Now laughed her lovely mouth in glee,[32]
That caused her back some agony.   20

For Steward Keyë, strong of hand,[33]
Seized Cunnewarë de Laland
All by her fair locks curly.
Her long braids then that surly
Warrior twisted round his hand
And tightened without iron band.[34]
Upon her back no oath was staved,[35]
Yet so on it a staff behaved
That ere its whizzing ceased to sound
Through clothes and skin a way it found.
This man unwise said loudly,   **152**
"The fame you bear so proudly
Your folly now dispatches:
But I'm the net that catches.
I'll pound it into you again,
Your limbs shall sense it by their pain.
See, to King Arthur there has come
Into his court, into his home,
So many a mounted knight, well fit;
On them you never laughed one whit,   10
And now your laugh is given a man
Who knows no knightliness, nor can."
In anger curious things occur.
The right to flog and punish her
Had never won the realm's consent,
And all her kin raised loud lament.
Though she'd no right to bear a shield,
'Twas hateful that she had to yield,
For she was born of princely line.
If Orilus and Laeheline,   20
Her brothers twain, had but been there,
No second blow she'd had to bear.

    Antanor,[36] who by choice was mute
And therefore had a fool's repute—
His speech and Cunnewarë's glee
Both sprang from one necessity:
Antanor his first word would say
When she laughed who was flogged today.
Now when her laughter had been heard
To Keyë then he said this word:

"Steward, God doth understand 153
That Cunnewarë de Laland
Was flogged because of yonder squire.
Your glee will turn to sorrow dire:
One day he'll make you stumble,
And were he ne'er so humble."
"Since your first speech is threatening,
Small joy, I think, to you 'twill bring."
His hide then got a tanning,
A thrashing and a panning: 10
This fool, less dumb than he appears,
Got fistlike whispers in his ears:
Thus Keyë smote without delay,
And Parzival, in great dismay,
Must see in plight so sorry
Antanor and Cunnewarë.
Their pain he pitied and chagrin:
Oft reached he for his javelin.
Throngs round the queen were swirling,
So he refrained from hurling. 20
And now his leave took Iwanet
From this young son of Gahmuret,
Who all alone went out to see
Knight Ither waiting on the lea.
To him he proffered this report,
That not a knight at Arthur's court
Would joust with him undaunted.
"My plea the king has granted.
I told him what thou saidst to me,
That thou without malignity
The wine-cup hast upsetted 154
With awkwardness regretted.
They all from strife are hiding.
Give me whereon thou'rt riding,
The harness too to me is owed,
For by the king it was bestowed:
In it, knight's honor will I earn.
I'll greet thee not, thy name will spurn,
If thou to give art not inclined.
Yield now if thou'st not lost thy mind." 10

The ruler of Kukumerland
Declared: "In case King Arthur's hand
Bestowed on thee my knightly dress,
He'd give my life to thee no less,
If all these trophies thou couldst win.
This shows thee how he loves his kin.[37]
Has he ere now been kind to thee?
Thy service soon its pay doth see."
"I dare deserve whate'er he pay,
And he's fulfilled my wish today.   20
Give here, thy silly talk forego:
No longer servitude I'll know,
Henceforth I crave to be a knight."
He seized the reins and held them tight:
"I think thou art that Laeheline[38]
Whom Mother called a foe of mine."
The knight reversed his lance's length[39]
And smote the lad with so much strength
That he and his frail steed as well
Perforce amid the flowers fell.
Sir Ither, quick in ire,   155
So stoutly smote the squire
That from his skin the shaft drew blood.
Parzival, the stripling good,
Stood all wrathful on the plain,
His javelin gripped with might and main.
Where helmet's end and beard-piece met
And against the ringed cap were set,
The javelin sped through his eye
And neck, so Ither had to die,   10
Who was the foe of false pretence.[40]

With the help of Iwanet, who must come to his aid, Parzival now strips Ither's body of its trappings and armor and appropriates these, as well as Ither's horse, as prizes allotted to him by King Arthur. He races the horse onward at breakneck speed until he reaches the well cultivated fields of Gurnemanz. (155, 12—161, 30)

"The tilling," so the young fool spoke,   162
"Is not so good mid Mother's folk.
So high their crops will never grow:

Whate'er in clearings they may sow,
Too heavy are the rains they boast."
Gurnemanz de Graharz was the host,
To his castle he was heading.
There stood a linden spreading
Upon a meadow green with grass:
Not longer nor more wide it was
Than suits a well-proportioned mead.
The highway and his doughty steed
Now bore him where he seated found
The man who owned both house and ground.
So tired he and all unstrung
That faultily his shield he swung
Too far before him or behind
And was to knightly customs blind
Which people hereabout adored.
Alone sat Gurnemanz, the lord,
The linden duly casting
Its shadows deep and lasting
Upon this chief of men well-bred.
He who from falseness always fled
Received the guest: such was his right.
With him no vassal was nor knight.
Parzival in his simple way
Replied to him without delay,
"Go seek advice, my mother said,
Of one with gray hair on his head.
In such desire I come to you,
Because my mother told me to."
"If counsel's your endeavor,
I must crave your favor
Upon the counsel I shall give
If you accordingly would live."
   The noble prince then jolted
A sparrow-hawk just moulted
From his hand. Inside it swang.
A golden bell upon it rang:[41]
This was a messenger; there came
Young men of good and noble name.
He bade them now escort the guest

Inside and give him a chance to rest.
Said he, "My mother I believe:
An old man's words will ne'er deceive."
Forthwith the honored guest was led
Where many worthy knights well-bred
At court had been together brought:
"Dismount," he was by all besought.　　　　20
His words showed his simplicity:
"A king has bid me knight to be;
Whatever fate for me's decreed,
I must decline to quit my steed.
My mother bade me greet each sir."
Thereon they thanked both him and her.
The greetings having run their course—
The man was tired, no less the horse—,
With pleas they all besought him
Ere from his horse they brought him
Into a room for resting.　　　　164
Then all began requesting:
"Doff your harness, fighter,
And let your limbs feel lighter."
　　Disarmed was he without ado.
But when they saw his coarse calf-shoe
And his fool's clothing scrutinized,
Those serving him were scandalized.
They told it in bewilderment,
The host was sick with embarrassment.　　　　10
Then a knight in courtly things astute
Said, "Truly, such a noble fruit
Has never blessed my seeing eyes:
In him ideal beauty lies,
With lofty breeding, pure and sweet;
How could they such a form maltreat?
I'm sick that such a paragon
Has such a silly raiment on.
Well for her that gave him birth:
He has enough of highest worth.　　　　20
His trappings all are sightly,
His harness looked most knightly
Ere his beauty was uncovered.

But on him I discovered
A bruise all stained and bloody
Inflicted by somebody."
The host thereon the knight addressed:
"'Tis worn at some fair dame's behest."
"Sir, no, for so he has been bred
That ne'er with a lady he'd have pled
That she accept his duty." **165**
"But for love he has the beauty,"
Said the host, "let us go and see
This man who's clothed so curiously."
   They went forthwith astounded
To Parzival as wounded
By Ither's yet unbroken lance:
Good care had he from Gurnemanz.
So fond was his attention,
No father could we mention, **10**
However fond and tender,
Who greater care could render:
The host himself now washed and bound
With loving care the stripling's wound.
And now the table had been spread;
The youthful guest felt need of bread,
For hunger great would he allay:
Fasting that morn he'd rid away,
Nor at the fisher's ate he.
His wound, his harness weighty, **20**
Which he at Nantes had acquired,
Increased his hunger, made him tired,
Not less his journeying wearily
From Arthur's court in Brittany,
Since everywhere he'd had to fast.
Now with his host he ate at last.
Rightly the guest refreshment craved,
And at the crib he so behaved[42]
That much food vanished from their sight.
The host saw this with some delight.
Gurnemanz, the kind and good, **166**
Egged on his guest in eager mood,
His appetite thus whetting,

To eat, fatigue forgetting.
　The board was raised at mealtime's end.⁴³
"I think you are fatigued, my friend;
"You woke betimes?" the host now said.
"My mother still had been in bed:
She can't stand such long waking."
The host, with laughter shaking,　　　　　　10
Now showed him to a room with bed
And bade him all his clothes to shed.
Perforce he did, though with regret.
A handsome ermine coverlet
Upon his naked form was spread:
A finer ne'er was born and bred.
Fatigue and sleep now held him bound,
And hardly once he turned around
To sleep upon the other side:
The daybreak thus he could abide.　　　　　20
And now the worthy prince took care
To bid his folk a bath prepare
About the mid of morn that day
Upon a rug near where he lay:
Each morning this must needs be done.
Into the bath were roses thrown.
Although the folk strict silence kept,
The guest awoke, as there he slept.
This worthy, sweet young man now sat
Him down inside the waiting vat.
　I know not who requested:　　　　　　**167**
Maidens⁴⁴ richly vested
And radiant in beauty
Entered for decorous duty.
Massaging him, they smoothed away
The bruise that on his body lay
With soft hands white and slender:
Home-feeling they could tender
Him, orphaned of all worldly sense;
His joy and easement were intense.　　　　10
They found his innocence not misplaced.
Maidens pert but truly chaste
Nursed him without cessation;

Whate'er their conversation,
'Twas not for him a word to say.
It seemed to him 'twas brightest day,
For they were like a sunshine bright,
And thus twin suns appeared to fight.
His beauty made them both seem dim:
There was no lack of that in him.
He was given a towel as cover
But would not slip it over:
Before these maids he felt such shame,
To dress before them were a blame.
The maidens had to go away,
No longer with him might they stay.
Methinks they would have liked to know
If he'd been injured down below,[45]
For women's love is generous:
They grieve when sorrow comes to us.

    And now the guest walked to the bed
Where shining raiment lay outspread:[46]
A belt of silk and yellow gold,
The breeches round the waist to hold.
Trousers of scarlet a squire drew
On him who naught but courage knew:
My, but his legs in them looked well!
Of handsome shape his limbs could tell.
Of darker red and modish fit
(Fur lining they did not omit
In both of snow-white ermine fur)
His flowing coat and mantle were.
A sable border, broad, black, gray,
Did these habiliments display.
His dressing being ended,
The noble hero splendid
Was with a handsome belt arrayed;
On it a buckle was displayed
Most costly, gracing his attire;
His lips the while burned red as fire.
The host in friendliness now nighed
And then the knights in lordly pride.
Now first the prince received the guest

And then the knights their views expressed:
On such a form they'd never gazed.
With warmth the woman they all praised
Who'd borne such fruit exceeding:
Truly, with courtly breeding
They said, "Where his endeavor
Is turned, he will find favor.
Both love and greeting he can gain: 169
May he enjoy his worthy reign!"
Each one for him made such a claim,
And later all men said the same.
   The host, with sociable intent,
Now took his hand and with him went;
The glorious prince then asked the lad
If sleep refreshing he had had
That night as there he rested.
"Sir, I'd have been divested   10
Of life, had not my mother sent
Me here, when from her house I went.[47]
May God reward you both, my lord:
To me great kindness you afford."
The witless lad now went along
Where hymns to God and host were sung.
At mass the host could teach him
How greater joy might reach him
If he himself would cross and bless
And foil the devil's viciousness.   20
When for the great hall now they made,
The table was already laid.
Beside the prince his host he ate
With zest the food upon his plate.
In courtly wise the host said this:
"Sir, pray you take it not amiss
If I should ask you whither
You rode as you came hither."
He told him how away he rode
And left his mother and her abode,
And of Jeschuté's ring and pin,   170
And how the armor he could win.
The host knew Ither well, the red,

And sighed, and mourned the hero dead,
Nor failed to tell the guest his name
And how the Red Knight he became.
  Now when the table was folded,
Wild ways were tamed and moulded.
The host forthwith the lad addressed:
"You speak just like a child, my guest.   10
Why of "mother" always chatter?
Seek out some other matter.
Henceforth counsel take from me,
Of mischief then you will be free.
This is the first: Be this your aim,
Ne'er sacrifice your sense of shame.
Without it, man's a worthless dolt,
A bird that must incessant moult:
His worthiness forsakes him,
To hell he soon betakes him.   20
You've beauty and nobility,
A people's leader you can be.
If high your race and rises higher,
To this then let your will aspire:
Compassion show to men in need,
Assuage their grief by word and deed
With kindness, generosity,
And cultivate humility.
A worthy person when distressed
By shame is oftentimes oppressed,
And bitter grief is then his lot: 171
'Twould be unkind to help him not.
If you will lighten such men's woe
His favor God to you will show:
They suffer even greater ills
Than those who beg at window-sills.
In proper manner and degree
Show riches both and poverty.[48]
A lord who's prone to squander
From lordliness doth wander,   10
But if excessive wealth he hoard
He will disgrace the name of lord.
Respect true moderation.

It's been my observation
That counsel you are needing.
Abandon boorish breeding.
From too much questioning refrain,[49]
But proper answer ne'er disdain
When asked, and speak out fairly
To meet all questions squarely, 20
If men would know what sort you be.
For you can hear and you can see,
And you can taste and you can smell:
All this should wake your wits full well.
Let pity be with courage blent:
Thus show regard for my intent.
When once a foe's surrendered,
Unless such woe he's tendered
That lasting grief your heart must know,
Accept surrender, let him go.
Right often weapons you must bear; 172
When laid aside, then wash with care
Your face and hands of dirt and dust
That comes from iron's grimy rust,
Then meet for love is your beauty rare.
Of this all women are aware.
Be manly, show men cheerfulness,
The world's good will you'll then possess.
Let women all be dear to you,
Then a young man's worth is higher too. 10
Toward women never fickle be,
For that's true manhood's quality.
If falsehood you'd be trying,
You'll win some hearts by lying;
But falsehood will not triumph long
Where true affection waxes strong.
Dry twigs upon the forest ground
Betray the thief who sneaks around:
Beneath his feet there breaking
They set the guard to waking. 20
In trackless spots, on rough detour,
Full many a strife you may endure—
Likeness to love you'll here detect.

Pure love itself can well protect
Gainst falsity and lying word.
If love's disfavor you've incurred,
Dishonor will be yours to face,
You'll always suffer keen disgrace.
This lesson take to heart and mind.
I'll tell you more of womankind.
Man and woman are but one,   173
As the sun which just has shone
Goes with the name and thing called day:
They're never parted, come what may.
From but a single seed they grow:
Observe it well, the truth to know."
The guest in thanks performed a bow.
Of his mother he was silent now
In words, but not within his heart:
That's of a loyal man the part.   10
    The host, due thanks returning,
Said, "More you should be learning,
In knightly ways abiding.
O, how you came here riding![50]
Full many a shield do I recall
That hung more neatly on a wall[51]
Than yours from off your shoulder.
Now ere the day grows older
To yonder meadow let's repair
And knightly arts I'll teach you there.   20
Bring him his steed, bring mine to me,
And mounted all the knights shall be.
The squires shall also join the throng,
And each of them shall bring along
A lance whose shaft is strong and true,
A lance that is unused and new."
The prince departed for the field,
Where horsemanship was first revealed.
He gave his guest the rules precise
To make his thighs grip like a vise
And with the aid of spurs that sting   174
To turn the steed when galloping
And forward dash upon the foe,

To bring his lance down somewhat low
And for the joust to chest his shield.
Said he, "Know how your arms to wield."
 He saved him thus from awkward slip
Far better than with supple whip
One breaks the skin of boys gone wrong.
And now he bade the knightly throng   10
To come and try the jousting.
He led the stripling trusting
To face a knight within the ring.
Such force to bear this youth did bring
That straightway through a shield he crashed—
From this they shrank and stood abashed—
And from his steed into the dust
A stout and sturdy knight he thrust.
Another jouster to advance
Made haste, and Parzival a lance   20
Picked up, both new and right in length.
O, but his youth had force and strength!
This young sweet lad without a beard,
His father's race his prowess steered,
And also inborn manliness.
Straight into gallop did he press
His horse and rode with all his might,
Keeping the shield's four nails in sight.⁵²
The other stayed not on his steed,
He fell and measured there the mead,
And from his lance the splinters there   175
They saw go flying through the air.
Thus five knights from their steeds he thrust;
The host then led him from the joust.
In sport this day he worked his will
And later grim frays showed his skill.
All those who saw him riding,
They found in him abiding
Both strength and great dexterity.
"Of worry now my lord is free,   10
Rejuvenated he can live.
As wife to him he ought to give
His daughter and our lady dear,

> If proper wit in him appear:
> Of all his grief he'll be relieved.
> For three dear sons whose death he's grieved
> This knight has now requited him,
> And no more joy has slighted him."

Gurnemanz introduces Parzival to his lovely daughter Liassë and hopes that he will accept her hand in marriage. This would compensate the unhappy host in part for the loss of his three sons. But Parzival puts this off to a time when he may have earned so high an honor, and leaves amid the lamentations of Gurnemanz. (175, 19—179, 12)

Book Four
Parzival and Condwiramur

Book Four

PARZIVAL AND CONDWIRAMUR

Parzival continues his journey aimlessly but filled with knightly ambition and much the wiser for Gurnemanz's teachings. Yet he also yearns for Liassë. (179, 13—180, 14)

  Little he rode astray,
Straight on and far away,
That day arriving from Graharz
Into the kingdom of Brobarz[1]
O'er mountain ranges wild and high.
The day was done and evening nigh.   20
He reached a stream of current strong,
And one could hear it rush along:
From rock to rock he saw it bound.
He rode adown it till he found
The town of Belrapeirë.[2]
The king, named Tampenteirë,
This town to his dear child had left:
Her numerous folk felt quite bereft.
Like bolts the water rushed and spumed,
Bolts that are neatly cut and plumed
And, placed upon a crossbow tense,   181
Are from its string directed thence.
A bridge across it led the way,
Upon which woven branches lay.
The stream was to the sea directed:
Belrapeirë was well protected.
Just as children rise so high
When a swing is made to fly,
Thus the ropeless bridge there swung,
But not because 'twas gay and young.   10
  Yonder, strong and sightly,
With helmets tied on tightly,[3]
Were sixty knights or even more.
"Turn back!" they shouted from the shore.
Their swords all vainly flailing,
They sought a battle ailing.[4]
Since oft they'd seen him there appear,

They thought that Clamidê was here,[5]
So royally he rode his horse
O'er the wide field, the bridge to cross.   20
So clamorous their cry and shout
Wherewith the youthful knight to rout,
Howe'er his rearing steed he spurred,
It shunned the bridge, by terror stirred.
This man who fear would never heed
Dismounted now and pulled his steed
Upon the bridge that swayed and swung.
A coward would have been unstrung
If into such a contest sent.
One thing besides he must prevent:
He feared his horse's falling.   182
The men now ceased their calling:
The bridge and shore these knights forsook,
Their helmets, shields, and swords they took,
Withdrew inside and closed the gate.
They feared an army strong and great.
   Thus crossing over, Parzival
Rode onward till he reached a wall
At which so many, seeking fame,
Had found that death had been their aim,   10
Out there before the portal wide
Of the castle high and fortified.
The portal bore a knocking-ring;
He pounded it with clattering,
But no one heeded or took a care
Except one maiden young and fair.
From out a window peered the maid
And saw our hero unafraid.
This sweet maid, rich in breeding,
Said, "If as foe proceeding   20
You come, sir, 'tis superfluous:
Without yours, hate has come to us
From off the land, from off the sea,
With strong and wrathful soldiery."
Said he, "My lady, here's a man
Who will serve you, if I can.
Your greeting my reward shall be;

PARZIVAL AND CONDWIRAMUR

Behold your loyal knight in me."
The prudent maid departed,
Before the queen she darted
And helped him gain an entrance there: 183
Ere long this saved them from despair.
To enter in he was allowed.
Along the streets he saw a crowd
Immense of fighters standing here
Equipped with all their battle-gear:
Slingers and skirmishers, each with bow,
Who stood there in extended row,
And javelin throwers he espied,
And there upon another side   10
Of lansquenets[6] a goodly host,
The very best the land could boast,
All with their lances sharp and long
And stoutly made and very strong.
If the story I've been told is true,
Full many a merchant stood there too
With axe and javelin in hand,
Whate'er their service might demand.
From hunger all of them were lean.
And now the marshal of the queen   20
Had trouble as he would escort
The knight through crowds into the court.
The court was well protected:
Towers o'er the rooms projected,
With bulwarks, gables, battlements
More numerous and more immense
Than he at any time had spied.
There came to him from every side
Knights to the stranger talking,
Some riding and some walking.
All this pitiable crew   184
Revealed a pale and ashen hue,
As though of yellow clay it be.
My lord, the Duke of Wertheim,[7] he
Would not have liked the service there:
He'd have starved on such a fare.
By hunger they were daunted,

Cheese, meat, and bread they wanted.
From picking teeth they long had ceased,
And with their lips they never greased[8] 10
The wine when they were drinking;
They found their bellies shrinking.
Their hips were high and very lean;
Like Magyar leather, shrivelled, mean,
The skin on their ribs was pasted,
Their flesh by hunger wasted.
From want they bore such suffering dire:
But little fat fell in their fire.
This brought on them a worthy man,
The haughty king of Brandigan: 20
Clamidê's suit thus wrought them ill.[9]
Mead[10] but seldom did they spill
From a two-handled jug or can.
A Trühendingen[11] stew-pan
With frying fritters rarely popped:
Long since had all such noises stopped.
If I'd reproach their need intense,
I'd show myself as lacking sense,
For where I've often sat at board
And where the servants call me lord,
I mean at home, in my own house, 185
There's not much fun for any mouse.
For mice their fodder have to steal,
And that's what no one need conceal:
E'en openly it's hid from me.
This happens all too frequently
To me, Wolfram von Eschenbach:
Such "comforts" rarely do I lack.[12]

   My many plaints have now been heard,
'Tis time my story had recurred 10
To Belrapeirë in grief immersed.
By joylessness the folk were cursed:
The heroes rich in loyalty
Were suffering bitter penury,
Impelled thereto by manliness.
Ye should bewail their dire distress:
Their very life is now at stake

Unless the Lord should pity take.
Of this unhappy city
I'll tell more, lend your pity. 20
Shamefaced the guest they greeted
To whom such strength was meted.
He seemed so worthy, anyway
He had no need of them to pray
A lodging, spite of all their woe:
Their great distress he did not know.
A rug upon the grass they laid
Where, walled and trained for better shade,
A linden tree spread branch and limb.
Of arms they now unburdened him.
He did not look the same as they 186
When once he'd washed the rust away
With water from a well near by:
He almost made the sun on high
Look pale, though it so brightly gleamed,
And hence a welcome guest he seemed.
Forthwith a cloak to him they bore
Of scarlet, like the cloak he wore
Before this town had met his view:
Its sable smelled both wild and new. 10
"Come see," said they in chorus,
"The lady ruling o'er us."
The hero bold and steady
Replied that he was ready.
Now to the palace he was bent,
Where up a lofty stairway went.
A lovely face all beaming bright
And eyes that shone with sweetest light,
This radiance issuing from the queen
Before she greeted him was seen. 20
   The Catalonian Kyot
And with him worthy Manpfilyot
(Each of them a duke and peer)
Had brought their brother's daughter[13] here
As queen o'er all the land to reign.
For love of God the noble twain
Their knightly swords had put away.

And now it was these princes gray,
But handsome men and worthy too,
Who led the queen with breeding true
Half down the stairs to meet him.   187
She kissed the knight to greet him;
Red lips each the other proffered,
Her hand the lady offered.
She now escorted Parzival
Till both were seated in the hall.
The ladies fair, the fighters good
Were weak and faint for lack of food.
Those standing there or sitting
All pleasure had been quitting,   10
The vassals and Condwiramur.[14]
With this young queen of high allure
No other maiden could compare,
Jeschutë or Enit the fair,
Or Cunnewarë de Laland;[15]
All those who the highest praise command
Where female beauty is admired
To no such merit e'er aspired:
She e'en surpassed the Isaldes[16] two.
The highest praise of all was due   20
To Condwiramurs:
She had the rightsome *bea curs*,
Which means the "body beautiful."
Those women were of merit full
That two such handsome children bare
As sat beside each other there.
The others present, woman or man,
Could nothing do but simply scan
Them sitting by each other.
They loved him like a brother.
What he was thinking I'll make clear: 188
"Liassë's there, Liassë's here.
Less grief God is decreeing:
Liassë here I'm seeing,
The maid whom I so lovely thought."
Liassë's beauty was as naught
Compared with hers now seated there,

In whom God left out naught that's fair
(She was the queen, this maiden):
As when with sweet dew laden 10
From out its dainty bud the rose
New loveliness and beauty shows,
Bearing the colors red and white.
This brought her guest to a grievous plight.
In manners he'd made much advance
E'er since the worthy Gurnemanz
His ignorance had exorcized
And said, to ask were ill-advised
Unless he did it prudently.
Before her royal majesty 20
His lips had now no word to say,
She close, and he not far away.
E'en now some men with words dispense
Who've had much more experience.

   The queen this way to think began:
"Methinks I'm scorned by this young man
Because my body is so spent—
But no, he does it with one intent:
The hostess I and he the guest,
'Twere right if he were first addressed.
With kindness did he on me look 189
So soon as here our seats we took:
His breeding he to me has bared,
And far too much my words I've spared.
My silence therefore I will break."
The queen now turned to him and spake:
"A hostess, sir, should speak her mind.
A kiss won me your greeting kind,
And you have offered me your aid;
I heard so from a little maid. 10
None of our guests have so behaved,
And yet my heart just this has craved.
Sir, this I would be knowing,
From where you have been going."
"Today, your ladyship, I went
From one I left to his lament,
A man of steadfast faith and fame.

This prince is Gurnemanz by name
And Graharz is the man's abode;
Queen, today from there I rode." 20
Again she spoke, the noble queen:
"If this another man had been,
I had not thought it could be true
That this in one day a man could do.
My fastest messenger would shun
That course in two whole days to run.
The sister of your host out there
My mother was. His daughter fair
May show the effect of grieving so.
Many days of bitter woe
We spent wet-eyed and wailing 190
In sorrow unavailing.
If you to him would be a friend,
This night with us in sorrow spend,
As we've done often, wives and men.
You'll do him thus a favor then.
Our grief and woe I'll tell you now:
To stern privation we must bow."
   Then her uncle Kyot[17] said,
"I'll send to you twelve loaves of bread, 10
Smoked hams and shoulders three,
Eight cheese besides, as you shall see,
Likewise a brace of jugs of wine.
What's more, I'll have this brother of mine
Send help today. The need we know."
Then said his brother Manpfiljot,
"Lady, as much again I'll send."
Her joy had reached a happy end:
Great thanks she did not fail to say.
They took their leave and rode away. 20
In their hunting lodge near by
In mountain passage wild and high
The two old men dwelt all unarmed
Yet by the hostile host unharmed.[18]
Their messenger returned with speed
And thus relieved the people's need.
For the city-dweller had no food

Except for this donation good:
Of hunger many a man was dead
Before the arrival of this bread.
"Divide it," said the queen discreet,   191
"All the cheese, the wine, the meat
Among the starving people all."
'Twas so advised by Parzival.
For them there scarce was left one bite:
They shared it without any fight.
   The food they'd got was all consumed,
Whereby they'd save a many doomed
Whom hunger had not yet struck dead.
The guest-friend now was given a bed   10
Most soft and good—or so I've heard.
Had the burgher been a hunting-bird,
Its crop not overstuffed had been,
As from their table could be seen.
The signs of hunger bore they all
Except the youthful Parzival.
He begged their leave to say good-night.
Was torch of straw his candle-light?
No, better far than that he had.
And now the young and handsome lad   20
Went to a bed most splendid,
As for a king intended:
No signs of poverty it bore.
A rug was spread upon the floor.
He bade the knights to go away,
No longer would he let them stay.
Unshod by pages soon he slept
Till summoned when true sorrow wept,
And tears from bright eyes streaming
Aroused him from his dreaming.
I'll tell you now how all this came:[19]   192
It was to womanhood no blame,
Constant was the maid and chaste,
Of whom some steps shall be retraced.
The stress of warfare on her weighed,
And dear friends' death upon her preyed,
So that her heart was breaking,

Her eyes perforce were waking.
And so the queen went roving,
But seeking not such loving
As is by people understood
When maidens turn to womanhood:
A friend's advice and help she sought.
Defensive raiment she had brought,
A shirt of silk, shining white:
What were more fit for loving fight[20]
Than a woman seeking thus a man?
She'd thrown around her, ere she ran,
A cloak of velvet, wide and long.
She was impelled by sorrow strong.
Her maids and servants many,
Of them she woke not any,
And where they lay she let them sleep.
Thus noiselessly she sought to creep
Where Parzival was sleeping.
Those who the rooms were keeping
Saw to it that alone he lay.
By candles lighted bright as day
The space before his bed was seen.
Up to his couch advanced the queen,
Then on the carpet kneeling.
Nor had those twain a feeling,
He and the queen, nor were inclined
To *Minnë* of the sensual kind.
Here then was such a wooing:
For grief had been undoing
Her joy, and hence she quailed with shame.
Would he embrace her to her blame?
Oh no, of such things naught he knew.
But what was done without ado,[21]
And guiltlessly as well, was such
That sinfully they did not touch
Each other, made no mention
Of any such intention.
  So deep was this poor maiden's woe,
It made the copious tears to flow
Upon the youthful Parzival.

He heard her weeping rise and fall
So loud, he looked at her, awake,
Felt joy and sorrow for her sake.
The young man sat up in his bed
And to the youthful queen he said,
"Lady, is this a mockery?
Kneel thus to God, but not to me.
I pray you on my bed to sit,"
(He wished it and requested it),
"Or lay you down here where I lay
And I will place me where I may."
Said she, "If honor schools you,
And moderation rules you,
So that no conquest you will try,
Forthwith beside you I will lie."
Words of asurance then he said
And so she crept into his bed.
So dark the night was showing
That still no cock was crowing;
'Tis true the perches all were bare:
Hard times had left no roosters there.
The queen, with sorrow sighing,
All chastely by him lying,
Asked if her lament he'd hear.
She said, "If I should speak, I fear
'Twill pain you, drive your sleep away.
My enemy, King Clamidê,
With Kingrun[22] his seneschal,
Has sacked my land and castles all
Right up to Belrapeirë.
My father Tampenteirë
Died, leaving me by error
In most atrocious terror.
Kinsmen, princes, and their men,
Rich and poor, they served me then
And were to me a powerful host.
Of brave defenders I have lost
Full half and even more than half.
What cause have wretched I to laugh?
And now so great has grown my ill

That I myself had rather kill
Than give my maidenhood and life
To Clamidê and be his wife.
For he it was who fought and slew   195
Schentaflur,[23] whose heart so true
Had every knightly quality.
The flower of manliness to me,
Of truth he was defender,
Liassë's brother tender."
   When Liassë's name was heard,
Once again deep sorrow stirred
In service-giving Parzival.
His buoyant spirit took a fall: 10
Such moods Liassë could evoke.
He now addressed the queen and spoke,
"Will comfort help you in your need?"
"Yes, sir, if I could be freed
Of Kingrun, that steward keen,
Whose jousting felled upon the green
Many a sturdy, valiant knight.
Tomorrow he'll return to fight,
Thinking to help his lord recline
Held in these two arms of mine.   20
Upon my palace you've laid eyes.
So loftly could it never rise
That I'd not leap into the moat
Ere Clamidê should ever dote
On me and rape my maidenhood;
His fame on me he'll not make good."
Said he, "My queen, if Kingrun be
A Frenchman or from Brittany,
No matter whence he's wended,
By me you'll be defended
With all my strength, as best I may."   196
The night was done and came the day.
The lady rose and bowed her head,
Nor were her great thanks left unsaid.
So gentle her tip-toeing
That no one could be knowing
That she was up and walking there,

Save only Parzival, the fair.
Not a moment more he slept.
The sun had swiftly upward crept,   10
Its gleam pressed through the cloudy shroud.
He heard bells ringing clear and loud:
Cathedral and church the people sought
Whose sorrow Clamidê had wrought.

Parzival visits the cathedral, then demands his armor and engages in single combat with Kingrun, the steward. He defeats him but instead of killing him sends him to King Arthur's court and to Cunnewarë, with the message to the latter that he, Parzival, will some day avenge the beating she received from Keyë for his sake. (196, 15—199, 14)

   He came on foot enraptured
To where his horse was captured,[24]
The burghers' battle-comfort he,
Through whom they later should be free.
The outside host was in suspense
Because Kingrun in his defence   20
Had been completely thwarted.
The queen's men now escorted
To her the hero Parzival.
The queen embraced the hero tall
And held him tightly as she said,
"Ne'er will I consent to wed
On earth a man in any case
Save him whom here I now embrace."
She helped disarm the hero bold
And offered kindnesses untold.
His labor had been great and keen;   200
Refreshment was but poor and lean.
Instead, the citizens were loud
In praise, and fealty they vowed,
Insisting he should be their lord.
With this the queen was in accord.
He was to be her *amis*,[25]
Since he had made the fame to cease
Of Kingrun, and won renown.
Now two sails of color brown   10
Were spied by watchers from the fort:

A strong wind drove them into port.
Their keels were laden so with freight
That everybody's joy was great.
'Twas only food they landed:
A wise God so commanded.
　From out the fort they scurried
And toward the vessels hurried
On pillage bent, the hungry crew.
As fast as withered leaves they flew,
The sunken and the meagre,
Whom hunger made more eager.
But little was their skin distent.
Thither the marshal also went
And the shipmen he protected:
He'd hang whom he detected
Stealing any food from thence.
Then the merchants led he hence
And to his lord he brought them all.
"Offer them," said Parzival,
"As pay twofold indemnity."
The merchants thought, "Too kind is he!"
They got more than they could require,
And grease dripped in the burghers' fire.[26]
I wish I'd been a soldier here:[27]
No one put up with simple beer,
They'd wine and food for everyone.
And now I'll tell you what was done
By Parzival, the pure and good.
First he himself gave little food
To each, for so he thought it meet.
He gave the worthiest a seat.
Stomachs by hunger goaded
Should not be overloaded,
So he gave a prudent ration:
They praised this dispensation.
That night more food did he provide,
This kindly man untouched by pride.
　Invited now to share one bed,
He and the queen said they would wed.[28]
He lay so chastely at her side,

His ways would not have satisfied
Many a woman treated so.
Oft teasing coyness a maid will show,
Good breeding thus betraying,
False diffidence displaying.
They act in public chaste and shy,
But oft their heart's desires belie
What by their acts they indicate.
In secret oft they irritate
Their friends by fond caresses.   202
Who moderation stresses,
The faithful and the constant man,
Will spare the loved one as he can.
He'll think, and he can truly vow,
"For many a year I've served her now,
To win true love's rewarding.
And now she is according
Love's solace: I am by her side.
Ere this I had been satisfied   10
If with bare hands I might caress
The hem of my beloved's dress.
Had I now unseemly craving,
Falsely I'd be behaving.
Making assault upon her,
Shall I spread our dishonor?
Sweet words when sleep is nearing
Suit women's gentle rearing."
'Twas thus he there was lying:
All fears he was defying.   20
He who as the Red Knight was seen,
He left her as a virgin queen.
She thought that now his wife she were:
Since this fair form was given to her,
Next morn she donned her wifely band.[29]
She gave him castle, gave him land,
This virgin who appeared as bride:
She loved him more than all beside.

   And they so shared togetherness
That true affection their hearts could bless[30]
For two days and of nights the third. 203

110   PARZIVAL

>Oft then the thought to him occurred
>Of fond embrace, as his mother taught.
>And Gurnemanz to show had sought
>How man and woman are one in kind.[31]
>Now arms and legs they intertwined.
>If I may say it with meetness,
>He found the waiting sweetness,
>And so the old love and the new
>Dwelt there within the lovers two.   10

Clamidê learns that his steward Kingrun has been defeated by Parzival and been sent as a prisoner to King Arthur and Cunnewarë. Thereupon Clamidê attacks the city and tries to take it by storm. The heroic resistance of Parzival and Condwiramur's men foils his efforts. Then, to Parzival's joy, Clamidê challenges him to a single combat. After a fierce fight Clamidê is exhausted and defeated by Parzival. He pleads for his life and Parzival, mindful of Gurnemanz's exhortation to mercy, spares his life. He would send him to Gurnemanz, but Clamidê begs to be excused because it was he who had slain Schentaflur, Gurnemanz's son. Thereupon he is dispatched instead to King Arthur and Cunnewarë, just as Kingrun had been. He goes and finds that all of Arthur's knights are agreed that the steward Keyë should be punished for having beaten Cunnewarë. (203,11—222, 9)

>This story we will now desert   222   10
>And of our hero we'll relate.
>The waste land he would cultivate
>When he the new-won crown assumed.
>Now joy and glad commotion boomed.
>Her father Tampenteirë
>Left him in Belrapeirë
>Sparkling gems and good red gold.
>He shared them so that men extolled
>Him for his generous manners.
>New shields and many banners,   20
>Thus was his land bedecked and dressed.
>They tourneyed much and oft with zest,
>The lord and those obeying:
>His strength he was oft displaying
>Along the march or boundary,
>This hero young, of terrors free.

'Twas learned by every hostile guest:
His deeds were proved the very best.
  Now let me tell about the queen:
Could greater happiness be seen?
The young, sweet, noble queen enjoyed   223
Earth's highest pleasure unalloyed.
So strong her love stood, and so true,
No wavering it ever knew.
For well she knew his loyalty,
And she was just as true as he.
She loved him, he loved her no less.
If with this tale I now progress
And tell you of his leaving,
'Twill cause them both much grieving.   10
I pity her, poor worthy wife.
Her people, land, and e'en her life
His hand had freed from trouble grave:
For this her love to him she gave.
One morning spoke he decorously
(Many a knight could hear and see),
"Lady, if I've permission,
I'll go forth on a mission
To see how my dear mother fares
And whether weal or woe she bears: 20
To know about her fate I'm lief.
To her I'll pay a visit brief
And then upon adventure go.
If service thus to you I show,
Your love will be my recompense."
Thus asked he leave to go from thence.
She loved him true, so runs the tale,
Hence to agree she could not fail.
Without his men he started
And all alone departed.

Book Five
Parzival At The Grail Castle

Book Five

PARZIVAL AT THE GRAIL CASTLE

Who fain would hear where he may stray 224
Whom lust for deeds has lured away,
Great acts of wondrous daring
To them we shall be bearing.
Let him his horse untether
Where the loyal live together:
They wish him well, for it must be
That he will suffer misery,
Though mixed with praise and pleasure.
He grieved beyond all measure 10
When this fair woman he forsook,
So fair that not in any book
Nor any tale related
As fairer e'er was rated.
Whenas of her he fondly thought
His mind appeared to be distraught.
He must have surely lost his mind
Had he not been of doughty kind.
Unreined his mighty steed must press
All through the swamp and wilderness: 20
The rider's guidance it must miss.
The narrative tells me of this:
That day he rode to such a length,
It would have taxed a birdling's strength
If e'er it such a distance flew.
Now if the story tells me true,
He rode not near so far that day
When Ither came to be his prey,
Nor since, when he from Graharz
Had reached the land of Brobarz.
   How he now fared shall I retell? 225
He reached a lake when evening fell
Where fishers had their anchor cast:
To them belonged these waters vast.
Now when they saw him riding,
So close were they abiding,

They heard his words quite audibly.
One of the men, as he could see,
Was clad in raiment rich and grand
As though he ruled o'er every land.
One sees no better garb than that.
Peacock plumes composed his hat.
This man who there was fishing
To question he was wishing:
"I beg you in God's holy name
And by the breeding that you claim
To say where I can shelter take."
This answer did the sad one make:
"Good sir," he said, "I understand
That not on water nor on land
For thirty miles a house doth lie
Except a single one near by.
'Tis there I'd counsel you to stay:
What other could you reach today?
Where yonder cliff comes to an end,
There sharply to the right hand bend;
Proceed until the moat you face
And that will be your stopping-place.
Bid them the bridge to lower
And entrance free implore."
Obeying what the fisher said,
He took his leave to forge ahead.
The fisher: "If you find the way
I'll care for you myself today.
Give thanks to match the care you find.
Take heed: some roads in there are blind;
You may ride false in coping
With paths so steeply sloping.
That's not my wish for you at all."
Away from him rode Parzival,
Along the proper road to ride
With speed until the moat he spied.
He found the bridge suspended,
The castle well defended:
It stood as by a turner wrought.
Unless on wing or wind 'twere brought,

Thus he dismounted from his steed.
The knights now begged him to proceed
And led him where he'd comfort find.
Quite swiftly then in manner kind
He was disarmed by men well-reared.
Naught entered there by power.
High walls and many a tower
Afforded wonderful defence.
E'en if besieged by host immense,   20
This castle would evince no fears
Of sieges lasting thirty years.

  A page saw him come nigher
And asked of his desire
And whence his wanderings began.
He answered, "By the fisherman
I was directed here and sent.
I thanked him for his kind intent:
A shelter I expected.
To drop the bridge he directed
And bade me enter the castle.   227
"Welcome," rejoined the vassal.
"Since the fisher bade you hither go,
Honor and comfort we will show
For his sake, sending you to us."
He lowered the bridge while speaking thus.
Then entered he of high emprise
Into a court of spacious size.
By battle-games it was not trod—
'Twas covered with a short green sod,   10
The *bohourt*[1] was forbidden—
Nor with banners[2] overridden,
As are the fields at Abenberg.[3]
No joyous knightly play and work
Had they enjoyed in many a day,
For in their hearts distress held sway.
And yet to him they were polite:
Both young and old received the knight,
And many squires came up who fain
Would seize his bridle, hold his rein,   20
And each with all the others vied

To grasp the stirrup at his side.
Now when this youth without a beard
They saw so winsome, they confessed
That truly he was richly blessed.
 Some water now the young man craved 228
And from his skin the rust he laved
Upon his hands and neath his eyes.
Now young and old deemed in surprise
Another sun was gleaming.[4]
Thus sat he, winsome seeming.
Of every flaw and blemish free
And made of silk from Araby,
A cloak they proffered now the lad,
With which his handsome form was clad; 10
The cords it had he wore unbound,[5]
Whereat applause and praise he found.
The prudent chamberlain now spoke:
"Repanse de Schoyë wore the cloak,
The queen, my gracious lady she:
It's lent by her and yours to be,
For not yet cut is your attire.[6]
'Twas right to tell her this desire,
For you are fit to be our guest,
If I your worthiness can test." 20
"Your kindness, sir, may God requite.
If what you say of me is right,
I've found good cheer and rapture then:
God grants such recompense to men."
They poured his drink and served him so;
The sad well-nigh concealed their woe.
High honor they could render
And better food could tender
Than Belrapeirë had that day
When he drove grief and care away.
 Straightway his armor was removed:[7] 229
Regrettable to him this proved
When a jest he failed to recognize.
A man at court in garrulous wise[8]
Too boldly now requested
The lad of valor tested,

As though in wrath, to join the host.
For that he lost his life, almost,
At the hands of Parzival.
Since his bright sword was not at all   10
Within his reach, its blade he missed,
He squeezed that hand into a fist
Till from the nails the red blood shot
And on his sleeve made many a spot.
"Nay, sir!" the knights regret expressed,
"This is a man who likes to jest,
However sad we're prone to be.
Pray show him your civility.
He merely wished to make it clear
That now the fisherman is here.   20
Go in! As guest you're dear to him:
Divest yourself of anger grim."
   A hall they entered huge and bright[9]
With a hundred chandeliers for light
And candles large provided
For those who there resided.
Small candles burned along the wall.
A hundred bedsteads in the hall
By serving vassals had been made;
One hundred quilts on them were laid.
Each bed for four knights had a place;   230
Between the beds was left a space,
There round rugs were spread out well.
Fil li roy Frimutel[10]
Such luxury could well provide.
Nor was this further thing denied:
E'en great expense not fearing,
Of marble they'd been rearing
Three fireplaces large and square;
Each bore what's known as fire there,   10
And wood called *lignum aloë*.[11]
Such fires not then or since I see
At Wildenberg,[12] my place to stay.
A costly work indeed were they.[13]
   The king was borne to where he'd face
The second, central fireplace

Upon a bed or litter.
A kind of bargain bitter
Was struck twixt him and happiness:
He lived toward death in dire distress. 20
Now striding to the palace
Came he who without malice
Was met by him who'd sent him there—
Parzival the young and fair.
Not long did he remain alone.
The host soon called in friendly tone,
"Pray come and sit here next to me.
If farther off your seat should be,
A lack of friendship I should show."
Thus said the host beset with woe.
This host, because of illness sore, **231**
Craved heat, and heavy clothes he wore.
Made of sable long and wide
Must be for him on either side
Robes of fur and outer cloak.
His poorest pelt high praise bespoke:[14]
It was of blackish hue and gray.
He also wore a fur beret,
Both sides of which were richly lined
With sable fur of costly kind. 10
A round Arabian border
Was sewed on to his order;
As button, quite apparent,
A ruby stone transparent.
There sat the knights for prudence known
The while their grief[15] to them was shown:
A squire came quickly through the door
And a lance with iron point he bore
(A rite that caused them bitter woe)
Which dripped with blood in steady flow, 20
Then down the shaft into the hand;
The sleeve its further progress banned.
All those assembled wept and cried
Throughout the spacious hall and wide.
The folk of thirty nations
Had made less lamentations.

PARZIVAL AT THE GRAIL CASTLE

He bore it upon his hands withal
Around the room along each wall,
Then back again toward the door
And out, as he had come before.
Those wails had now abated,   232
By deepest grief dictated,
As by the lance they had been taught
That in his hand the squire had brought.
  If now I do not bore you,
The tale I'll set before you,
Until with your own eyes you see
The service done there decorously.
Along the great hall's other side
A door of steel was opened wide.   10
From it two maidens came to sight:
Now mark and know how they were dight.
They could have given love's reward[16]
To him who service would accord:
Maidens were they pure and fair
With garlands laid upon their hair.[17]
Their coiffure was of flowers.
On the hand of each there towers
Of gold a handsome candlestick.
Their curls were long, blond, and thick.   20
They carried candles burning.
By all means let's be turning
Our eyes their raiment fine to view
As they came in and nearer drew.
The countess fine of Tenabroc,[18]
Of brown wool was her skirt and frock;
The same wore her companion there,
And girded was the noble pair
Each with a belt around her waist
And well above the hip-line placed.
A duchess entered now the hall   233
With escort. Each a pedestal
They bore of finest ivory.
Their lips were red as fire to see.
The four maids bowed politely,
Then two of them set rightly

The pedestals before the host.
Of perfect service they could boast.
They stood together as a group
And were indeed a beauteous troop. 10
These four, all dressed alike were they.
Now look, in come without delay
Yet other maidens, four times two,[19]
Who did what they were called to do.
Four carried candles great and tall,
The others did not mind at all
To bear a precious stone and fine
Through which by day the sun could shine.
This gave the name by which 'twas known:
A garnet-hyacinth.[20] The stone 20
Was amply wide and amply long,
Cut thin, for lightness' sake, but strong,
To make a table of it.
The rich host ate above it.
Advancing now direct and straight,
Before the host appeared the eight;
With lowered heads deep bows they made.
By four this table-top[21] was laid
Upon the pedestals well-wrought
Of ivory white that they had brought.
Then stepping back with modesty 234
They bore the first four company.
On these eight maidens could be seen
Skirts like grass so bright and green
Of Azagouc's[22] velvet fine,
Long and ample in design.
The maidens' waists were confined
By narrow belts of costly kind.
These maidens eight, trim and fair,
Had each adorned her flowing hair 10
With flower chaplets from the dell.
The count Ivan de Nonel,
Also Jernis de Rile[23]
(They both lived distant many a mile),
'Twas their daughters had come here to serve.
These princesses one could observe

In clothes of rich and beauteous sheen.
Two knives[24] that cut like fish-bones keen
They brought, a miracle to see,
Upon two towels separately.   20
These were silver, hard and white.
A dainty skill there came to light:
That silver was so sharp and true
That steel it could have cleft in two.
Before these knives proceeded
More maids for service needed.
Four maids of pure and blameless lives
Held up candles o'er the knives.
All six then forward wended:
Now hear what was intended.
   They bowed, and two of them now bare **235**
Upon the jewel-table rare
The silver, where they let it lie,
And with decorum then did hie
To join the other twelve ere long.
Unless it be that I am wrong,
Of maidens there should be eighteen.
Aha, six more maids now are seen
In garb of costliness untold,
One half of silk all wrought with gold,   10
The other silk from Ninniveh.
These and the six of whom I say[25]
Wore twelve skirts of twofold hue,
The costliest you'd ever view.
After them appeared the queen.
So bright the maiden's face and mien,
All thought the dawn was breaking.
The clothes her raiment making
Were costly silks of Araby.
Upon a deep green Achmardi[26]   20
She bore the pride of Paradise,
Root and branch, beyond all price.
That was a thing men call the Grail,[27]
Which makes all earthly glory pale.
Repanse de Schoyë was her name
Who bore the Grail of highest fame.

The Grail was such that she must be
Possessed of purest chastity
Who would fulfill its service high:
All false pretense she must deny.
   Before the Grail there was more light   236
Of costly kind, a wondrous sight:
Six goblets tall came nigher,
In each a balsam fire.[28]
When they'd entered by the door
And ta'en their proper place before,
The queen bowed low in decorousness
And all the maidens there no less
Who'd brought the flaming balsam near.
The queen, of all deception clear,   10
Before the host set down the Grail.
Parzival, so goes the tale,[29]
With thought to her was clinging
As she the Grail was bringing:
Her cloak he wore, as well ye know.
In seemly wise the seven now go
To join up with the first eighteen,
Admitting then the noble queen
Between them, and, unless I err,
Twelve stood on either side of her.   20
Thus with the crown the maiden
With beauty rare was laden.
To all the knights attending,
And thus their presence lending,
Servants with basins were assigned
Of heavy gold and well designed:
Each steward served a group of four.
A handsome noble, helping, bore
A towel of snow-white radiance.
It was a scene of opulence.
A hundred tables must have been   237
Through the entrance carried in:
One table they completed
For each four knights there seated,
On each a white cloth laying
And thus their zeal displaying.

The host then washing water took;[30]
Joy long since his soul forsook.
With him then Parzival washed too:
A silken towel of brightest hue
Was offered by a county's son,
Who knelt as service there was done.
Where any table one could find,
Four youthful squires were assigned,
That service good be meted
To those who there were seated.
Of these, two knelt and cut the food,
The other two, in serving mood,
Food and drink they richly bore
And served as oft they'd done before.
Hear more of luxury untold.
Four carts into the hall were rolled
And bore gold vessels rich and dear
To all the knights assembled here,
Along the walls progressing.
Four knights, to serve professing,
Set the vessels on the board.
A clerk[31] each item must record,
For it was his to be concerned
That all the vessels be returned
When once the sumptuous meal was o'er.
Now let me tell you something more:
One hundred squires, nobly led,
In snow-white cloths accepted bread
In reverence there from the Grail.
Then each one took a different trail
And to the several tables came.
'Twas said to me, I'll say the same—
That is, if on your oaths ye'll swear
The Grail of everyone took care
(If truth I am denying,
Perforce ye too are lying!)[32]—
Whatever someone wanted,
That by the Grail was granted:
Dishes warm, dishes cold,
Dishes new and dishes old,

Meat that's tame and meat that's game.
"It can't have happened as you claim,"
I hear some men objecting.
Their rancor needs correcting.[33]
The Grail, the fruit of highest bliss,
The plethora of sweetnesses,
Well-nigh possessed the attributes
That man to heaven's realm imputes.
  They served in golden vessels small
The proper savors one and all:
Pepper, fruit-juice, every sauce.
The moderate and the gluttonous,
Both had just enough to eat.
Service was courteous and meet.
Mulberry juice, wine red or white[34]
To please the cup of every knight—
Whatever beverage came to mind
The knight within his cup would find,
All from the Grail's capacity.
This noble, worthy company
Was served completely by the Grail.
Parzival could hardly fail
These costly wonders to admire,
But he'd been taught: Do not inquire.
"Prince Gurnemanz admonished me,"
He thought, "in steadfast loyalty
That I should not inquire too much.
What if my visit here be such
As when to his abode I turned?[35]
Without a question I'll have learned
How stands the situation here."
Bearing a sword whose sheath alone
'Twould cost a thousand marks to own.
While thus he thought, a squire drew near,
Its hilt was of one ruby made
And then it seemed as if the blade
Were a source of many wonders blest.
The host bestowed it on the guest.
Said he, "I used it, sir, in need
In many a fight, ere God decreed

To wound me past all measure.
This sword shall be your pleasure
And make up for our faulty care.
You're fit to bear it anywhere.
When its full merit you have tried   240
'Twill keep you safe whate'er betide."
   Woe's me that he did not inquire!
For him I still feel sorrow dire.[36]
When with this sword invested,
A question was suggested.
And his sweet host I pity there,
Whom God's displeasure did not spare:[37]
A question this had mended.
The banquet now was ended.   10
Those who were charged with serving neared,
Equipment soon away was cleared.
They loaded all four rolling carts,
The women also played their parts.
Who entered last now went out first.
Once more they led the queen, who durst
Approach the Grail there in the hall.
Before the host and Parzival
The queen bowed low in courteousness,
And all the other maids no less.   20
Again they took out through the door
The things they'd carried in before.
Parzival these actions eyed,
Thus on a litter he espied,
Within a room reposing,
Ere they the door were closing,
The handsomest old man[38] that e'er
He'd laid his eyes on anywhere.
With moderation I insist
That he was whiter than the mist.
   Of this old man's identity   241
Hereafter you may question me.[39]
What's more, the host, his house, his land,
I'll name so you will understand,
When later on the time is due,
Clearly and orderly and true,

And no digression will I show:
Straight string and not the curving bow.[40]
The string is but a simile.
You think bent bows shoot speedily?   10
More speed have arrows sped by a string.
If I've just said a truthful thing,
The string is like a straightened tale:
To satisfy 'twill never fail.
Who speaks like bows all curving
From his straight course is swerving.
When the bent bow you contemplate,
You must admit the string is straight,
Unless it's to an angle bent
So that an arrow may be sent.   20
But if a tale goes soaring
To one who finds it boring,
'Twill nowhere find a resting place
But wander through wide-open space,
In one ear, out the other.
In vain my work and pother
If to such ears I'm winging:
My saying or my singing
As well might at a goat be shot
Or at a tree-stump filled with rot.

   Yet further would I have you know   242
Of these poor folk so full of woe.
Where Parzival came riding,
Glad din was seldom abiding:
No dance nor *bohourt* could one see.
These people grieved so constantly,
Amusement was not their concern.
E'en where less folk you may discern,
You find them fond of sunny cheer;
Yet every nook was crowded here,[41]   10
And e'en the hall did they congest.
And now the host addressed the guest:
"I think your bed is ready.
If you are weary," said he,
'Tis best you should be sleeping."
Oh, I could burst out weeping

Parzival at the Grail Castle

That thus they separated:
For both great woe is fated.
From off the couch departing,
Upon the carpet darting,   20
Stood Parzival, the handsome wight:
The kindly host bade him good-night.
His vassals sprang up rightly
And some advanced politely,
And then their youthful guest they led
Into a chamber with a bed.
So well was it outfitted,
For comfort naught omitted,
That I am irked by all my dearth
Since wealth like this is found on earth.
   All this bed lacked was poverty.   243
As bright as any fire you'd see
A silk quilt on it rested.
The knights he now requested
To go where they resided:
One bed was here provided.
They took their leave and left the room,
Then servants could their tasks assume.
Candles and his complexion bright
In emulation shed their light.   10
Could greater brightness be shed by day?
Before his bed another lay,
On it a quilt, where he sat down.
Young nimble pages of renown
With eagerness came into sight:
The legs and feet they stripped were white.
Of other clothes was he unclad
By many a noble, well-born lad:
These youths were handsome all and trim.
And now there entered, greeting him,   20
Four maidens fair and demure:
They came to make doubly sure
That comfort was afforded
And kindliness accorded.
The story tells me one thing more:
A squire before each maiden bore

A candle burning brightly.
So Parzival the sprightly
Beneath the quilt receded.
"Wake yet a while," they pleaded,
"Let us enjoy your sweetness." 244
A nimble race with fleetness
He ran and won, but still his face,
Which from the bed lit up the place,
Afforded them a sweet delight
Before he bade them all good night.
Heart's distress in them was bred
On seeing how his lips were red,
And how his youth was such that there
No one could spy e'en half a hair. 10
These fair and clever maidens four,
Now hear me tell what each one bore.
Mulberry, wine, and claret clear
Three maids with white hands carried here;
The fourth of these young maidens wise
Brought fruit like that of Paradise
Upon a towel white as snow
And knelt before him, bowing low.
He begged that she should take a seat.
She said, "That would be indiscreet: 20
Such service I'd fail to tender
As my lord bids me render."
Sweet converse he could cultivate.
He drank, some food he also ate.
They took their leave and went away
And down young Parzival then lay.
The candles they were holding yet
The squires upon the carpet set
When once they knew the stranger slept,
Then softly from the room they stepped.

 Parzival lay not alone: 245
Beside him till the new day shone
Abode extremest worriment,
For bitter future woe had sent
Its messengers in sleep to him,
So that the stripling fair of limb

PARZIVAL AT THE GRAIL CASTLE 131

Had such a dream as once beset
His mother touching Gahmuret.[42]
His dream was like a tapestry
Where sword-blows round the hem ye see, 10
And edged with many a doughty joust.
Of chargers dashing through the dust
He dreamt in agony untold.
He had preferred death thirty-fold
Had all his senses been awake.
Such dreadful toil did worry take.
By this dire dreaming shaken,
He need must soon awaken:
He was asweat in vein and bone.
The daylight through the window shone. 20
Said he, "The pages, where are they,
That here no more with me they stay?
Who'll bring my raiment now to me?"
The hero waited patiently,
Until again he fell asleep.
He heard no calling, not a peep,
For all of them had disappeared.
Much later, when mid-morning neared,
The youth awakened once again
And sat up straight where he had lain.
    Upon the carpet at his side 246
His harness and two swords he spied:
The host had given him one of these,
The other was from Kahaviez.
Then to himself he said this word:
"O me, why has this thing occurred?
To arm myself must be my will.
In sleep I suffered so much ill
That in my waking state today
I doubtless shall incur dismay. 10
If by a war this king's oppressed,
I'll gladly serve his interest,
And her commandments I will heed
Who lent her new cloak at my need
In kindness without measure.
I would it were her pleasure

A knight as devotee to take:
That I'd welcome for her sake,
But not to win her love I mean.[43]
My wife, Condwiramur, the queen,   20
Is just as fair as this one here,
Or even fairer, that is clear."
The hero acted meetly:
He armed himself completely,
For any strife preparing;
Two swords he now was wearing.
The noble man went through the door
And tethered found his steed before
The steps; beside it spear and shield
Were leaning, this to him appealed.

   Ere Parzival stouthearted   247
Bestrode his horse and parted,
He ran through many rooms with speed
And called upon the folk to heed;
No one did he hear or see,
He deemed this monstrous injury,
With rage he was exploding.
He ran, some ill foreboding,
Where he'd dismounted when he came:
The earth and grass were not the same,   10
The sod was trampled all around
And no more dew was to be found.
Shouting the youth retraced his course
To where he found his waiting horse.
With angry words of scolding
He mounted. Who was holding
The castle portals open wide?
Hoof-tracks leading out he spied.
No longer here he halted
But o'er the bridge he vaulted.   20
The rope a hidden vassal drew:
So swiftly up the drawbridge flew,
Its end almost the charger felled.
When Parzival this thing beheld,
He fain would ask, but 'twas too late.
"Be off and bear the sunshine's hate,"

Said the squire, "you are a goose.
Had you your mouth but shaken loose
And asked your host his story!
You've spurned the greatest glory."
   He yelled for explanation
But got no information.
However loud his screaming,
The squire on foot was seeming
To sleep, and slammed the portals to:
Too soon for him, but what to do?
How great the joys he now had lost
Who had to pay the heavy cost:
His joys henceforth are hidden.
For "care" he had been bidden
To dice, whenas he found the Grail,
With eyes, and not with fingers frail,
Nor with real dice as shaken.
If grief his soul awaken,
Unwonted dole on him is thrown,
For little longing has he known.
Parzival rode off amain
Adown the trail made by the train.
He thought, "Those who went speeding,
Today they may be bleeding
To serve my host here manfully.
If they agreed, their company
No weaker I would render.
Unwavering as defender,
I'd help defeat the foemen dread
And thus would I deserve my bread
And rightly claim this wondrous sword
Bestowed upon me by their lord.
I bear it, unempowered.
Shall I be deemed a coward?"
   He who gainst falsity was proof
Pursued the trail of many a hoof.
I grieve because he went from thence:
Now first his trials will commence.
The track began to fade from sight:
Some had turned left and others right.

The trail grew narrow, once so wide,
At last 'twas lost: for grief he cried.
And now the young man tidings heard
Whereby his heart to woe was stirred. 10
The dauntless fighter, free of fear,
A woman's wailing voice could hear.
The dew still lay upon the ground.
There in a linden tree[44] he found
A faithful maid whose joy had fled:
A knight who was embalmed and dead
Clasped in her arms was lying.
Who'd pity not her sighing
On seeing her thus sitting
Would lack compassion fitting. 20
He turned his charger toward the spot,
Although he recognized her not;[45]
Yet daughter to his aunt was she.
No other earthly loyalty
With hers could fitly be compared.
Greeting her, Parzival declared,
"Dame, my spirit you oppress
By your longing and distress.
If of my service you have need,
I'll serve you with my every deed."
   She thanked him as a mourner may 250
And asked him whence he'd come that day.
Said she, "It's known as baneful
That to this wasteland painful
A stranger pay a visit:
If unfamiliar is it,
The guest may suffer damage great.
I've seen, and people oft relate,
That many lost their lives who nighed
And fighting hard were felled and died.[46] 10
If you would live, then take to flight,
But first say where you spent the night."
"It is a mile away or more.
So brave a castle ne'er before
I've seen, with such an opulence.
'Tis only now I rode from thence."
Said she, "Men who your words believe

You should not purposely deceive.
It is a foreign shield you bear,[47]
And if from planted land you fare,   20
This wood might have been too much for you.
For thirty miles men never hew
Wood for a house or build of stone.
There's just one castle stands alone
All full of earth's perfection.
Who *seeks* its bold detection,
Alas for him, he'll find it not.
Yet many people seek the spot.
It must be done unwittingly,
If any man the castle see.
    That you don't know it I'll aver.   251
They call it Munsalvaeschë, sir.[48]
The kingdom of this lord of fame,
Terre de Salvaeschë is its name.[49]
Bequeathed was it by Tyturel[50]
To *his* son, called rois Frimutel:
He was the hero ruled this land,
And many a prize acquired his hand.
At love's command he fought and bled
And in a joust at last lay dead.   10
Four children fine to him were born:[51]
Though wealthy, three of them now mourn.
The fourth has chosen poverty,
For sins atoning ruefully.
The name he bears is Trevrizent.[52]
His brother Anfortas is bent:[53]
He cannot walk, he cannot ride,
He cannot lie or standing bide.
There he has jurisdiction.
From God is his affliction.   20
O sir, if you had come," she spoke,
"To these unhappy, troubled folk,
The host would now at last be free
Of great and lasting misery."
To her said this Valaisan bold,
"Great wonders there did I behold
And many ladies wondrous fair."

His voice betrayed him then and there.
    She said, "Why, thou art Parzival.[54]
Speak, sawest thou the Grail at all,
The host bereft of pleasure?
Give me of joy that measure.
Blest is thy hither journey,
If from his terror turn he!
Of all things breathed on by the air
Thou shalt the highest station bear,
Thou wilt be served by wild and tame,
Earth's greatest glory grace thy name."
The hero brave thus made reply:
"You recognized me then? Whereby?"
She answered straight, "I am the maid
Who once her grief before thee laid
And told thee of thy race and name,
Whereof thou needest feel no shame:
Thy mother, she is aunt to me,
A flower of female chastity,
As pure as buds untouched by dew.
God bless thee that thou feelest rue
For him I loved, in joust laid low.
I have him here; canst weigh the woe
Which God the Lord to me doth give
By letting him no longer live?
As man he had high merit;
Now sorrow I inherit,
And as day follows after day
My grieving is renewed alway."
"Alack, where are thy lips so red?
Art thou Sigunë, then, who said
Just who I was, without deceit?
That curly hair, long, brown, and neat,
Thy head no longer can command.
There in the woods of Breceliand
I saw thee full of loveliness
For all the wealth of thy distress.
Complexion thou hast lost, and strength;
To such an escort dread, at length—
If he were mine—I should demur:

This dead man let's at once inter."
Sigunë's eyes bedewed her cloak.
The counsel that Lunetë spoke[55]
Was nowhere in Sigunë's mind.
(She bade her ladyship, "Be kind
To him, though he your husband killed.
You may by him with joy be filled.")
On joy this maid was not intent,
Like womenfolk of fickle bent
Whose names at present I'll suppress—;
Hark to Sigunë's faithfulness.
Said she, "If joy I ever know[56]
'Twill be at this, that all the woe
Of that sad king has found an end.
If thou didst part as helpful friend,
Thou art the greatest glory worth.
I see his sword hangs on thy girth:
If of its blessing thou'rt aware,
Thou mayest fight without a care.
Keen-cutting is its either edge.
Its maker, high of heritage,
Was Trebuchet;[57] 'tis by his hand.
A well-spring[58] flows hard by Karnant,
From which King Lac his name doth bear.
One blow this sword will not impair.
A second blow will break it.
But if to that spring thou take it,
'Twill mend itself in the water's flow.
But seek the source, be sure to go
Before the dawn beneath the rock.
The name of yonder spring is Lac.
The parts, if thou'lt not lose them,
And if thou rightly fuse them,
When in the water they're immersed,
Will yield a stronger sword than first
It was, in groove and double blade,
Nor will the bright engraving fade.
The sword doth words of blessing need,[59]
To which I fear thou gav'st no heed.

If once thy tongue has learned them well,
Good fortune's power will sprout and swell,
Thy happiness obeying.
Dear Cousin, trust my saying: 20
What there thou saw'st of wonders all
Will then be at *thy* beck and call,
And thou wilt e'er go faring,
The crown of gladness wearing,
A man whom all respect, admire,
For then earth's loftiest desire
Thou'lt be in full attaining.
No other, power gaining,
Could equal thee in anything.
Didst thou do proper questioning?"
 "I asked no questions," answered he. 255
"O woe that you my eye must see,"
Exclaimed the sorrow-laden maid,
"Since you to question were afraid!
Did you not see great wonders done?
To think that questions you would shun,
There in the Grail's proximity,
Where ladies dwell of probity,
The noble Garciloyë,[60]
The fair Repanse de Schoyë, 10
The cutting knives, the bloody spear.
Alack, why have you journeyed here?
Dishonored and accursed your youth!
You bore the wolf's envenomed tooth,[61]
Since gall within your loyalty
Took root in you luxuriantly.
The host your pity should have moved
Whom God so wondrously reproved.
You asked naught of his suffering dread?
Your body lives, your bliss is dead!" 20
Said Parzival, "Dear cousin mine,
To greater friendliness incline.
If I have erred, I will atone."
"Not so, the chance for that is gone,"
The maid retorted. "I must say
At Munsalvaeschë you threw away

Your honor and your knighthood's prize.
Henceforth no answer in no wise[62]
You get from me, say what you may."
Parzival now rode away.
   That he from questions had abstained   256
While sitting by the king so pained,
That he regretted greatly,
This hero stout and stately.
From heat and perturbation
He dripped with perspiration.
He loosed his helmet, seeking air,
And in his hand he held it there.
The visor also he untied.
But rust his radiance could not hide.   10

Parzival continues his journey and comes upon the tracks of a knight's steed. He meets Jeschutë who is riding a miserable white nag and is clad in tattered garments. Her husband, Orilus, suspecting her of infidelity with Parzival, has been mistreating her most cruelly. Orilus and Parzival engage in combat. After a bitter struggle Orilus, who has never been defeated before, is completely overpowered by Parzival. Now Parzival rides with him to the cell of Trevrizent, the hermit-brother of Anfortas, and on a holy relic swears that Jeschutë is quite innocent of any wrong-doing. This finally convinces Orilus of his wife's devotion. Thereupon he is sent by Parzival to Cunnewarë, who recognizes him as her brother. Both he and his wife are hospitably received by King Arthur, who has pitched camp with his knights on the banks of the Plimizoel River. A painted spear which Parzival takes along from Trevrizent's altar later serves him well. (256, 11—279, 30)

Book Six
Parzival At King Arthur's Court

Book Six

PARZIVAL AT KING ARTHUR'S COURT

Will ye the tidings now receive,   280
Why Arthur Karidoel[1] would leave
And bade his house and land adieu?
As counselled by his retinue,
With all the best he could command
And those of many another land
He'd fared eight days, the story goes,
Making a search without repose
For him who called himself Red Knight,
Who honored the king with all his might,   10
And freed him from unhappy lot
Whenas his spear King Ither shot.
(Kingrun as well and Clamidê
He'd[2] singly sent upon their way
To Brittany and the court renowned.)
With those who formed the Table Round
He wished that hero to abide,
Hence after him the king did ride,
But this condition he expressed:
Whoever knightly ways professed,   20
The lowly and the lofty both,
Should promise Arthur on his oath,
Whene'er a challenge he espied
He surely would refrain to ride
Into a joust alluring
Unless before securing
The king's express permission.
Said he, "We've many a mission
To do in lands whose fighters bold
Might offer challenges untold:
Erected spears we well may see.   281
Would ye advance in rivalry,
Just as unleashed a pack of hounds
In wild disorder forward bounds?
To see this I'm not willing,
Such tumult I'd be stilling.

If fight ye must, I shall not fail,
Then let my valor e'er prevail."
  About this oath I've told you true.
Will ye now hear me tell to you
Where Parzival had chanced to go?
A blanket dense of fallen snow
Had freshly covered him that night;
Yet for snow the time was hardly right.
If I may judge what poets say,
King Arthur's time is merry May:
Whate'er to do or say he tried,
It all occurred at Whitsuntide,
Or in May's flowery glory.
How sweet he smells in story!
This tale is variegated:
With snow it is related.
The falconers of Karidoel
At sundown reached the Plimizoel
For fowling, but at heavy cost:
Their finest falcon there they lost.
Sudden it left them, flying
And to the forest hieing.
That was because 'twas overfed
And from their bait it simply fled.
All night with Parzival it stood,
Since neither of them knew the wood
And with the cold they nearly froze.
But when next day the sun arose,
With snow the paths were overspread.
So Parzival must ride ahead
Without a trail o'er stock and stone,
The while the sun e'er higher shone.
The forest sparser he beheld
And saw a single tree-trunk felled
Upon a mead, toward which he crept;
Beside him Arthur's falcon kept.
A thousand geese sat on the ground
And made a most tremendous sound.
Into their midst the falcon flew
And one of them it almost slew:

The goose just barely got away.
Beneath the fallen tree it lay,
Unable lofty flight to show,
And from its wound upon the snow
Three drops of red blood came to fall,
They brought distress to Parzival.
This came from his fidelity,[3]
For when the blood he came to see
Upon the snow (all gleaming white),
He thought, "Who made this color bright?
What man to it applied his skill?
Condwiramur, with thee I will
Compare this red and whiteness.
God enriches me with brightness,
Since here the like of thee I spy.
I praise the hand of God on high
And all the creatures that are His.
Condwiramur, thine image 'tis,
Since white snow under the blood doth show
And blood has rendered red the snow.
Condwiramurs,
Like this I find thy *bea curs*,[4]
Thou canst not but admit it."
Unable now to quit it,
His glances, as the matter stood,
Pictured as cheeks two drops of blood,
To the third her chin comparing.
True love his heart was bearing
Devoid of vacillation.
A prey to meditation,
At last unconscious there he stood,
Strong *Minnë* forced his servitude.
His wife had caused him such a plight:
The same complexion, red and white,
Did Belrapeirë's queen possess.
Him she withdrew from consciousness.

In this dazed condition Parzival, still girded for battle, is found by a squire of Cunnewarë, who fails to recognize him and hastens back to Arthur and his retinue to report the presence of the intruder. The knight Segramors asks Arthur's permission to go out and fight the impudent interloper. He is granted this privilege, finds Parzival still in a daze, and challenges him. Parzival remains mute but turns away from the drops of blood to face the speaker. Thus he regains consciousness for the time being and, after warding off Segramors' spear, unhorses him with the lance from Trevrizent's altar. Then Parzival turns and lapses into his dream-state once more, while Segramors goes back to his fellow-knights. (283, 23—290, 2)

    Sir Keyë, as a valiant man,
To Arthur with the story ran:
How Segramors had just been felled,
And how out there a fellow held
The field and fain would joust still more.
Said he, " 'Twould grieve me evermore
Should he unpunished go his way.
If you have faith in me, then pray   10
Let me essay this cavalier,
Since he with his uptilted spear
Before your wife is posted.[5]
I'll leave your service boasted,
Unless my wish assent has found.
Dishonored is the Table Round,
If he's not swiftly brought to shame:
His challenge weakens our good name.
O let me fight, o be so kind!
Were all the others deaf and blind,   20
Right soon yourself would have to fight."
The king then granted him the right.
The seneschal was armed in haste:
The forest he would fain lay waste[6]
Upon this new unbidden guest.
But he, by *Minnë* sore oppressed,
Was held in ban by blood and snow;
A sin to add more to his woe!
And *Minnë's* prize would be but slim:
Her wand already waved o'er him.
    O *Minnë*, wherefore do you so,   291
Now making glad the man of woe
With joy and pleasure fleeting,

With death his life completing?
My Lady *Minnë*, is it meet
A manly spirit thus to treat
And cause a heart so brave and chaste
To be dishonored and abased?
The lowly and the high in worth
And every living thing on earth 10
Will never join in strife with you
But that you win the day anew.
To you we must the power allow;
That this is truth we all avow.
One honor only you may claim,
Dame *Minnë*, else your praise is lame:
Dame *Liebë's*[7] your associate,
Alone you're in a hapless state.
Dame *Minnë*, you can be untrue
In customs old but ever new: 20
You rob some women of their name,
Drive others to incestuous shame.
Masters by you have been beguiled
That they their vassals' beds defiled,
And friend to friend has shown despite
(Your works can easily come to light),
With vassals their lords deceiving.
You, *Minnë*, should be grieving;
You bring the body to lecherous lust:
The soul will mourn at this, and must.

 Dame *Minnë*, since you have the power 292
To age the young with every hour,
That have at best such fleeting years,
How treacherous your work appears!
 Such words can only befit the wight
Who ne'er through you has had delight.[8]
Had you been of more help to me,
I'd praise you not so listlessly.
To make me lose you've fixed the dice
And rigged the play to a miss precise, 10
Till I've no confidence in you.
Pity for me you never knew.

But you are far too nobly born
That e'er my puny rage or scorn
Against you any charge should bring.
Your spurring has so many a sting
That heavy loads fall on the heart.
Heinrich von Veldekë showed his art,
He likened your nature to a tree;[9]
Had he but told how you might be   20
Successfully and long retained![10]
Instead, he split his tree, explained
How you're to be securely won.
Stupidity has oft undone
A great find unexpected.
If such is in me detected,
Dame *Minnë*, you to blame will be
Who prudence keep under lock and key.
Against you shield and sword lack powers,
Fleet horses, castles high, and towers:
You triumph over all defence.   293
On sea or all the continents,
What can resist your stinging
By swimming or by winging?
Minnë, you showed the power you hold
When Parzival, the fighter bold,
Through you his wits completely lost
By being faithful to his cost.
His wife, so noble and so fair,
Sent you to be her envoy there,   10
The queen of Belrapeirë.
Kardeiz,[11] son of Tampenteirë,
Her brother, him you also killed.
If you to take such toll are willed,
I'm glad I'm not your debtor,
Unless you'd treat me better.
For all of us I've said this word,
Now let me tell what else occurred.
    Keyë, the bold and sightly,
Came out in harness knightly,   20
As if a joust he wanted.
And this I ween had granted

Of Gahmuret the doughty son.
All ladies who have smiled and won
Men's hearts should wish him all success,
For a woman caused him such distress
That *Minnë* took his wits away.
But Keyë still postponed the fray
Till this he'd let the stranger know:
"Sir, since your fate has willed it so,
That you've brought our king to infamy,   294
My counsel, if you'll hark to me,
Is that from danger you abstain
By putting on a good dog-chain,
That I to him may take you.
Be sure I'll not forsake you
Till conquered you are brought to him:
Your treatment will be rather grim."
Still *Minnë* kept the young man dazed
And mute, but valiant Keyë raised   10
His spear and smote with such a swing
His head as made his helmet ring.
Said he, "It's time to be waking:
Without sheets for its making
A bed for thee I'm going to name;
My hand will choose a different aim.
I'll lay thee on the snow, I will.
The beast that bears the sacks to mill,[12]
If he got such a beating,
No slackness were repeating."   20
Dame *Minnë*, look to this! " 'Tis you,
I ween, whom they insult anew,
Peasants would speak of one accord:
Let this be done as to my lord!"[12a]
He would cry out if he could speak.
Dame *Minnë*, let him vengeance wreak,
This hero chained by error.
If you'd withdraw your terror,
The bitter burden on his breast,
Defence he'd find, this noble guest.
   Keyë charged him with a bound   295

And forced his horse to turn around,,
So this Valaisan must forego
His ever sweet but bitter woe:
The image of her dainty sheen,
His wife, of Belrapeirë the queen.
I mean the snow with bloody stain.
Dame Consciousness returned again
And once again his senses stirred.
His steed for jousting Keyë spurred   10
To gallop on in full career:
Lowered was each one's mighty spear.
Keyë's jousting brought him,
As his keen eye had taught him,
In the other's shield a window wide,
But this success was nullified,
For Keyë, steward of the crown,
In the counterthrust went crashing down
Across the log where the goose was forced,
So that the steed and man unhorsed   20
Found a most unhappy bed:
The rider hurt, the charger dead.
Between his pommel and a stone
The man's right arm and left leg-bone
Were broken by the mighty fall;
The girth, the saddle, bells, and all
Were shattered by the hurtling flight.
Two blows the guest could thus requite:
One given a maiden for his sake,[13]
And one that he had had to take.

   Parzival, who falseness slew,   **296**
Was taught by loyalty anew
To find the snowy blood-drops three
That brought insensibility.
Thoughts of the Grail that caused his plight,
His wife's complexion, red and white,
Each was a grief and burden dread,
But heaviest weighed Dame *Minnë's* lead.
Sadness and love's madness
Break down the stoutest gladness: 10

Parzival at King Arthur's Court

Adventure would ye call the twain?
Rather let us call them pain.
Brave folk the seneschal's distress
Should pity, for by manliness
He was impelled to many a strife.
In many lands the tales are rife
That Keyë, Arthur's seneschal,
Had no true courtesy at all;[14]
But my reports exonerate
The man and call him virtue's mate.　　20
However few with me agree,
Good faith and noble bravery
Had Key', on that I would insist.
I'll tell still more, if ye will list.
A gathering place was Arthur's home:
From far away did many come,
The worthless and the worthy,
The showoffs and the earthy.
Those who in honesty were loose,
For such men Keyë had no use;
But he who cared for *courtoisie*　　297
And valued worthy company—
Keyë that man respected,
To serve him ne'er neglected.
I'll say this of the seneschal:
He was indeed quite critical.
But oft he feigned such ugliness
To shield King Arthur from distress.
Those who deceive or idly prate
From noble folk he'd separate:　　10
On them he'd fall like deadly hail,
No bee could sting so with his tail.
Look, these have vilified his name.
Good faith and virtue were his fame,
But hate to him did men accord.
Thuringia's Herman, noble lord,[15]
Among thy *inmates* I have seen
Some who had better *outmates* been.
A Keyë thou as well wouldst need,
Since thy known charity must lead　　20

To thee a motley retinue,
In part a base and lowly crew,
In part a noble, worthy throng.
This will explain Sir Walther's song:
"Bad men and good, I greet you!"[16]
Where such a song can meet you,
False men are there abided.
Such songs Key' would have chided,
No less Sir Heinrich von Rispach.[17]
Now listen while I take you back
To Plimizoël upon the plain.   298
Keyë now was borne amain
To where the king was tented;
Loudly his friends lamented,
Many ladies and many a man.
Along came my lord Gawan
And joined them where the steward lay.
Said he, "Alas, unhappy day
On which thou didst to jousting wend,
Whereby I've lost a trusted friend."   10
Loud was his lamenting.
Said Keyë, his anger venting,
"Are you lamenting thus my life?
If so, you're like a wailing wife.
You are King Arthur's sister's son:[18]
O, could your will by me be done,
As oft by you was spoken!
When God gave me limbs unbroken,
My hand no truce has given,
And oft for you I've striven   20
And would still do so, could it be.
Lament no more, leave pain to me.
Your uncle there, our ruler high,
Will find no Keyë such as I.
To venge me you're too nobly born,
But if one finger you had lorn,
To risk life would not grieve me.
I trust you will believe me.
Heed it not that I'd incite you,
For he[19] out there can bite you,

Who abides there still and flee will not,   299
Not galloping nor at a trot.
Nor is there here a lady's hair,
And were it twice as fine and fair,
But it were like an iron band
To stay from fight your good right hand.
A man with gentleness like this
A credit to his mother is:[20]
Strength from his father gets a man.
Turn to your mother, Sir Gawan!   10
Then at a sword-flash you will pale,
Your manly hardness softly quail."
Thus was this man of eminence
Attacked where he had no defence,
With words: these he could not requite.
'Tis so with men who're bred aright:
Shame keeps them from an answering word;
Of that the shameless never heard.
   Gawan then to Keyë spoke:
"Where swords or lances smote or broke,   20
Whate'er of that was done to me,
If one my color fain would see,
I ween he'd find no paling
At thrusting or at flailing.
Thy rage has little reason,
I've served thee in every season."
Sir Gawan left forthwith the tent
And bade the men his steed present
Without a spur, without a sword;
Thus mounted rode the noble lord.
He sought the young Valaisan man   300
Whose wits were still in *Minnë's* ban.
By three big rents his shield was lamed
Where heroes' spears at it had aimed
And Orilus slashed it with his sword.
Thus Gawan rode across the sward,
Not galloping nor plunging
With lowered lance for lunging:
He wished to find out peacefully
The unknown knight's identity.   10

He greeted with good breeding
This Parzival unheeding.
So he behaved without his will:
Dame *Minnë* wielded power still
O'er him whom Herzeloydë bore.
Uncounted[21] ancestry before
Withdrew him from his common sense,
Likewise a suffering intense
From parents both inherited.
Thus Parzival appeared as dead
To all that Gawan's lips would say,
To every message he'd convey.

   King's Lot's son now essayed anew:
"Sir, you would injure me, since you
Refuse me salutation.
I feel no trepidation
Another question to begin.
King Arthur's vassals and his kin
And e'en himself you've brought disgrace,
And our dishonor grows apace.
Yet I'll win for you his favor,
Forgiveness of your endeavor,
If you my counsel will obey:
Let me to Arthur lead the way!"
The offspring of King Gahmuret
Paid no head to plea or threat.
The Table Round's best knight and true,
Gawan, the pangs of *Minnë* knew:
What helped him now to understand[22]
Was that he once pierced his own hand
As into *Minnë's* power he fell
And love of woman cast its spell.
From death a queen once saved Gawan
When Laeheline, the valiant man,
With him in a joust competed
And he was quite defeated.
The gentle maiden more than fair
Had given as pledge her head and hair:
Reine Inguse de Bahtarliez,[23]
Thus was the queen's name, if you please.

Thus pondered then my lord Gawan:
"What if Dame *Minnë* holds this man
In ban as she did then with me,
And so his mind in loyalty
Must let love over him hold sway?"
He marked the stranger's eyes, how they
Gazed steadily with absent mind.
A scarf of faille from Syria,[24] lined
With yellow taffeta, Gawan slipped
Across the spots where blood had dripped.

   When the scarf fell on them like a roof,   302
So Parzival was kept aloof,
Once more did Belrapeirë's queen
Restore to him his senses keen;
His heart however she retained.
Now hear the words he had regained:
"Alas, my lady and my wife,
Who's ta'en from me thy beauteous life?[25]
Did not with knightly deed my hand
Acquire thy love, thy crown and land?   10
Did I not free from Clamidê
Thyself, and others in dismay
And sighing, that were serving thee?
And now with clouded eyes I see
Thee not, though bright the sun as aye.
But how this came I cannot say."
And then, "Alas, where is my spear?
I know with me I brought it here."
Sir Gawan answered in a word:
"You lost the spear in jousting, lord."   20
"With whom?" the hero bold replied.
"No shield or sword is at your side,
What fame, by fighting you, were gained?
But when your mockery I've sustained,
Then better you may treat me.
No man could yet unseat me
In joust. If such with you is denied,
I ween the lands around are wide
Enough for seeking toil and fame,
The joys that cheer, the fears that lame."

My lord Gawan replied anew, 303
"In all that I have said to you
Lucid and kind I mean to seem,
Not turbid like a muddy stream.
I ask but that for which I'd serve.
Here bide a king and knights of verve
And many a beauteous damsel fair.
Right willingly I'd guide you there;
If with me you'll be riding,
I'll save you from all chiding." 10
"You're gracious, sir, and are so kind,
To serve you I am well inclined.
But since to guide me I've your word,
Pray who are you, and who's your lord?"
"He whom I serve at his command
Has given me many a boon and land,
A part of which I'll mention.
So kind is his intention
That knightly gifts from him I've got.
It was his sister wed King Lot, 20
And she it was that gave me birth.
Whatever God to me on earth
Has granted, serves my master's fame:
King Arthur is the monarch's name.
My name as well is unconcealed,
And everywhere it is revealed:
Those who as acquaintance claim me
Are wont Gawan to name me.
My name and I will serve you aye
If shame from me you'll turn away."[26]
"Art thou Gawan?" he cried aloud. 304
"I ween I scarcely can be proud
To hear from thee so kind a word,
For of thee often I have heard
That *all* men kindly thou dost treat.
For me, such kindness were not meet
Unless I can repay it.
Tell me, if thou canst say it,
Whose are the many tents there set?
If Arthur's there, I must regret 10

That in honor I may not be seen,
Either by him or by the queen,
Till I avenge a thrashing
At which my teeth I'm gnashing
E'en yet, with sorrow laden.
On me a noble maiden
Bestowed a laugh: the steward rude
Splintered on her a forest of wood."[27]
"Vengeance is done, he's broken" —
This was by Gawan spoken— 20
"His right arm and his left leg-bone.
Ride hither, see both horse and stone,
And here lie splinters on the snow:
Thy spear, whose fate thou fain wouldst know."
When Parzival saw this was true,
To Gawan he put questions new:
"Upon thee I rely, Gawan,
That yonder fell the selfsame man
By whom disgrace on me was spilt.
And now I'll follow where thou wilt."
"I'll never lie to thee or cheat," 305
Said Gawan, "here didst thou defeat
Sir Segramors, a hero bold
Of whom most valiant deeds are told.
'Twas done by thee ere Key' went down.
In both fights thou hast gained renown."
   They rode together, man and man,
The young Valaisan and Gawan.
On horse and foot a goodly crowd
Uttered a welcome kind and loud 10
To Gawan and the knight in red,
For they were courtly folk, well bred.
His tent sought Gawan there at hand.
Dame Cunnewarë de Laland
Tented beside him in the row.
What joy the gentle maid must know
To greet and thank her valiant knight
For avenging Keyë's cruel slight.
She took her brother[28] by the hand
And Dame Jeschutë of Karnant; 20

'Twas thus he saw her coming there.
No rust his beauty could impair,
Like dewy roses hither blown.
His harness swiftly from him thrown,
He sprang up, as the three he spied.
Now hear what Cunnewarë cried:
  "By God to start with, then by me
Be welcomed, since with you I see
True manliness has still remained.
From laughter I had e'er refrained
Until with you acquainted. 306
But Keyë then attainted
My joy in you with beating rough.
This you have now avenged enough.
I'd kiss you, were I worth a kiss,"
"I should myself have wished for this,"
Replied her champion, "if I might:
Your greeting fills me with delight."
She kissed him, bade him sit again
And sent a maiden from her train 10
With orders splendid clothes to bring,
All tailored, suited for a king
And made of silk from Ninivê.
Her prisoner, King Clamidê,
For him 'twas planned to wear it.
The maid complained who bare it,
Saying the mantle had no cord.[29]
Cunnewarë said no word,
But from her dress a string she drew
And took the cloak and pulled it through. 20
He asked her leave to go, and scrubbed
His face, the rust from it he rubbed:
Red-lipped, fair-skinned returned the guest
And in his raiment new was dressed:
Ha, but he was both proud and fair!
Whoever saw him must declare
He was of living men the flower:
Such rightful praise was beauty's dower.
Becoming to him were his clothes.
And now an emerald they chose,

Which fastened at his throat he wore.   307
But Cunnewarë gave him more:
A costly girdle for his own;
Beasts formed by many a precious stone
Along the outer edge were sewed,
A ruby as the buckle glowed.
How looked the youth without a beard
When in his finery he appeared?
Why, well enough, this tale doth tell.
The people's hearts were neath his spell.   10
Those who saw him, man or maid,
High respect to him they paid.
   The king had listened to the Mass
And from the church they saw him pass:
With Knights of the Table Round he came,
Not one a prey to fraud and blame.
They all by now had heard it said
That he had come, the knight in red,
In Gawan's tent his guest to be.
So Arthur neared of Brittany.   20
Antanor, once so soundly thrashed,
Before King Arthur swiftly dashed
Till this Valaisan guest he spied.
"Did you avenge both me," he cried,
"And Cunnewarë de Laland?
For that men highly praise your hand.
Keyë's pawn is stranded,
His threats on a reef have landed.
I little fear his mighty stroke
For now his good right arm is broke."
   The youthful Parzival now stood,   308
Though wingless, as an angel would
That blossomed into earthly sight.
The king and many a noble knight
Greeted him full sweetly.
Filled with good will completely
Were all who saw his winsomeness.
To him their hearts all answered Yes,
To praise of him none answered No.
So winning was his youthful glow.   10

The king addressed the valiant lad:
"You've done to me both good and bad,
But the honor you have lent me,
Brought to me and sent me,
Is more than man e'er gave to me.
I've paid for that but scantily,
E'en though naught else you had attained
But for Jeschut' the duchess gained
Her husband's love and confidence.
Be sure, Sir Keyë's grave offense[30]
Avengèd and atoned had been
If I your face ere now had seen."
King Arthur, answering him, declared
Why he and his had hither fared[31]
And had through many countries pressed.
Then of him all made this request:
That by his oath he should be bound
Henceforth to all of the Table Round,
With each associated.
By this he felt elated,
And his delight was justified.
So their request was not denied.

 Now listen, counsel me, and say
If this Round Table can today
That old tradition well observe
From which King Arthur ne'er would swerve.
To eat with him no knight might sit
If e'er Adventure should omit
Her daily visit steady.
But Adventure's here already;
This honor the Table must maintain.
Though at Nantes the Table must remain,
Its rights they gave to a flowery mead:[32]
No bush or tent was there to impede.
This should be done, King Arthur said,
In honor of the knight called red:
His true desert was thus made known.
A silken cloth from Acraton,[33]
From a heathen country far away,
Served as the Table Round that day,

Not wide but cut to make it round,
Matching the table far renowned.
This rule equality must bring:
No knight might claim to face the king,
Thus none was hinder, none was fore.
King Arthur ordered something more:
That noble knights and ladies too
Around the circle one should view:
All those accorded high estate,
Maid, wife, and man at table ate.
 And now Queen Guinevere came there   310
With many ladies of beauty rare
And noble princesses as well,
All fairer than the tongue could tell.
They made the ring so wide and free
As not to crowd: in harmony
Each lady sat beside her lord.
The king who falsity abhorred
Led the Valaisan by the hand.
Dame Cunnewarë de Laland   10
Walked upon his other side:
No more her heart for sorrow cried.
King Arthur eyed the knight called red,
And you shall hear the words he said:
"Of my old wife I ask for this,
That she your fair young face shall kiss.
True, *you*'d not need to beg us here
For kisses, coming from Belrapeir',
Where sweetest kisses wait for you.
But there's one thing for which I'd sue: 20
Should I come to your home some day,
Your wife this kiss shall then repay."
"I'll gladly meet your wishes there,"
Said Parzival, "or otherwhere."
With but a few steps to meet him
The queen gave her kiss to greet him:
"I now forgive you truly,"
Said she, "the pain that newly
Was put into my heart by you,
What time your hand King Ither slew."

While pardoning, her eyes grew wet, 311
For Ither's dying grieved her yet,
And her ladies all had felt dismay.
And now they placed King Clamidê
On the bank of River Plimizoël.
With him sat Jofreit fiz Idoël.
Twixt Clamidê and Gawan
They set the young Valaisan man:
Assurance doth the story bring
That no one sat around the ring 10
Of all who'd sucked a mother's breast
Who stood so well each knightly test.
For blest with youth yet passing strong
This young Valaisan came along.
Regard him well with proper mien:[34]
Full many a wife herself has seen
In a glass less bright than his lips of red.
Now let this of his skin be said
That there on chin and cheek you'd view:
His winsomeness as tongs might do[35] 20
To clasp and hold attention
As fickleness' prevention.
I think of women who waver,
Who give and withdraw their favor.
His handsomeness held women bound,
Toward him no fickleness was found:
They greeted him with loyalty,
Through eyes into their hearts went he.
 Men and women wished him well;
Thus of esteem his life could tell,
Until a time for sighing came. 312
Now she approached whom I will name,
A maid whose loyalty was great,
But now fanatic in her hate,
She said things woe betiding.
I'll tell you what she was riding:
A mule it was, a horse in height,
'Twas fallow and a curious sight,
For its nose was slit, and brands it bare,
Like a true Hungarian battle-mare. 10

Her bridle and accoutrements
Were neatly wrought in every sense,
A rich and costly dower.
Her mule-horse paced with power.
Like a lady she did not appear:
Alas, what meant her coming here?
And yet she came, it had to be:
She brought the king's men misery.
The maid was master of such skill
That all the tongues she spoke at will: 20
French, Latin, Arabic she'd learned.
The highest knowledge in her burned
As of logic and geometry,
And e'en the skill commanded she
Of what is called astronomy.
By name they called her Cundry,[36]
Surziere was her second name.
Her mouth and tongue were far from lame
And talkative enough they were.
Much joy was now cast down by her.

    The maid, howe'er intelligent,   **313**
In looks she was quite different
From those we know as *bea gent*.[37]
A garment exquisite from Ghent,
Bluer than lapis lazuli,
This kill-joy wore for all to see,
A hooded cape, well cut and sewed,
And French according to its mode;
Beneath, a silken dress well-groomed.
A hat from London, peacock-plumed 10
And lined with costly cloth of gold
(The hat was new, the strings not old),
Was hanging down the maiden's back.
Her story was a bridge, alack!
Across their joy great grief it bore,
And no one jested any more.
Over the hat one hair-braid swung
And down upon the mule it hung,
Black and hard and not too fine,
Soft as the bristles on a swine. 20

Her nose was like a canine snout
And from her mouth two teeth stood out
Like boar-tusks, each a half-foot long.
She thrust her braided eyebrows strong
Beneath the ribbon on her head.
The truth has made me seem ill-bred
A woman to limn with words so plain.
Of me no others need complain.
   Cundry had ears just like a bear.
No lover for her face could care,
For it revealed a hairy hide.   **314**
A whip she carried at her side:
Of silk the thongs that lashed the mule,
The handle was a ruby jewel.
As monkey-skin one well might class
The hands of this attractive lass.
Her finger-nails were not too white,
And if my source records it right
More like a lion's claws were they.
For *her* love few knights risked a fray.   10
'Twas thus into the ring she rode,
The source of woe, of joy the goad.
Seeking the host she took her stand.
Cunnewarë de Laland
At Arthur's side did sit and eat;
The Queen of Janfuse,[38] as was meet,
Beside Queen Guinevere she ate;
King Arthur dined in royal state.
Cundry approached the Breton lord
And all in French she spoke her word.   20
All this for you I must translate:
My joy therein is none too great.
"Fil li roy Utpandragon,
Thyself and many a Breton's son
Thou hast disgraced with thy own hand.
The best of men from any land
Would gather here in honor all,
Were not that honor mixed with gall.
The Table Round is nullified:
Falseness is now with it allied.

King, men thy name were praising,   315
Above all others raising,
But fate thy pride is taming,
Thy rising glory laming,
Thy lofty fame is drooping:
To falseness thou'st been stooping.
The glamor of this Table Round
Has dwindled now that it has found
The company of Parzival,
Though outwardly he's knight withal.   10
'Tis him ye call the Knight in Red,
From him who there at Nantes lay dead.
Their lives must shed unequal light:
No lips e'er told us of a knight
To equal him in nobleness."[39]
Then Parzival she would address.
Said she, " 'Tis you who are to blame
That proper greeting I disclaim
To Arthur and his company.
May your fair face accursèd be,   20
Your manly body strong and fine.
If peace and clemency were mine,
I'd never let them serve your need.
You think I'm of uncanny breed,
Yet I'm far cannier than you.
Sir Parzival, now tell me true
And give me explanation:
When without consolation
The fisher sat, could only grieve,
Why would you not his pain relieve?
   He showed how much he was oppressed.   316
You faithless, inconsiderate guest!
Had you ta'en pity on his woe!
I hope your mouth a void will show,
Reft of your tongue there slacking,
As your heart true sense is lacking!
To hell your name's been given
By God on high in heaven,
And so it will be here on earth
When this is known to men of worth.   10

You curse of bliss, salvation's ban,
You blight on all the worth of man!
So lacking in all manly will,
In nobleness profoundly ill,
No cure for you brings doctor's care.
I'm willing on your head to swear,
If one will grant me such an oath,
That beauty and greater falseness both
To no one else are so innate.
You adder's fang, you fish-hook bait![40]   20
The host gave you a sword to wear,
With which your worth could not compare.
Your silence wrought great evil,
You're the playmate of the devil.
Accursèd man, Sir Parzival,
You saw the Grail borne in the hall,
The silver knives, the bloody spear,
You joy-thief, bringer of sorrows drear!
If you'd but asked—alas the pity!—
Famed Tabronite,[41] the heathen city,
In every glory basking,   317
Could not have matched this asking.
Yonder country's noble queen[42]
Feirefiz Anshevîn
Won in arduous knightly fray.
He's kept that valor to this day
Which in your common sire began.
Your brother is a wondrous man.
As black and white his skin is seen,
The son of Zazamanc's noble queen.   10
Of Gahmuret I think anew:
In his heart falseness never grew.
Your father, who from Anjou came,
Left you no heritage of shame,
As now is your election.
Your fame has found rejection.
Had e'er your mother acted wrong,
Then my suspicion would be strong
That you another's son might be.
But no, she pined in loyalty: 20

Give her your approbation.
Your sire by reputation
From manly honor never swerved
And ever highest praise deserved.
Right merrily his voice could bawl.
A mighty heart, but little gall[43]
His breast encompassed; 'twould appear
A dam was he, a fishing weir:
His virile and courageous ways
Could catch the fish of public praise.
Your glories now to falseness turn.   318
Woe's me that e'er I had to learn
That Herzeloydë's only son[44]
His prize and praise has so undone!"
   By sorrow Cundry was unstrung:
Weeping aloud her hands she wrung,
That tear on tear fell on her breast;
Great wailing from her eyes she pressed.
Devotion 'twas that taught her
To show the grief this brought her.   10
Returning to King Arthur's side,
Her messages she amplified.
Said she, "Is here no noble knight
Who craves reward for all his might
And lofty *Minnë's* glowing?
Four queens[45] I could be showing,
Besides four hundred maidens sweet,
For any knightly eye a treat.
Chastel Merveil's their domicile.[46]
All high adventure seems as nil   20
Compared with what may there be won,
If *Minnë's* will is duly done.
Despite all hardships, far from slight,
I mean to get there by tonight."
The mournful damsel full of rue
Forsook the ring without adieu;
Weeping she often turned her head,
Now hear the final words she said:
"Oh, Munsalvaesch', thou sorrow's goal!
Alas that none will thee console!"

        Cundry called the Sorceress,   319
        Unlovely, and yet proud no less,
        Had burdened the Valaisan lad.
        What availed the doughty heart he had?
        True breeding in a manly breast,
        Yet even more this man possessed,
        That ruled all else—a sense of shame:
        To shun all falseness was his aim.
        A sense of shame will merit praise
        And crown the soul for all men's days.   10
        In all our virtues shame stands high.
        Cunnewarë began to cry
        That Cundry in this wise should scold
        Young Parzival, the hero bold,
        Cundry that strange creation.
        Now heartfelt tribulation
        Brought flowing tears to many eyes
        Of noble ladies full of sighs.

    Cundry departs and immediately thereafter a well accoutered knight appears on a hostile mission. His name is Kingrimursel (in Crestien Guigambresil). He asks to see King Arthur and Sir Gawan; the latter he accuses of the murder of his lord Kingrisin—a charge of which Gawan is later cleared. Kingrimursel summons Gawan to appear in two weeks in Schanpfanzun before King Vergulaht of Ascalun. In vain does Beacurs, Gawan's brother, try to intercede for him; Gawan agrees to heed the summons and to fight Kingrimursel. Now Clamidê appears before Parzival and asks him to favor his suit for Cunnewarë. This Parzival does. Through the heathen queen Ekuba Parzival learns more about his half-brother Feirefiz, the mighty king of Zazamanc and Azagouc. Ekuba herself, it turns out, is related to Feirefiz on her mother's side. Parzival, who is more dejected even than King Arthur and his knights as a result of Cundry's disclosures and execrations, has now decided to leave the Round Table and to go out in order to make amends for his remissness and to seek the Grail once more. However, he does not depart without emphasizing that it was Gurnemanz who had advised him not to ask questions:

        If I a mockery am made   330
        Because good breeding I obeyed,

His counsel was not wholly wise:
'Twas Gurnemanz who did advise
With questions ne'er to be too free,
Thus fighting impropriety.   (Lines 1-6)
His farewell from King Arthur and the knights is touching.
(319, 19—331, 21)
>There kissed him now my lord Gawan,
These manly thoughts expressing
To him such strength possessing:
"I know that wheresoe'er thou fare
Much opposition thou must bear.
God grant thee all success in this,
And help me too, lest I should miss
The chance to serve thee as I would:
God grant me this, my wish is good!"
He of Valois: "Woe, what is God?   332
Were He almighty, scorn so odd
To thee and me He'd not have sent,
If He had been omnipotent.
To serve Him e'er was in my mind,
Since I had hoped His grace to find.
But now His service I forswear.
If me He hate, that hate I'll bear.
Friend, when thy time has come for strife,
Then may some lady pledge her life   10
And e'er to thee her guidance show—
Her virtue thou must surely know—
With woman's kindness toward thee,
And may her loving guard thee.
Will e'er our paths together run?
At least my wish for thee be done."
Their parting was harsh labor,
And sorrow was their neighbor.
With him Dame Cunnewarë went,
Escorting him into her tent.   20
To bring his gear was her command,
And she herself with gentle hand
Equipped the son of Gahmuret.
Said she, "By right I pay this debt,
Since Brandigan's king,[47] high in fame,

Because of you my hand would claim.
Care for your reputation
Brings me to tribulation.
So long as you must bear distress,
Your grief gnaws at my happiness."
    The harnessed steed they brought him   333
And now new sorrow sought him.
This handsome, well accoutered knight
Wore armor that was gleaming white:
Its costliness all eyes bespoke.
His corselet and his outer cloak
With precious stones were richly set.
One thing he had not donned as yet:
His helmet still beside him lay.
He kissed her who behind must stay,   10
Cunnewarë the beauteous maid:
This tale to me has been conveyed.
In sadness, heavy-hearted,
These loving friends now parted.
The son of Gahmuret rode away.

Gawan prepares for his journey to Schanpfanzun. Ekuba returns home. Arthur goes back to Karidoêl, while Orilus and Jeschutë accompany Clamidê to his home in Brandigan, where he is to marry Cunnewarë. In some manuscripts Wolfram indicates a break here and invites other writers to take up the tale. (333, 16 —337, 30)

Book Seven
Gawan and Obilot

Book Seven

GAWAN AND OBILOT

Who never yielded to disgrace, 338
For some time he shall claim first place
In these adventures high, a man
To all as noble known: Gawan.
In this tale many a man is seen
Beside the hero, above him e'en,
Who plays the chief role—Parzival.
Who gives his friend[1] no faults at all
But to the highest height would raise,
Must not expect the hearers' praise. 10
But men's approval is his due
Who only praises when it's true:
Else all that then or now is said
Will find no shelter o'er its head.
What man has prudence guide him
If the wise stand not beside him?
Who tells a lying narrative,
'Twould serve him right if he must live
All homeless out upon the snow,
So that the mouth would suffer woe 20
Which claims the truth it's saying.
Thus God would be repaying
That crime, as wished by men whose truth
Brings them but care with carking tooth.
Should a poet aim at tales like these,
Which bring reproof and never please—
If a noble patron him sustain,
He must be lacking in his brain.
He'd shun that if possessed of shame:
Let shame control! Be that his aim.[2]

    Gawan the warrior wary, 339
Of too much fighting chary,
Saw to't that cowardice was ne'er
Allowed his glory to impair.
In strife, a castle was his heart,
And sharp attack so made it smart

> That into the thickest fight he pressed.
> Friend and foreman both confessed:
> His battle-cry re-echoed loud,
> What though Kingrimursel the proud   10
> Fain had reduced his just renown.

Leaving King Arthur and passing through a wooded valley, Gawan discovers a martial host on the march, accompanied by numerous camp followers. Gawan mingles with the crowd and learns from a squire that King Meljanz of Liz is one of the leaders of the expedition, which is bound for Beärosche to punish Duke Lyppaut, Meljanz's tutor and liegeman. Lyppaut's daughter Obie had flippantly rejected the amorous advances of Meljanz, whom she really loves. Gawan is undecided whether to remain and perhaps take a part in the adventure because he fears he may miss his appointment in Schanpfanzun. Finally he decides to remain. Approaching Beärosche and the castle, he sees Lyppaut's wife and two daughters, Obie and Obilot. They wonder who he may be. (339, 12—352, 11)

> Said they, "Who's coming here to us?"   352
> The duchess mother spoke and said,
> "By what troop are we visited?"
> The older girl[3] said presently,
> " 'Tis a merchant, mother, don't you see?"
> "But shields his men are bearing, too."
> "That's what many merchants do."
> The younger girl[4] was heard to cry,
> "Thy charge his bearing doth belie.   20
> Sister, thou shouldst be ashamed,
> A merchant he was never named.
> He is so beauteous to see,
> My warrior the knight shall be.
> His service well may crave reward:
> Favor and love I will accord."

Gawan finds an olive tree and a linden at the wall. Dismounting, he camps there with his squires. His chamberlain provides a mattress and a pillow. (352, 27—353, 12)

> The mother-duchess spoke her mind: 353
> "What merchant, daughter, wouldst thou find
> With such behavior knightly?
> Pray treat him more politely."

Then said the youthful Obilot,
"Worse than that's come from her throat:
Toward King Meljanz of Liz she showed
The foolish pride that in her glowed,   20
When he her love requested.
Such feelings I detested!"
Obie made protestation,
Not free from irritation:[5]
"I find his ways unfitting:
A merchant there is sitting,
A host of goods he hopes to sell.
He's watching all his boxes well:
Thy knight, thou silly sister mine,
He makes himself a watchman fine."

Gawan overhears this conversation. The besieged town receives reinforcements, and Duke Lyppaut and his men sally forth to do battle. A part of the invading host joins in the battle, Gawan looking on. (354, 1—357, 30)

"Look here," Obie said, "sister mine,   358
I ween my champion[6] and thine
Quite different types of battle choose.
Thine seems to think that we shall lose[7]
Castle and hill in yonder fight.
We'll have to find some other knight."
The young one bore her mockery:
"He'll make amends for this," said she.
"I still expect his valiant deed,
That from thy scorn he will be freed.   10
To me his service he'll accord,
I'll give him joy as his reward.
Since he's a merchant, by thy tale,
I'll offer my reward for sale."

Gawan hears these words, too. Meanwhile the battle continues and Meljanz is hard pressed. Obie sends a page to Gawan to ask him what he offers for sale, but is sternly rebuffed. Now she dispatches the burgrave Scherules to Gawan, but he, noticing the stranger's noble appearance, invites him as a guest. Gawan accepts the invitation but meanwhile Obie reports to her father Lyppaut that he is a money-changer and counterfeiter in possession of rich treasures. Lyppaut, thinking that such a person might be of help to him in his feud, sets out to accost him but is advised by Scherules that Obie's description of him is not true. Now Lyppaut is more eager than ever to meet the stranger and goes with Scherules to meet him. (358, 15—364, 25)

        His eyesight and his heart confessed
        (Which Lyppaut with him took along)
        That handsome was this guest and strong,
        And that his manners and his face
        Of manliness showed every trace.
          Whom true love e'er has brought to this,   365
        That he has suffered *Minnë's* bliss,
        He's learned that every loving heart
        Is forfeit from the very start
        To love, is mortgaged, pledged, and sold.
        No tongue has e'er completely told
        The wonders love will do, and can.
        Be it a woman or a man,
        True love will oft deceive them,
        Of noble sense relieve them.   10
        Meljanz and the maid Obie,
        Their love was true to such degree,
        So faithfully adoring,
        That ye should be deploring
        The wrath that made him from her ride.
        Her grief was then so magnified
        That wrath grew out of gentleness.
        This Gawan suffered, though errorless,
        And others too who bore with her.
        From womanly ways she oft would err.   20
        Thus wrath from tenderness was born.
        In both her eyes it thrust a thorn
        Whene'er she saw a man esteemed:
        Her heart as to her Meljanz deemed
        That *he* must be the best of all.
        She thought, "Should sorrow me befall
        Through him, I'll suffer it with joy.
        This noble, sweet, and precious boy,
        I'd set no man before him,
        My heart and soul adore him."
        Oft love as the cause of wrath we see,   366

So don't be hard on poor Obie.⁸

Lyppaut bids Gawan welcome and asks him to be his ally, but Gawan tells him of his engagement in Schanpfanzun. Disappointed, Lyppaut explains how he is torn between love for his daughters and loyalty to his lord. He hopes he will some day have a son-in-law. Gawan politely assures him of his good will and asks for more time before reaching a decision. (366, 3—368, 9)

In the courtyard there was Obilot,   10
With her the burgrave's little girl,⁹
Playing a game, small rings to hurl.¹⁰
The father put the question mild,
"Tell me, whence comst thou here, my child?"
"From the castle, father, for I think
From my request he will not shrink.
I'm going to beg the stranger-lord
To serve me for my love's reward."
"Daughter, I regret to say
He told me neither yea nor nay.   20
Get his consent to my request."
Off ran the child to find the guest.
When she into his chamber sped,
Gawan sprang up. With greeting said,
He sat down by the sweet young maid
And thanked her that respect she paid
To him when he had been maligned.
Said he, "If e'er a knight must find
Distress for such a damsel small,
For your sake I should bear it all."

    This maiden sweet, endearing,   **369**
Said, frank and true appearing,
"God will aver, as well He can,
That you, sir, are the firstest man
With whom as now I'm pleading.
If thus I show good breeding
And keep my woman's modesty,
'Twill be a gain in joy to me.
For this is what my teacher taught:
That speech should be the roof of thought.   10
Sir, I would plead for me and you:¹¹

A real distress brings me thereto.
I'll speak of this if you permit.
E'en though you censure me for it,
Decorum I'm not ceding,
For with myself I'm pleading.[12]
Actually, you are I,
No matter what our names reply.
You shall have my identity
And maid and man at once shall be.
Of you and me I've made request:
If, sir, you fail to meet the test,
So I must go from you in shame,
Your own repute will suffer blame
As judged by honor you've been taught,[13]
Since as a maid I refuge sought,
That you my need be stilling.
Sir, if you are willing,
Henceforth my love to you I'll give,
For you with all my heart I'll live.
If you true manliness will use,
I ween that you will not refuse
Me service: I am worth your deeds.
The fact that father also needs
The help of friends, the help of kin,
Need not affect what you begin:
For my reward you'll serve us both."
Said Gawan, "Lady, from my troth
I'd part, should I obey you.[14]
Such unfaith should dismay you.
My faith is pledged with heart and head,
If it's unredeemed, my name is dead.
But were my service and my mind
To gain your *Minne* well inclined,
Ere you are ready love to give
Some five more years you have to live.[15]
So long you'll have to wait love's call."
But then he thought how Parzival
In women more than God would trust.[16]
This thought the maiden's pleading thrust

GAWAN AND OBILOT

Into Gawan's heart as messenger.
His promise then he gave to her
That thenceforth in her name he'd fight.
And this assurance gave the knight:
"Into your hand my sword be placed.[17]
If e'er with jousting I am faced,
My gallop you'll be riding,
The strife for me deciding.
What though I'm *seen* in any fray,
'Tis yours to win or lose the day."
   Said she, "I've no objection,   371
For I am your protection,
I am your solace and your heart.
Since you my soul from doubting part,
Whate'er ill-luck betide you,
I will escort and guide you,
A roof gainst threatening shower,
A comfort-bringing bower.
My love shall be a source of peace
And from anxiety surcease,   10
So that your valor ne'er will slack,
E'en though to the castle you fall back.[18]
Both host and hostess I shall play
And stay by you in every fray.
If you have confidence in this,
Both strength and luck you'll never miss."
Then noble Gawan spoke again:
"Lady, from you I'll have these twain,
Since I shall live at your command
With love and solace from your hand."   20
Meanwhile, the hands of the little maid
Between his mighty ones were laid.
She said then, "Sir, pray let me go,
For I too must some effort show.
Could you without my gift appear?
For that I hold you far too dear.
I must forgo all leisure
To work for you a treasure.
When this you wear, the fame you gain

No other knight can overstrain."
  The damsel and her playmate went,   372
Both maidens much on service bent
To Gawan, who would save them.
With bows his thanks he gave them,
Saying, "When you have come to years,
If forests yielded only spears
And no wood else that's growing there,
You'd need them all with none to spare.[19]
If *now* such force as this is yours
And when you're older still endures,   10
Your love will show full many a knight
How spears can shatter shields in fight."
The little maids departed,
Right joyful, not downhearted.
The burgrave's daughter, young and fine,
Said, "Pray you, tell me, lady mine,
To give him what do you intend?
Since we have naught but dolls to send.
If yours are not as fair as mine,
Give them to him, I'll not repine.   20
Of quarrels that will be no source."
Prince Lippaut rode up on his horse
And on the hill he spied her,
Claudittë there beside her.
As they were climbing to the top,
He asked the two young girls to stop.
Young Obilot knew how to plead:
"Father, I never had such need
Of thee. Advice is wanted:
The knight my plea has granted."
"Daughter, whatsoe'er thy will,   373
If I have it, I'll fulfill.
Blest was the fruit that in thee lay!
Thy birthday was a happy day."
"Father, then I'll tell to thee
In private just what troubles me.
Thy kind advice I'd like to get."
Upon his steed he had her set.
Said she, "What of my playmate then?"

GAWAN AND OBILOT

With him were many mounted men;
Each one to take the maiden teased:
To have her, none had been displeased.
To one the maid was handed there:
Clauditte too was passing fair.
  Her father said while riding,
"Let's hark to thy confiding:
Give me a hint of thy distress."
"A guerdon, father, I confess
I promised to the stranger-knight.
I fear my mind was not quite right.
If I've no gift for giving,
Of what use is my living,
Since he's agreed to serve me?
Deep shame would quite unnerve me,
If I have naught to give him here.
No man was to a maid so dear."
He answered, "Child, on me rely:
What thou desirest, I'll supply.
Since service from him is thy aim,
I'll give thee such as he might claim,
If thy mother grant permission.
May this help my position.
Oh my, that proud and noble knight,
What hopes with him come into sight!
Yet not a word to him I've said.
Last night I dreamt of him in bed."[20]
  To see the duchess went Lippaut,
There too was daughter Obilot.
Said Lippaut, "Mistress, help us twain.
My heart cried out, but not with pain,
Since God on me this child bestowed
And freed me from a heavy load."
The mother-duchess answered straight,
"What would ye have of my estate?"
"Madam, if you're in readiness,
Our daughter wants a better dress.
She thinks that she deserves it too:
A noble man for her love doth sue

>   Who'd serve her without measure
>   And would her guerdon treasure." 20
>   Then said the maiden's mother,
>   "A sweet, good man, none other!
>   I ween you mean the stranger guest:
>   His glance is like the springtime blest."

Costly clothes are now prepared for Obilot, but one sleeve of her precious garment is sent to Gawan as her guerdon. He attaches it to one of his shields. During the night fortifications are prepared. Gawan and Scherules are to defend one of the gates. The city itself is alive with bustle and colorful attire. The knight Poydiconjunz has so many spears prepared that the Black Forest could scarcely have furnished enough timber to make them. The ground was so cut up by horses' hoofs that it looked like the Erfurt vineyard after King Philip had been besieged there by Landgrave Herman of Thuringia in 1203. Fierce fighting ensues, in which Gawan acquits himself nobly. He rides against the army of Meljanz, one of whose companions is an unidentified Red Knight. Gawan overpowers Meljanz and takes him prisoner. Of the defenders Gawan proves the doughtiest, and of the attackers the Red Knight, but they never meet. When the latter learns of the capture of Meljanz, he orders some of his own prisoners to try to secure Meljanz's release or to lead him to the Grail. Of the Grail, however, they know only that Anfortas is its king. Then the Red Knight asks them to seek Belrapeirë and surrender to its queen, bringing her news about himself. Gawan takes the tattered sleeve from his shield and sends it to Obilot, who is overjoyed. The battle is now over. Meljanz confesses that he has been in the wrong and asks forgiveness of Gawan and Lyppaut. Now the captives of the Red Knight also come and from their description of him Gawan realizes that he is Parzival. Meljanz is turned over to Obilot. There is a general reconciliation. The wedding of Meljanz is celebrated with much pomp. Gawan, well escorted, now takes his leave, much to Obilot's disappointment. (374, 25—397, 30)

Book Eight
Gawan and Antikonie

Book Eight

GAWAN AND ANTIKONIE

Gawan travels through a vast forest and finally reaches the land of Ascalun. Here he notices a splendid castle (Schanpfanzun), more elaborate than Carthage in the days of Eneas (Aeneas) and Tydo (Dido) and comparable to the heathen castles of Acraton (Agra?) and Babylon. He encounters King Vergulaht and five hundred knights, who are hunting herons. Vergulaht's family had been sent by Mazadan from the mountain of Famorgan. He was as handsome as Parzival and resembled Gahmuret, to whom, it turns out later, he is indeed related. Gawan is received more graciously than was Erec (the hero of one of Hartman von Aue's romances) at Karidoël, whither Lady Enite accompanied him. Vergulaht sends Gawan ahead to Schanpfanzun, where he says his sister Antikonie (name not in Crestien) will treat him well. He arrives at the castle. (398, 1—403, 20)

    The castle's praise I must cut short,
For I have much that I'd report
Of the sister of the king, a maid.
Of buildings plenty has been made.
The maid I'll paint as best I should:[1]
If she was fair, then she looked good,
And that her sentiments were right,
That gave her merit greater height,
So that her mind and her address
Were like those of the Margravess
Who from her castle Heitstein[2]   404
O'er all the land was wont to shine.
Blest he who may live close to her
And learn to know her character:
Trust me, he'll find enjoyment there,
And better there than otherwhere.
To speak of ladies I've the right
According to what meets my sight;
But she whom I shall choose to praise,
Let her adhere to virtuous ways.   10
Now may all hearers true and kind
To this adventure turn their mind:

I care naught for the faithless souls;
Their decency is full of holes,
They've lost their chance of heavenly bliss,
They'll feel the wrath of God for this.

Gawan is received in courtly fashion by Antikonie; she is so beautiful that one must regret the death of the poet Heinrich von Veldeke, who alone could have described her. They engage in a long, intimate conversation which ends in his proposal of love. To her question about his identity he answers evasively. She is just about to accept his proposal when an old knight enters and accuses him not only of having slain his master but also of now trying to seduce that master's daughter. For Antikonie is the daughter of Kingrisin. The old man's call to arms is heard by the knights, who come to attack Gawan. He, unable to find his sword, flees with Antikonie to a tower, where he wards off his attackers with a bolt from a door, and a huge chess board. She pelts them with chessmen and fights more furiously than do the women of Dollenstein, near Eschenbach, during their mock battle at Shrovetide. (404, 1—40, 21)

What Gawan there was doing?
Whene'er he found the leisure,
His eyes the maid would measure,
Her mouth, her eyes, her nose compare.
Upon a spit no slenderer hare,
I ween, to you could e'er appear
Than she was fashioned there and here:
I mean between the hips and breast.
A hot desire for *Minnë's* quest
Her body could engender.   410
I ween no ant so slender
You ever saw, with such a waist
As hers where she her girdle placed.
'Twas for her fellow-fighter,
Gawan, a greed inciter.
With him the fighting she endured.
His death alone release insured,
No other terms they wanted.
Their hatred little daunted   10
Gawan, when he beheld her then:
That cost the lives of many men.

GAWAN AND ANTIKONIE   187

King Vergulaht returns and, forgetful of his duties as host, joins in the fight against Gawan. The latter, though yielding to numbers, continues the struggle in the doorway of the tower. Landgrave Kingrimursel, who had summoned Gawan hither, comes and, feeling guilty because of the unchivalrous treatment accorded his guest, aids him in the battle. After much persuasion Vergulaht finally declares an armistice until the charge against Gawan can be investigated. Antikonie, now recognizing a kinsman in the guest, kisses him and reprimands her brother Vergulaht. (410, 13—414, 13)

> "Sir Vergulaht, had I a sword
> And were a man by God's decree
> To bear a shield in chivalry,
> Your fighting quickly had been stayed.[3]
> But I was a defenceless maid,
> Save that a certain shield I bore
> Which honor as its symbol wore.   20
> The coat-of-arms I'll name to you,
> If this you will consent to view:
> Good conduct and a spirit pure,
> These two in constancy endure.
> This shield I held before the knight
> Whom you had sent into my sight.
> That was our sole protection.
> Though now you change direction,[4]
> A wrong to me you tried to do—
> If womanly honor finds its due.
> When it's occurred, I've heard it said,   415
> That one to a maid's protection fled,
> The eagerest pursuing
> Should cease from battle-doing,
> If bravery were paired with right.
> Sir Vergulaht, the desperate flight
> Of Gawan here, his life to keep,
> Upon your head disgrace will heap."
>   Kingrimursel took up the word:
> "Through trust in you this thing occurred,[5]   10
> That I assured Sir Gawan
> Where Plimizoel's waters ran
> Safe entry here into your land.

Upon your honor it must stand
That if courageously he came
I'd guarantee in your good name
That more than *one* he need not fight.
Upon *my* name this puts a blight.
My peers have seen and judge the case:
Too soon to us comes this disgrace.   20
If thus the princes you will spurn,
We'll scorn the monarch in our turn.
If you'd abide by courtliness,
Your courtly honor must confess
That we twain are related.
E'en if it can be stated
A concubine gave birth to me,[6]
Your deed would still an insult be,
For I'm a knight with knightly aim,
In whom naught has been found to blame.
I wish my fame in this to lie: 416
Blameless to live and blameless die.
For this in God I put my trust:
My bliss will beg for it, and must.
What if the word goes yon and thither
That Arthur's sister's son came hither
In my escort to Schanpfanzun:
The Frenchmen and the Bertun,
The Provençals and Burgunjoys,[7]
Galicians[8] and the Punturtoys,   10
When they find out how Gawan bled,
If I've a name, 'twill then be dead.
His struggle anxious and intense
Curtails my praise, my shame augments.
Of joy it will deprive me,
Away from honor drive me."

   While these last words were echoing,
A royal knight stood near the king,
His name was known as Liddamus.
Kyot himself doth call him thus.   20
Kyot is L'aschantiure named.[9]
By art his soul was so inflamed
That stories he must tell and sing,

Much joy to many hearts to bring.
Kyot is a Provençal
Who all this tale of Parzival
Saw written in the heathen tongue.[10]
What he thereof in French has sung,
If I am not devoid of wit,
I'll tell in German more of it.

Liddamus objects to harboring Gawan, whom he calls the murderer of his master's father. However, Kingrimursel chides Liddamus and implies that he is cowardly; he adds that with Gawan's consent he will postpone the duel with him for a year. Gawan agrees. Liddamus nevertheless continues his tirade and reminds Vergulaht that he is descended from Gahmuret and Galões. He, Liddamus, however, does not wish to fight. (417, 1 —420, 14)

"Who fain would fight, let him do so.
Though I at fighting am but slow,
I'll find out what the outcome be.
Whoe'er in strife wins victory
Will win the praise of some proud wife.
For no one would I risk my life   20
Or put my limbs in jeopardy.
Shall I another Wolfhart[11] be?
My warpath by a moat is barred,
Upon my head is a falcon-guard.
Though always your respect I lacked,
Like Rumolt[12] I would choose to act:
To Gunther he had this to say,
Ere the king to Hunland rode away:
He bade him slices long to stew
In oil, and turn them in the brew."

    The landgrave brave retorted,   421
"Your speech is as distorted
As all that many a man could hear
You saying now for many a year.
You *counsel* what to do I've *willed*,[13]
And say that's what a cook instilled
In the Nibelungen vaunted,
Who started out undaunted
And suffered vengeance, every one,
For what to Siegfried had been done.   10

Gawan will have to strike me dead,
Or I'll teach him revenge to dread."
"Agreed," did Liddamus reply.
"His uncle Arthur's wealth piled high,
And all that India can display:
If this before me one would lay
And over to me turn it,
Before I'd fight, I'd spurn it.
Retain the fame that's yours of course.
I'm not a second Segramors,[14]   20
Whom one must chain to keep from fight;
Yet from the king I'll get no slight.
Take Sibech,[15] who a sword ne'er drew
And stuck to those who fled and flew:
Yet high in favor went he,
Great gifts and fiefs in plenty
From Ermenrich he could receive,
Though ne'er his sword did a helmet cleave.
Of scars my skin will never tell
Because of you, Kingrimursel.
That's my resolve concerning you."   422

Vergulaht instructs Antikonie to take Gawan and the landgrave unto herself while he deliberates with his friends. At nightfall maidens bring Antikonie costly food, which she offers her guests. Meanwhile Vergulaht tells his counselors how he recently fought a knight (he means Parzival) who defeated him and spared his life only after he had promised to win the Grail for him, or, failing in this, to offer himself as prisoner to the queen of Belrapeire. Liddamus craftily advises Vergulaht to send Gawan on the mission in search of the Grail. Thus he will rid himself of this unwelcome guest, and perhaps Gawan will lose his life in the attempt. All applaud this counsel. On the next day Antikonie appears in all her beauty before Vergulaht with Gawan. Vergulaht makes his sly proposal to Gawan and effects a reconciliation with him. Gawan's companions, who had been held as prisoners, are restored to him. Antikonie feasts them all royally and then bids Gawan a tearful farewell. Kingrismursel escorts Gawan out of the city and promises to see that his retinue will reach King Arthur safely. Gawan sets out to seek the castle of the Grail. (422, 2—432, 30)

Book Nine
Parzival Visits Trevrizent

Book Nine

PARZIVAL VISITS TREVRIZENT

"Open!"—To whom? Who are *you*?   **433**
"For entrance to thy heart I sue."
For narrow space you're pining.
"What if it be confining,
Of crowding thou needst not complain:
To tell thee wonders I am fain."
Ah, Dame Adventure, is it *you*?
Our charming friend, how does he do?
I mean the noble Parzival,
Whom Cundry drove with words of gall   10
That he should find the holy Grail,
When many a lady[1] must bewail
That naught could halt his journeying.
From Arthur then, the Breton king,
He went: what fortune bore he?
Pray tell me all his story:
Is he of joy despairing,
Is he high honor sharing?
Say, is his reputation
Widespread in estimation,   20
Or is it only scant and short?
Pray give to us a full report
Of what meantime his hands attained,
If Munsalvaeschë he has gained,
And if he's seen dear Anfortas,
Whose heart with sighing cried Alas!
Be kind to us, our hearts console:
Is he released from bitter dole?
Do let's have the news you bear,
If Parzival was really there.
Of him, your lord and mine, relate,   **434**
Enlighten me about his fate;
Sweet Herzeloydë's offspring rare,
Gahmuret's son, how did he fare
Since he from Arthur rode away?
Was pleasure or was pain his pay

For taking part in battle?
Did he stray off like cattle,
Or did he spend his time in sloth?
His deeds, his conduct, tell me both! 10
   Adventure tells to me and you
That many a land he traveled through
On horseback or in ships at sea.
Kin or stranger it might be:
Whoso him in joust might meet,
Our friend his foeman would unseat.
And thus in the balance, day by day,
His fame more heavily must weigh,
While others fell clear out of sight,
Though hard and bitter were the fight. 20
To defeat he never yielded,
His body ne'er he shielded.
Who from him fame would borrow,
Tried it to his sorrow.
The sword[2] that king Anfortas laid
Into his hands when there he stayed,
Was shattered once in an attack,
But then the waters of the Lac,
Hard by Karnant, restored the blade.[3]
   In winning fame it was his aid.

An incident now follows which is not in Crestien. Parzival reaches a hermitage, where he finds Sigunë, who is still mourning her dead lover Schionatulander. After mutual recognition she asks him whether he has rediscovered the Grail. He tells her of his profound dejection, while she forgives him his remissness in not asking Anfortas the question. Then she urges him to continue his search for the Grail, advising him to pursue Cundry, who has just left and who comes to Sigunë every Saturday with a week's supply of food from the Grail. Parzival follows this advice but soon loses her trail. He meets a knight of the Grail whom he defeats but does not kill, while he himself skillfully avoids a bad fall. His own horse is killed in the encounter, and Parzival appropriates his enemy's steed. (435, 1—445, 30)

   To him who'll hark, the tale I'll tell 446
Of things that now our friend befell.
The days and weeks I cannot count

That Parzival upon his mount
Sought adventure, as before.
One morn the earth a blanket bore
Of snow, just thick enough to make
The people yonder freeze and shake.
'Twas in a forest great and cold.
On foot toward him came an old   10
Knight with beard gray as could be,[4]
Whose skin was soft and fair to see.
His wife was also gray but fair.
They both, upon their bodies bare,
Wore garments coarse, harsh, and gray
Upon their penitential way.
Two maids, their daughters, followed on,
And winsome they to look upon.
They wore the selfsame sort of clothes.
This rede from humble hearts arose.   20
All wore nothing on their feet.
Parzival was fain to greet
The gray knight in his pilgrim's dress,
Whose counsel brought him happiness;
Like a noble lord he nighed.
The ladies' poodles ran beside.
In gentle wise and far from proud
Came knights and squires, a goodly crowd,
And courteous, on their pilgrimage,
Some beardless, being young of age.
   Parzival, the noble knight,   447
Was outwardly so well bedight
That all his trappings sightly
Made an appearance knightly.
In such a harness now he fared
As could by no one be compared
With what was worn by him in gray.
His horse he drew out of the way
By pulling on the bridle.
Attentive, not just idle,   10
He asked these good folks where and why.
In friendliness he got reply.
The knight in gray expressed regret

That from these holy days not yet
He'd learned to cease from riding,[5]
And, not in arms abiding,
To walk unshod upon his way
And celebrate the holy day.[6]
To him responded Parzival,
"Sir, I do not know at all   20
When the present year began,
Or how the weeks in number ran.
I could not name the days for you,
Of this I lack all knowledge true.
One time I served a lord called God,
Ere I upon His scornful nod
With deep disgrace was favored.[7]
My loyalty had not wavered
To Him who I was told would bless:
His help has now grown powerless."

    Then said the old knight, gray of hair,   448
"You mean our God, whom the Virgin bare?
Think you that He a man became,
And suffered today to heal our shame,
Wherefore this day we celebrate?
Then wrongful is your armored state.
Good Friday 'tis, as you should know,
When all the world its joy may show,
Yet also sigh in fear, and moan.
What greater love was ever shown   10
Than toward us was exemplified
When Christ for us was crucified?
Sir, if you've been baptizèd,
This sacrifice be prizèd:
His precious life He gave away,
With His own death our guilt to pay,
Through which mankind was wholly lost,
A guilt whereof hell was the cost.
If you are not a heathen, sir,
Then to this holy day defer.   20
Keep riding farther on our track.
There dwells on it,[8] not too far back,
A holy man; seek his advice

How you for sin may sacrifice.
If penitence beseem you,
From sin he will redeem you."
  His daughters spoke protesting:
"Why, father, such molesting?
When we in such bad weather live,
Is it proper such advice to give?
Lead him to where he'll warm him. 449
His limbs, though iron arm him,
And knightly they and pleasing,
We think they must be freezing.[9]
He'd freeze if he were thrice as strong.
Remember, thou hast brought along
Both pilgrims' cloaks and tents withal.
E'en if King Arthur came to call,
Thou'st plenty to regale him.
As host thou must not fail him. 10
Take him there, with thee to stay."
Responding said the man in gray,
"Sir, they are right: not far from here
I've visited year after year,
Dwelling in this forest old,
Were it warm or bitter cold,
Just at the time He suffered pain[10]
Who gives for service heavenly gain.
The food which I for God's sake bear
With thee I honestly will share." 20
Then begged of him each maiden—
With good will they were laden—
That he decide on staying.
"Much honor," they were saying,
" 'Twill bring." No interest did they feign.
Parzival surveyed the twain:
Albeit heat oppressed them not,
Their lips were red, full, and hot;
They did not look like weeping,
As with this day in keeping.
If they deserved some punishment, 450
To drop my grudge I'd not consent,
But as atonement take a kiss,—

Provided they'd agree to this.
Woman always is the same:
E'en a doughty man she'll tame
When victory is needed:
Often that's succeeded.
  Parzival around him heard
The pleading and the kindly word   10
Of father, mother, daughters twain.
He thought, "If I should join their train,
To walk with them I could not bear.
These maidens are so sweet and fair,
If I should ride, it would seem odd,
Since all these pilgrims are unshod.
'Twere better I should separate,
Since in my heart I harbor hate
For Him they are adoring,
His helpfulness imploring.   20
To me His help He has denied,
Nor banished sorrow from my side."
Parzival addressed them so:
"Sir and lady, let me go
With your leave. —May favoring fate
Grant you health and pleasures great.
Sweet maidens, I address you:
Your virtuousness should bless you,[11]
That for my weal you were concerned.
Your leave to go I think I've earned."
He bowed, the others bowed again,   451
Nor did they from lament refrain.
  Away rides Herzeloydë's son,
Led by the manliness he's won,
By virtue and compassion:
Since his mother in her fashion
Bequeathed him faith as heritage,
Regret must now his heart engage.
So first he meditated
On Him who the world created,   10
Who gave His life its dower:
How mighty was His power!
Said he, "What if God help should lend

And bring my sadness to an end?
If e'er He favored knight and lord,
If e'er a knight earned His reward,
Or if it be that shield and blade
Are thought so worthy of His aid—
Also a manly battle-deed—
That His aid might help me in need,   20
If this is His help-giving day,
Then let Him help, if help He may."
He turned, his pathway leaving;
The pilgrims still were grieving
That he no longer sought them:
'Twas this their kindness taught them.
The maidens watched him ride away,
And his own heart was bound to say
That gladly he'd behold them,
Such beauty did enfold them.[12]

    Said he, "If God commands such force   452
That He can guide both beast and horse,
And show men right behavior,
I'll praise Him as a savior.
If God have help for such a deed
As pointing this Castilian steed
Upon the best of roads for me,
A test of His help in that I'll see.—
Now take the road that God ordains!"
Forward then he laid the reins   10
And kept the charger stirring,
By energetic spurring,
To Funtan' la Salvatschë[13] thus,
Where the oath was heard by Orilus.[14]
The pious Trevrizent lived there,
On Mondays[15] used to humble fare:
All week such was his doing.
For years he'd been eschewing
Mulberry, wine, and bread as well;
So much restraint in him did dwell,   20
That no desire for foods he'd show
Like fish or flesh, where blood doth flow.
Thus holily the man would live:

'Twas God's, this spirit him to give.
He was preparing, more than most,
To join the blessed heavenly host.
With suffering was his fasting done:
His continence fought the Evil One.
He'll tell to Parzival the tale
Of secret things about the Grail.
Whoever formerly might ask[16]   453
Me this, and then take me to task
Because no tale I'd venture,
He'd merit naught but censure.
I should withhold it, begged Kyot,
And Dame Adventure he would quote,
Who said, "Pay no attention,
Till at my intervention
The story will itself unfold."
Which then no more I might withold.   10
   Kyot, the bard known far and wide,
Found in Toledo, cast aside,
Set down in heathen writing,
This story's source exciting.
First of course it had to be
That he had mastered a, b, c.
But necromancy he despised.
'Twas good that he had been baptized,[17]
Or this tale were unknown this hour:
No heathen arts could give us power   20
To tell of the Grail's high properties,
Or how were unveiled its mysteries.
   A heathen, Flegetanis by name,[18]
In learning won the highest fame.
This man, as nature-student known,
Had his descent from Solomon,
Of Jewish stock arising
Long years before baptizing
Protected us from fire of hell.
He wrote the Grail's adventures well.
Of pagan faith paternally,   454
Before a calf worshipped he,[19]
As if he thought it were his god.

How could the Devil ever prod
So shamefully a folk so wise,
That no distinction it descries
From Him who sits on the highest throne,
To whom all miracles are known?
Flegetanis, the heathen sage,
Could predict through every stage   10
Each star's withdrawal from mortal view,
Then its reappearance new,
How long each planet goes around
Until its highest point is found.
The course in which each planet swings
Is the touchstone of all human things.
Flegetanis, the heathen, saw
What he described with timorous awe:
The stars revealed it to his eyes,
Though hidden in mysterious wise.   20
He spoke of something called the Grail:
This very name he could not fail
To read upon the starry sphere.
"It was a host that left it here,[20]
And then beyond the stars they flew.
If them their innocence withdrew,
Then men of Christian discipline
Must guard it now—chaste, free of sin;
As noble men respected
Are those for the Grail selected."
   Thus Flegetanis wrote of it.   455
Kyot, the master, dowed with wit,
Was driven by this story
To Latin volumes hoary:
Where could there have been ever
A folk of such endeavor
As to cling to virtuous living,
The Grail due nurture giving?
The chronicles he read with care
In Brittany and otherwhere,   10
In France and also Ireland;—
In Anjou, there it came to hand.
He read there about Mazadan,[21]

And truth in all the record ran:
About his whole relation
There was full information.
On the other hand, how Tyturel
And the latter's offspring Frimutel
Passed on the Grail to Anfortas,
Whose sister Herzeloydë was.   20
A son by Gahmuret she bore
Of whose tale you will hear still more.
He's riding now the new-found way
On which he met the knight in gray.
He recognized, despite the snow,
A spot where fair blooms used to grow.
A mountain wall shut off the land,
Where on a time his powerful hand
For Dame Jeschut' won favor new,
And Orilus his wrath withdrew.
Then he went on until he came   **456**
To Funtan' la Salvatsch—the name
Of a dwelling where his course was bound:
A host and greeting there he found.

  To him the hermit spoke and said,
"Sir, woe that such a fortune dread
Be yours on such a holy day!
Is it some fear-inspiring fray
That made you don this armored dress
Or does no quarrel on you press?   10
Then other garb were better fit,
If pride in you permitted it.
Pray you, dismount at present
(You'll find that not unpleasant!)
Here by the fire to warm you.
If Adventure, perhaps to charm you,
Has sent you out for love's reward,
And true love is what you've adored,
Then love the love true love decrees,
The love that reigns on days like these.[22]   20
Hereafter serve for women's pay.
Deign to dismount, if ask I may."
Parzival, the hero bold,

Dismounted, as he had been told.
With great decorum there he stood
And told him of the people good
Who gave him this direction,
Praising counsel and protection.
Quoth he, "For counsel I'll come in.
Sir, I am a man of sin."
   When this speech had thus been made,   457
The hermit answered unafraid,
"Advice I'll give you, have no fear.
But tell me first, who sent you here?"
"Sir, I met in the forest there
A gray man who bespoke me fair.
His train gave a like reception.
He said without deception
That I had best be hither bound.
I rode his trail, till you I found."   10
The host said, "That is Kahenise,[23]
A man in worthy conduct wise.
This prince was born a Punturteis;
The powerful king of Kareis
Took his sister as his wife.
No purer fruit of human life
Was ever born than his daughters fair,
Who met you on the pathway there.
This prince, though of a royal race,
Each year he seeks this humble place."   20
   Parzival this question put:
"When I saw you standing there on foot,
I wondered, did you feel some fear,
Weren't you displeased when I drew near?"
The host replied, "Believe me, sir,
A bear or e'en a stag can stir
More fear in me than any man.
This truth I'll say, as well I can:
There's naught I fear that's born of men,
For human ways are in my ken.
Think not to boast I have the will: 458
In fleeing I'm a virgin still.
My heart has never grown so weak

That flight from battle I would seek
In days when I was wont to fight.
For just like you I was a knight,
Like you for noble *Minnë* fought.
But once I mingled a sinful thought
With virtue that hung in the balance.
I swelled like other gallants   10
To think I'd a lady's favor.
I've forgotten that forever.—
Put the reins into my hand,
I think your steed had better stand
Beneath yon rocky cliff and rest.
Then afterward, as you think best,
We twain will gather ferns and greens:
For other fodder I've no means.
But amply fed 'twill surely be."
Parzival would not agree:[24]   20
The hermit should not lead the horse.
"Good manners won't permit this course:
Your host you never must gainsay,
If courtesy's not gone astray."
The holy man spoke in this vein.
So Parzival gave him the rein.
He led the steed neath cliff and stone,
Where rarely any sunshine shone.
That was indeed a savage stall.
Close by there leaped a waterfall.
   Parzival stood in the snow.   459
A weakling would have suffered woe
If in armor he'd array him
And the frost thus came to slay him.
The host then led him to a cave,
Where the winds but rarely drave:
There was a fire of glowing coal,
The guest found this a pleasant dole.
The hermit furnished candle-light:
Now his armor doffed the knight.   10
On straw and ferns lay his youthful form,
Soon his members all grew warm,
So that his skin was bright again.

Of forest-travel he showed the strain:
Through trackless woods he'd made his way
And roofless waited for the day.
Thus had many a dawn aroused him.
A kindly host now housed him.
There lay a coat. To put it on
The host requested, and anon
Into another cave he led
Where lay the books the hermit read.
To keep this day, an altar-stone
Stood bare.[25] Upon the top was shown
A relic he could well recall.
'Twas that upon which Parzival
An oath unfalsified had sworn,[26]
Whereby Jeschut' the duchess lorn
Through love found sorrow ceasing,
Her joys henceforth increasing.

   Said Parzival with some surprise, **460**
"This relic, sir, I recognize,
For 'twas thereon an oath I swore
One time when I was here before.
I saw a painted spear here stand.[27]
Sir, that was taken by my hand.
With it the praise of men I earned,
As later on from men I learned.
Such thoughts of my wife came o'er me,
That all was blank before me.
Two glorious jousts with it were run,[28]
But naught I knew of what I'd done.
Then, honors I had won me,
Now, cares are weighing on me,
More than a mortal ever knew.
Sir, in your kindness tell me true:
How long is't since away I rode
And took the spear from your abode?"

   Again replied the holy man,
" 'Twas left here by friend Taurian,[29]
Who later came lament to raise.
Four years, six months, and three more days
'Tis since you took from him the spear.

I'll prove it to you, if you'll hear."
He read him the psalter:[30] there were shown
How many years and weeks had flown
And filled the passing time since then.
"Ah me, 'tis only now I ken
How long I've wandered leaderless,
While joy denied me all redress.
Joy is a dream," quoth Parzival.   461
"Upon me sorrow's weight must fall.
I'll tell you more that is not good:
Wherever church or minster stood,
Wherever men God's praise declare,
No eye has ever seen me there
Since away from here I wended.
To fighting I've attended.
Then too, 'tis hate toward God I bear,
For He's godfather of my care.   10
This He's exalted all too high,
My joys beneath it buried lie.
If the power of God a help could be,
What anchorage my joy would see!
Instead, it sinks into sorrow's ground.
If my brave spirit bears a wound,
Or if it could remain untorn,
While sorrow sets its crown of thorn
Upon the great and glorious fame
That chivalry has won my name   20
In battle's high endeavor,—
This speaks in His disfavor,
Who gives all help and wields the power,
Whose help is ready every hour,
And yet who gives no help to me,
Though helper of all He's said to be."
   The hermit, sighing, at him stared:
"Sir, if your mind is not impaired,
In God you ought to put your trust,
For He will help you, since He must.
God grant us both assistance!   462
Tell me, on my insistence
(I pray you first be seated),

With words sincere, not heated,
The starting of your wrath relate
Toward God, which then turned into hate.
Let your breeding teach you patient sense
To learn from me God's innocence,
Ere you to me of Him complain.
His radiant help will never wane.   10
Though a layman in my training,
From the Bible I've been gaining
The truth—for I could read and write—
How man should serve with all his might
Our God, whose help is great and true,
Whose help no flagging ever knew
To keep men's souls from sinking.
Be faithful without shrinking,
Since God Himself is loyalty[31]
And hates all falsity to see.   20
To God we must show gratitude:
For our sake He has done much good,
Since His noble, lofty race
For us put on a human face.
God's name and essence is the truth:
False doing finds in Him no ruth.
Let this be your reflection:
God cannot show defection.
This thought take for your guiding,
In God show faith abiding.
   From God no wrath will win you aught.   463
Should you be seen with hate thus fraught,
'Twill seem your mind is not quite well.
Think what to Lucifer befell
And those who shared his fighting,
Erst not in gall delighting.
Ah sir, whence came their hating,
Till for conflicts ne'er abating
Hell's bitter wages must atone?
Astiroth and Belcimon,[32]   10
Belet, and Radamand,
And others, men whose names I've scanned,
Once glorious in heaven's light,

Through hate fell into hellish night.
When Lucifer to hell was brought,
A man was in his image wrought.[33]
From earth, God created
Adam the celebrated;
From Adam's body Eve was ta'en,
Who caused us mortals endless pain, 20
Not heeding our Creator,
Which brought much sorrow later.
From these twain comes all human seed.
One man, impelled by monstrous greed,
Took in haughty, lustful mood
His grandmother's maidenhood.[34]
Some make interrogation,
Not waiting for explanation,
And ask how such a thing could be.
The cause of it: iniquity."
   Parzival responded, "Sir, 464
I ween this thing could not occur.
From whom was that man ever born,
Whose granddam had by his fault lorn
Her maidenhood, as you just said?
You'd have good cause to hush instead."
The hermit turned to him to say,
"The doubt in you I'll take away.
If truth I speak not truthfully,
Then chide me for mendacity. 10
'Twas Mother Earth gave Adam birth,
And Adam lived on the fruits of earth.
As yet the earth was a maid.
Till now to tell you I've delayed
By whom the maidenhood was ta'en.
Adam's oldest son was Cain,
Who for scant profit Abel slew.
When blood the pure earth did bedew,
At once her maidenhood was gone,
Ta'en from her by Adam's son. 20
Then first the hate of man arose.
Since then it no cessation knows.
There's naught upon the earth so pure

As maidens void of false allure.
Behold, how maids are pure as morn:
God was himself from a virgin born.
From maiden-earth were born two men,³⁵
And God took human stature then
From this first maiden's fruit and breed—
Exalted God's benignant deed!
From Adam's race are descended   **465**
Both grief and rapture blended,
Since through him kinship man maintains
With God who o'er the angels reigns;
But sinful are all Adam's kin,
So we must bear the load of sin.
Be this His pity compelling
With whom all pity's dwelling,
Since lovingly in mortal guise
With love He fought unlove and lies.—   10
Have done with further spurning,
Thus the bliss of heaven earning.
Atone for your iniquity,
Of words and acts be not so free.
Who for woe revenge is seeking
By means of blasphemous speaking,
What wage has such a man incurred?
He damns himself with every word!
Let teachings old be teachings new
And teach you this: be ever true.   20
The famous prophet Plato³⁶
Said in days of long ago,
And Sibyl, the prophetess,
Who knew no deceitfulness,
Years ago they spoke it out
To us would come without a doubt
Salvation from our sin and wrong.
In hell God's mighty hand and strong³⁷
Seized on us with love divine.
The wicked he left there to pine.
  Of Him whose love is true and great   **466**
These gracious prophecies relate.
He's a transcendent light above

And never wavers in His love.
On whom our Lord His love bestows,
True happiness that mortal knows.
But here there's a division;[38]
Each one must make a decision:
Here's His love and there's His hate.
Decide which is the better fate. 10
The guilty, by not repenting,
To love is not consenting;
Who for sin makes restitution,
Of God seeks absolution.
'Tis His who through our thoughts can break,
Thoughts e'en in sunlight are opaque.
Without a lock our thoughts are sure,
Against all creatures they're secure.
Thought is a darkness lacking light.
Only God can be so bright 20
As into our darkest heart to shine,
Our secret leaping to divine,
Which makes no noise or ringing
When in our heart upspringing.
No thought of ours such speed can win
That ere from the heart it pass our skin
By Him it's not detected.
Good thoughts are by Him respected.
Since God sees through our every thought,
Alas for the evil deeds we've wrought!
When one for his acts by God is blamed, 467
So that of him God is ashamed,
To whom is he left by *courtoisie*?
Whither can the poor soul flee?
But if to God you would do ill,
Who can be kind or stern at will,
Who's prone to wrath or favor,
Then you are lost for ever.
Now turn to Him your spirit,
That He reward your merit." 10
   Parzival replied to him,
"Sir, my joy will ne'er grow dim
That the truth of Him you would accord

Who leaves no act without reward,
Be it virtue or a deed uncouth.
In sorrow I have spent my youth,
And to this day I've lived it so:
That faithful striving brought but woe."
Again the host replied in turn,
"Conceal it not, I'd gladly learn
The grief and sins that on you rest.
If you'll allow, I'll try my best
And may perhaps some counsel find
That is not present to your mind."
Parzival resumed his tale:
"My greatest grief involves the Grail,
My second one concerns my wife.
No fairer creature in this life
Has ever sucked a mother's breast.
These twain are my longing quest."
    The host said, "Sir, you speak aright,   **468**
You're truly in unhappy plight,
Since for your wife you're grieving,
Thus woe for your own heart weaving.
If you are true to your marriage tie,[39]
What though in hell you come to lie,
Your suffering there will swiftly cease,
From the bonds of hell you'll find release
Through God's assistance, without fail.
You say you're yearning for the Grail?
This, foolish man, I must regret.[40]
The Grail is something none can get
Who's not of the world's anointed,
And thus to the Grail appointed.
This of the Grail I say: I know
It's true, for I have seen it so."
Parzival said, "Were you there?"
"I was," he heard his host declare.
To tell him Parzival forbore,
He too had been there once before.
Instead, he begged narration
Of the Grail and its relation.
    The hermit said, "I know right well

That many doughty warriors dwell
Around the Grail at Munsalvaesch'.
They often seek adventure fresh
As chivalrous exemplars,
And all these many templars
No victory or defeat may win
But that they bear it for their sin.
There dwells a valiant multitude.   **469**
Let me tell you of their food.
By a wondrous stone they're nourished,
Whose purity e'er has flourished.
If you've no information
I'll give you its appellation:
'Tis called the *lapsit exillis*.[41]
One power the stone employs is this:
To ashes it helps the Phoenix burn,
But his ash gives him new life in turn.   **10**
Thus moults the Phoenix, so to say,
But then he shines as bright as day:
He once was fair, he is so still.
Let a man be ailing as he will,
If he one day this stone can eye,
For one whole week he cannot die,
So long will Death its claims abate,
Nor will his looks deteriorate.
That beauty he may call his own
In which he first beheld the stone,   **20**
And, be he maiden or a man,
The same as when his prime began,
Though he saw it through two hundred years—
Save that gray his hair appears.
To man such power gives the stone,
That in his flesh and in his bone
Youth will suddenly prevail.
This is the stone men call the Grail.

   A message comes to it today,
Which doth its power well display.[42]
Good Friday 'tis, as I have said,   **470**
And there they now observe o'erhead
A dove from heaven winging,

That to the Grail is bringing
A wafer white and full of grace
Which on the stone the dove will place.
The dove is of pellucid white;
To heaven again it takes its flight.
And always on this holy day
It brings to the Grail, as I say,   10
That whence the stone's deriving
Good things that on earth are thriving,
The best for drinking and eating
That Eden once was meting.
I mean whate'er is born on earth.
The stone won't let them[43] suffer dearth
Of game that lives beneath the sky,
Whether it run or swim or fly.
On this knightly brotherhood
The Grail bestows this prebend good.   20
   How those men to the Grail ordained
Are heralded, will be explained.
Upon the Grail-stone's end we see
In letters writ mysteriously
The name and family of those[44]
Whom heaven for this mission chose,
And lads and maids 'twill indicate.
No name need one obliterate,
For once they've read the name aright,
At once it vanishes from sight.
They entered there as children small,   471
Now they're people, grown and tall.
Blest she who a son or daughter bare
To be ordained for service there!
The poor and the wealthy,
Their joy is great and healthy,
When their child is summoned to be sent
To join this group pre-eminent.
In many lands beginning,
From evil shame and sinning   10
They're evermore protected,
So in heaven reward's expected:
For when on earth their life must die,

Perfection waits them there on high.
Those who stood with neither faction,
When in belligerent action
Lucifer fought the Trinity,
Whate'er of angels one could see,[45]
The noble and the worthy,
Must share existence earthy   20
In service of the Holy Grail.
Its purity can never fail.
I know not if God their sin forgave,[46]
Or into destruction these angels drave.
If He deemed it right, He took them back.[47]
Since then the stone doth never lack
Men by Him nominated,
On whom His angel waited.
About the Grail I've told you all."
To this responded Parzival,
   "If chivalry an earthly crown,   472
Together with the soul's renown,
Can capture with the sword and shield—
Knighthood has e'er to me appealed.
I fought where'er I found a fight,
So that my merit as a knight
Had almost won the highest prize.
If God is truly battle-wise,
On the Grail let him bestow me,
That they[48] may get to know me.   10
My hand in fighting will not fail."
The pious host resumed the tale:
"But there you'd have to lay aside
With humbleness your vaunting pride.
Your youth might tempt you easily
To burst the bonds of modesty.
Pride always rose, but also fell,"
The host said. Tears began to well,
The while he meditated
The tale he now narrated.   20
   He said then, "Sir, a king there was,
Who was and is named Anfortas.[49]
We, wretched in our fashion,

Should both feel great compassion
For him, since his heart-rending woe
From overweening pride doth flow.
His youth, his power, and his wealth
On earth, brought him to unhealth,
Since a love he was pursuing
That led to unchaste doing.
Such living must displease the Grail: 473
There, knight and squire must never fail
To flee from all frivolity.
Pride yields to meekness the victory.
There dwells a noble brotherhood:
They have with valiant fortitude,
And fighting hands, defended
Gainst all who thither wended
The Grail, that it be unprofaned,
Reserved for those by God ordained 10
At Munsalvaesch' to guard the Grail.
Unbidden, *one* man reached its pale,[50]
But this one was a foolish man,
And weighed with sin away he ran,
Since ne'er his host he questioned there
About the woe he saw him bear.
No man I am indicting,
But *he* must be requiting
The sin, that he ignored distress.
Such suffering did his host oppress, 20
That more a man could never pine.
Before that time, King Laeheline
Came riding to the lake Brumbane,[51]
Where Libbeäls,[52] the noble thane,
Awaited him, a joust to make,
Which his own life was soon to take.
This knight was born of Prienlascors.
Laeheline took the hero's horse
And with his hand led it away.
This theft was known without delay.[53]
  Sir, are you Laeheline?[54] 474
There stands in that stall of mine
A horse that's very like the steeds

Which none but that Grail-castle breeds.
A turtle-dove[55] on the saddle shows
That the steed from Munsalvaeschë goes.
Anfortas chose these saddle-arms
When he was joyful, free of harms.
'Twas on their shields, long ago;
Tyturel bequeathed it so 10
To his son, rois Frimutel.
Under it the hero fell
In jousting, lost it and his life.
So much he loved his wedded wife,
No wife of a man's selection
E'er knew so much affection,
I mean so faithfully and true.
Such love as his should dwell in you.
Love your wife with all your heart,
From his example ne'er depart: 20
You're like to him in all detail.
He too was master of the Grail.
Ah, pray you, tell me whence you came,
Reveal to me your race and name."

  Each man the other firmly eyed.
Parzival to him replied,
"I am the offspring of a knight
Who lost his life in jousting fight
And through knightly disposition.
Sir, by your kind volition
In prayer he should your notice get: 475
My father's name was Gahmuret,
By race he was an Anshevine:
Sir, I am *not* that Laeheline.
Did I a body-theft commit,
That was when I was lacking wit.[56]
But after all I did it, yes,
This very sin I must confess.
Ither of Kukumerland
Was slain by this my sinful hand. 10
I laid him dead upon the grass
And took all that upon him was."

  "Alas, o world, why doest thou so?"

The host exclaimed: this caused him woe.
"The hearts of all thou makest sore,
Of sorry grief thou giv'st them more
Than joy. What givest thou as boon?[57]
Thus ends at last thy every tune.
Dear sister's son," continued he,
"What counsel could I give to thee?
Thy own flesh[58] thou hast foully slain.
If thou'lt fore God the guilt retain,
Since ye were one in kindred blood,
And if God decrees a judgment good,
Thou'rt forfeit now with life and limb.
What wergild wilt thou give for him,
Ither, lord of Kahaviez?
Of highest worth without surcease,
Which is the world's purgation,
God made him the revelation.
Misdeeds to him were scatheful,
This paragon of the faithful;
All worldly shame before him fled,
Virtue entered his heart instead.
Women all will bear thee hate[59]
For this beloved hero's fate.
His service was so wholly right
That every woman's eyes grew bright,
His handsome countenance viewing.
God have pity on this doing,
That thou hast wrought such havoc dread!
For thee, my sister too lay dead,
Herzëloyd', thy mother dear."
"No, God's forbid, what's this I hear!"
Cried Parzival, "What is this tale?
Were I now master o'er the Grail,
Its glory could not compensate
For what your lips to me relate.
If I'm indeed your sister's son,
Then treat me as by kin is done;
Speak honestly, I beg of you:
Are both the things you tell me true?"
    The holy hermit made reply:

"I'm not the one to tell a lie.
Thy mother's love was so sorely tried:
When thou hadst gone, forthwith she died.
Thou wast the beast that sucked her breast,[60]
The dragon thou that fled her nest:
Of dreams like these there was no dearth
Before the dear one gave thee birth.
Two other sisters still I have.   477
My sister Schoysianë gave
Birth,[61] but of the birth she died.
She had become lord Kyot's bride:
From Catalonia was he.
Thenceforth no joyance could he see.[62]
Sigunë, the infant daughter,
To thy mother's care they brought her.
Schoysianë's death bereaves me,
In my deepest heart it grieves me.   10
How kind her woman's heart had been,
An ark against the flood of sin!
One sister is a virgin, she
Lives a life of purity.
Queen Repanse de Schoy' holds sway
O'er the Grail, which is found to weigh[63]
So much, that no wicked race
Can remove it from its place.
Her brother and mine is Anfortas,
Who is and long already was   20
By race the Grail's commander.
All joys from him must wander.
But this hope he can borrow,
That all his pain and sorrow
May bring him to peace forever.
'Twas by most strange endeavor
He got to suffering's highest height,
As, nephew, I will now recite.
If thou'st a heart that's faithful,
Thou'lt deplore his fortune scatheful.
When Frimutel, my father, died,   478
The men took counsel to decide
To give his eldest son command

Of Grail and castle, folk and land.
My brother Anfortas was king,
Both crown and kingdom meriting.
We still were young, we others.
But with the years my brother's
Beard began to sprout and grow.
Youth and *Minne* conflict know: 10
Her friend she's then compelling,
Thus her dishonor swelling.
The Grail-king who a love desires
Other than what the Grail requires,[64]
Is thereby led into distress
With sighing and unhappiness.
My brother, as king elected,
A loved one now selected;
He thought her worthy of his flame,
At present I'll withhold her name.[65] 20
In serving her, he acted so
That never cowardice he'd show.
Thus, by his stout hand battered,
Full many a shield was shattered.
In adventurous deeds he won this fame,
The precious man of splendid name:
Has ever higher praise been told
In lands where knightly customs hold?
Such question could he well deny.
"God Cupid!" was his battle-cry.
But when humility's the test, 479
Such battle-cries are not the best.
   One day the king rode out alone
(That made his friends thereafter moan),
On some adventure hieing,
And on *Minne's* aid relying.
Desire for love impelled him thus.
From a sharp spear poisonous
In jousting he received a wound,
So that he ne'er again was sound. 10
That was thy uncle, be it said.
Through his testicles the spear had sped.
A heathen 'twas who fought the fray

And rode the fateful joust that day,
Born in faraway Ethnise,[66]
Where, flowing out from Paradise,
The river Tigris rises new.
The pagan warrior took as true:
He'd win to the Grail as haven.
His name on the spear was graven.
Such distant chivalry for naught
But the power of the Grail he sought,
Thus roving over sea and land:
By his fight thenceforth our joy was banned.
Thy uncle's valiant fighting
I laud: the spear-tip biting
He bore from there within his flesh.
When this fine youth, no longer fresh,
Came home to his retainers,
Of grief they were the gainers.
Out there the pagan he had slain:
Thereof we should—not much—complain.

 But when the king approached so pale,
And all his strength appeared to fail,
A doctor's fingers probed the wound
Until the iron tip he found.
A piece of shaft—'twas made of cane—[67]
Also in the wound had lain;
The doctor pulled out both of these.
I fell in prayer upon my knees,
And made a vow to God's great might
That ne'er again as armored knight
Love-service I would render,
If God in all His splendor
Would succor lend that brother mine.
Forswearing meat, bread, and wine,
I shunned all blood-containing food:
Henceforth for such I'd have no mood.
This caused the Grail-band's other woe—
Dear nephew, I can tell thee so—
That I parted from my sword.
They asked me, 'Who shall here be lord,
The Grail's high secret keeping?'

Bright eyes there were weeping.
  Forthwith the ailing king they laid
Before the Grail that God might aid.
When the king the Grail beheld,
A second grief within him swelled,
That death could not enshroud him.
But death was not allowed him,[68]
Since I had vowed myself to give   481
To poverty, and poorly live;
Thus our noble line, while ruling still,
Was reduced to *one* man, weak and ill.
The wound of the king was suppurous:
In doctors' writings numerous
No help of any kind was known.
Against aspis, ecidemon,[69]
Ehcontius and lisis,
The snakes jecis and meatris—   10
These bear deadly poisons hot—
Whatever cures a person wot—
Or the other vermin bearing pus,
Whate'er wise doctors have for us
Secured with aid of herb or wort—
But let us to our tale revert:
No one any help provided.
For thus God had decided.
Seeking the help of Geon,[70]
Also that of Fison,   20
Eufrates and the Tigris,
We neared these streams, to Paradise
So close, that all their redolence
Could hardly yet have vanished hence:
Could we an herb there borrow
To rid us of our sorrow?
Success our toil would still elude,
And so our grieving was renewed.
In different ways we tried again.
The selfsame branch we could obtain[71]
That on a time, the Sibyl said,   482
Would spare Aeneas hellfire dread,
Save him from Phlegethon[72] in flame,

And other streams of hellish fame.
On search we went, enduring
Till the branch we found for curing,
To see if the spear so dire
Was put in the hellish fire
For poisoning or annealing,
Our happiness thus stealing.   10
That branch the poison did not ban.
A certain bird, the Pelican,[73]
In its young takes too much pleasure,
It loves them beyond measure.
Its parent-love is so expressed
That it bites a hole into its breast,
Its offspring with its blood to feed:
Straightway the bird to death must bleed.
We sought and found the Pelican's blood,
In hope its love would do us good:[74]   20
Upon the wound we'd smear it
As best we could, and near it.
But that was of no help to us.
A beast there is, Monicirus,[75]
Which deems young maids so innocent
That on their laps 'twill sleep content.
The heart of such a beast we found,
To lay upon our ruler's wound.
Also the garnet from the horn
We took, of such a unicorn:[76]
Beneath the horn it develops there.   483
We rubbed the edge of the wound with care,
And buried the garnet in the pus,
Because the wound looked poisonous.
The king was no less grieved than we.
We found an herb called trachontë[77]—
Of this herb we hear it said
That where men strike a dragon dead,
Its blood this herb will nourish;
In this way does it flourish: 10
It has the nature of the air[78]—
We hoped the Scorpion's[79] course up there
Might be of some assistance

Against the stars' resistance,
What time the moon should change again,
Which was the time of greatest pain.
But all this herb's great power
Gave us no painless hour.
  Kneeling before the Grail in prayer,
Sudden we witnessed writing there,
Saying: one day there'd come a knight.
If he should question us aright,
Our sorrow would be at an end.
But if child, maid, or man intend
To prompt the question, or hint at it—
The question would not help one whit:
The damage would be as before,
And cause us grieving even more.
Said the writing, 'Have you understood?
Warning won't do any good.
If naught he asks on that first night,
The question's power will vanish quite.
But, if he asks in time that day,
The kingdom shall his word obey,
And sorrow will be ended,
As God on high intended.
With that Anfortas will be healed,
But the scepter no more shall he wield.'
We read thus the prediction
That Anfortas' affliction
By a question would be mended
And thus forever ended.
Always we were smearing
His wound with ointments cheering,
As oil of nards, and any salve
With theriac, and oft we have
Smoked it with *lignum aloë*.[80]
But always in pain the king we'd see.
Then I withdrew me hither,
To see years joyless wither.
Meantime a rider came one day:
'Twere better had he stayed away.
I told thee how he came there

And reaped naught else but blame there.
He saw the grief, the tears they shed,
But not once to the host he said,
'Sir, how does your trouble stand?'
Since his folly was in command
That question he omitted,
Great happiness he quitted."
 Both men fell to sighing.   485
Meanwhile, midday was nighing.
"Let's eat," the host decided.
"Thy horse is unprovided.
Of food I've none to offer,
Save God some help will proffer.
My kitchen's never smoking:
No meat is there for poking—
Thy loss today and some days more.
I'd gladly teach to thee the lore   10
Of herbs, if but there were no snow.
God grant that soon it melt and go!
Meanwhile let's find yew-leaves and weed.
Methinks thy horse saw better feed
At Munsalvaesch' than here with me.
No host thou'lt find more fain—nor he—
For thy comfort, or the horse's;
Had I but more resources!"
They sallied forth as was agreed;
Parzival foraged for his steed.   20
The host dug roots from out the ground:
No better food was to be found.
His vows the hermit ne'er forgot:
Much as he dug, he ate them not
Till the nones,[81] when bells had rung them.
On bushes there he hung them,
And more he sought for storing.
To show his love adoring,
He fasted many a livelong day,—
When he missed what he had hung away.
 They did not fail, these comrades twain,   486
To seek the brook across the plain.
They washed the roots and herbs the while,

But never did they laugh or smile.
Then, after they'd been washing
Their hands, together lashing
Yew-leaves, the guest now fed his horse.
Thereafter, they retraced their course:
The straw-couch by the fire they sought.
To feed them, naught else need be brought: 10
No meat was boiled or roasted,
No food their kitchen boasted.
Parzival's reflection,
Because of the true affection
His heart now to the hermit bore,
Was this: "Methinks that here I've more
Than when I stayed with Gurnemanz,
Or at Munsalvaesch', when in sweet advance
So many beauties did past me glide,
And where the Grail my food supplied."   20
The hermit, wise and truly good,
Said, "Nephew mine, I trust this food
Thou'lt not consider spurning.
Where'er thou mayst be turning,
No host in any place thou'lt find
Who to treat thee better were inclined."
"Sir," Parzival to him replied,
"God's favor be to me denied,
If a host has e'er appeased me
With food that better pleased me."

   Whate'er of food was served the twain,   487
Should their hands unwashed remain,[82]
Rubbing their eyes would harm them naught,
Though damage by fishy hands be wrought.
But I, for my own self talking,
Were I as falcon hawking,[83]
And men to use me so had planned,
Voraciously I'd leave their hand,
Were my food so poor and meager:
I'd show them flying eager.   10
But why do I mock these virtuous folk?
My old perverseness prompts the joke.[84]
For well ye've apprehended

What all their wealth suspended,
Why they for joy must suffer harm,
Often cold and seldom warm.
At heart they both were grieving,
In loyalty believing,
Although their hearts were free of blame.
From the hands of God, and in His name,   20
Reward for sorrow they would find.
God then and later to both was kind.[85]
They rose and went out to the stall,
The holy man and Parzival,
To see how fared the latter's horse.
It sounded very like remorse,
As the holy man the steed addressed:
"I'm sorry thou'rt by hunger pressed,
Since the saddle thou art wearing
Anfortas' symbol is bearing."

   When for the horse they thus had cared, 488
Renewed laments the two men shared.
Parzival, with some design,
Spoke, "Beloved uncle mine,
For shame I hardly dare confess,
But let me bare my great distress.
Forgive it for your kindness' sake:
In *you* my faith can refuge take.
So grievously I've misbehaved,
If by *your* help I can't be saved,   10
I'll part from consolation,
And ne'er find liberation
In all my days from bitter rue.
Uncle, with your counsel true
Help me my folly to bewail.
He who saw the Holy Grail,
Saw that woe and still sat by,
And never thought to question why,
That was I, unhappy son:
Sir, 'tis thus I have misdone."   20
   The host said, "Nephew, what say'st thou?
For both of us 'twere fitting now
With all our hearts to make lament,

And say farewell to heart's content.
Thou'st slain thine own felicity.
Since God five senses gave to thee—
They'd left thee hitherto inept—
How was by them thy duty kept
When thou wert all unheeding
Anfortas' grievous bleeding?
Yet help to seek I will not fail. 489
Nor shouldst thou to excess bewail.
Lament and its cessation
Should both show moderation.
Mankind much oddity betrays:
Youth sometimes strives for wisdom's praise.
If age such effort's spoiling,
Pure youthful waters roiling,
Then whiteness gets a dirty shade,
And the green of virtue is bound to fade, 10
Where, else, those forces might take root
Which the growth of nobleness would suit.
Could I help thee to new greening,
Thy heart to courage leaning,
So that, in triumph faring,
Of God there was no despairing,
Thou still mightst make connection
With deed of such perfection
As well might compensate thee.
God would not leave or hate thee. 20
As God-sent counselor I appear.
Now tell me, sawest thou the spear
At Munsalvaesch' the marvellous?
When the planet Saturnus
Had reached the zenith of its round,
We knew it by the festering wound,
And by the snow that summer brought.
No frost had e'er such suffering wrought
As this time to thy uncle dear.
The wound perforce took in the spear;[86]
One pain the other comforted, 490
And thus the lance turned bloody red.
   The rising light of certain stars

The Grail-folk's peace most sorely mars;
'Tis those which o'er each other rise
And unharmonious cross the skies.
From the moon's periodic changes
The wound's pain higher ranges.
In the time that I have named to thee,
Without or sleep or rest is he.   10
A frost severe will cause such woe,
His flesh grows colder than the snow.
Since it's well known that poison hot
The iron spear-point still doth clot,
At this time on the wound it's held.
The body's frost, by it dispelled,
Forms glass around the spear, like ice.
But no man knew the way precise
How this from the spear could be removed.
Then Trebuchet,[87] of wisdom proved,   20
Wrought, to cut the glass away,
Two knives of silver bright as day.
This skill a charm to him had taught
Which on Anfortas' sword was wrought.
There's many a man who's prone to claim
That wood of asbestos knows no flame.
When a piece of the glass upon it fell,
A flame of fire was seen to swell,[88]
And thus asbestos burned right through.
This poison wondrous things can do!

    He cannot walk, he cannot ride,[89]   491
He cannot lie or standing bide.
He crouches, never sitting,
His sighs are not unwitting.
At the change of moon new pain has he.[90]
Brumbane is called an inland sea.
There he's conveyed to breathe sweet air
And find relief from pain and care.
He calls such a time his hunting-day,
But all he'll catch and take away   10
Is scant, with a wound so painful,
For his castle not too gainful.[91]
Thence the rumor once began:

He is but a fisherman.
This rumor goes against his wish,
But of lampreys,[92] salmon, or other fish
He has not many for selling,
This man in sadness dwelling."
Quoth Parzival, response to make,
"I saw the king upon the lake,[93]
His skiff in the lake at anchor lay.
He'd hoped to catch some fish that day,
Or sought some pastime hidden.
For many miles I'd ridden,
Which all day long had taken.
Belrapeir' I had forsaken
In the morning, quite unhurried.
Toward evening I was worried:
Where might there a shelter be?
It was my uncle counselled me."

"A perilous way for thee to fare;"
The host said,, "guard-posts everywhere,
Each with fighters so well manned,
Not many manage through that land
To reach their journey's ending.
Whoe'er may there be wending,
In terror he must learn to live:
To no man do they pardon give,
Staking against his life their own.
'Tis for their sins they thus atone."
"But I, then, without fighting,
Or anything exciting,
To where I saw the king rode on,"
Said Parzival. "His house anon
I saw that evening full of grief.
It seemed that wailing brought relief.
A squire into the great hall sprang,
Whereat the hall with wailing rang.
The squire's hands were bearing,
Past all the four walls faring,
A shaft that held a bloody spear:
Then heartfelt wailing did I hear."

"Nephew, later nor before

Such suffering our ruler bore
As when its coming ominous
Announced the planet Saturnus.
It often comes with frost and ice.
To lay the spear would not suffice
Upon the wound, as oft we must:
Into the wound the spear was thrust.
Saturnus sails so very high, **493**
The wound can tell that he is nigh
Before the second frost is here.[94]
Nor did the snow in haste appear,[95]
It only fell the second night
When summer's force was at its height.
Though they dispelled the ruler's chill,[96]
His vassals suffered greater ill."
Then added the holy Trevrizent,
"From Grief they got emolument. 10
The spear robbed them of happiness,
When it touched their deepest heart's recess.
Their lamentation strong and true[97]
Taught them the Christian faith anew."
  To him spoke Parzival again:
"Maids five-and-twenty saw I then[98]
Before the ruler standing,
Behavior good commanding."
"In maidens' care the Grail should be,"
The host said, "this is God's decree. 20
They came before the Grail to serve.
From nobleness they dare not swerve.
By such knights it is attended,
By the chaste and good defended.
The high planets' rising brings them all
The greatest woe that could befall,
Which young and old is paining.
God is His wrath retaining
Against them far too long a term.
Whenever can they joy affirm?
Nephew, I will tell to thee **494**
What thou well mayest credit me:
An ever changing life they live,

For gains they take, but also give.[99]
Young children they initiate
Of handsome form and noble state.
If rulerless grows any land
Which sees therein God's mighty hand,
So that the folk a king request
From the Grail's own band, they get the best.   10
But they must show due respect:[100]
God's hand their ruler will protect.
In secret God sends the men away,
But maids depart in the light of day.
Certain mayst thou be of this:
A king whose name was Castis[101]
Queen Herzeloydë wanted,
So his wish was granted.
He wed thy mother Herzeloyd',
But yet her love he ne'er enjoyed.   20
Ere that, death laid him in the grave,
But first he to thy mother gave
Waleis and Norgals,
Kanvoleis and Kingrivals,
Which legally were his to give.
The king had little time to live:
While journeying homeward with his bride,[102]
The king then laid him down and died.
She wore the crown of a double land:
There she was won by thy father's hand.
  Thus, maidens leave quite openly;   495
Men depart in secrecy,
That children they may have and rear,
In hopes these one day will appear
To swell the Grail's attendance.
God teaches them such dependence.
Who'd give the Grail his service pure,
All love for women must abjure.
The king alone has a right to wed
A wife who is by virtue led,   10
And the other knights whom God commands
To wear the crown in kingless lands.
This rule I violated,

To *Minnë* dedicated.
My dashing youth, so bold and smart,
And a virtuous maid, who took my heart,
Demanded service chivalrous.
My jousts were many and arduous.
In wild and venturous fighting
So oft was I delighting,   20
I mostly shunned the tourney.[103]
Her love sent on a journey
Into my heart the joy it wrought:
For her sake many a fight I fought.
Her *Minnë* drove me far away
To many a wild and knightly fray.
'Twas thus I sought her *Minnë* prized:
If heathen foe or if baptized,
They looked alike to spear or sword.
She seemed to promise rich reward.
 By love of her I thus was sent   496
To every major continent,
To Europe and to Asia,
And far away to Africa.
And when I craved rich jousting's boon,
I rode to distant Gariun.[104]
Then, many a joust I stoutly ran
Before the mount of Famorgan.[105]
In numerous splendid jousts I've been
Before the mountain Agremontin.[106]   10

Trevrizent continues his reminiscences, mentioning various other places where he has fought, among them Rohitsch and Cilli, both in present-day Jugoslavia, and Friuli and Aquileja in Italy. He also tells how he used to be sent on secret missions by King Anfortas and once met Gahmuret, Parzival's father, whose wife, Herzelyodë, turned out to be Trevrizent's sister and Parzival's mother. The two became fast friends, and Gahmuret gave Trevrizent his nephew and squire, Ither, who was later to become the Red Knight and the victim of young Parzival. Trevrizent warns Parzival that he will have to atone to God for Ither's death, as well as for that of his own mother. Now Trevrizent inquires how Parzival came into possession of the Grail horse which he has, and Parzival declares that he won it fairly in battle. Trevrizent also explains that Repanse de Schoyë is Parzival's aunt and that she loaned him her cloak when he visited the Grail because she expected him to become the next king of the Grail. After Trevrizent mentions the sword which Anfortas gave Parzival—a visible symbol of the latter's failure to ask the question of pity—, the two men prepare for sleep. (496, 11—501,6)

> Without bed or cover for sleeping,
> They lay on a pile of sweeping.
> Their resting-place was not designed
> For folk of their illustrious kind.   10
> He stayed until the fifteenth day.
> The hermit cared for him as I say:
> Herbs and rootlets out of the ground,
> For food that was the best they found.
> These hardships he was enduring,
> Because of works reassuring:
> Of sin the host relieved him quite,
> Yet counseled him to be a knight.
>   "Who was the man," he asked one day,
> "Out there before the Grail that lay?   20
> All gray he was, though his skin looked well."
> The host said, "That was Tyturel.
> Thy mother is daughter of his son.
> He was the king who first begun
> To guard the Grail, both in and out.
> He has an illness called the gout,
> Is paralysed, cannot be cured.
> But fair looks are to him assured,
> Because the Grail he oft doth eye,
> And, thus revived, he cannot die.
> They value him for counsel's sake.   502
> In youth he rode through ford and brake
> In search of jousting's relish.
> Wouldst thou thy life embellish,
> And live in truly noble state,
> Then never show a woman hate,
> For woman and priest, as well is known,
> Bear no weapons of their own.
> Yet priests the love of God possess:
> Serve them with constant faithfulness;   10

If thou wouldst have thine ending good,
Show priests an ever trustful mood.
Whatever thou on earth canst see,
Unlike to priests that thing must be.
Their lips Christ's martyrdom proclaim,
That saves us all from hellish flame.
Their consecrated fingers take
The highest pledge and holiest stake[107]
That e'er for guilt the Lord could give.
The priest who such a life can live,　　　　20
That toward this pledge is reverent—
Could he a holier life have spent?"
This was the day the twain must part.
Trevrizent the host took heart
And said, "Give all thy sin to me:[108]
Atonement to God I'll guarantee.
And do what I have on thee laid,
Nor let thy will e'er be dismayed."
Each from the other parted now.
If 'tis your will, imagine how.

Book Ten
Gawan and Orgeluse

Book Ten

GAWAN AND ORGELUSE

Again the author turns away from Parzival to follow the fortunes of Gawan, who is now released from his obligation to fight Kingrimursel because it has turned out that it was not he who had killed Kingrisin. It also develops that Gawan and Vergulaht are kinsmen. Now Gawan encounters a lady who holds a wounded, unconscious knight in her lap. He restores him to consciousness and proceeds to Logroys in pursuit of the wounded knight's adversary, Lischoys Gwelljus. Logroys turns out to be one of the finest castles he has ever seen, well-nigh impregnable. Here he meets Orgeluse, next to Condwiramur the most beautiful woman he has ever seen. He makes advances to her, but she taunts him and says that it is dangerous to woo her. She bids him go to the orchard, pass through the crowds of merrymakers he will find there, and fetch her horse, whereupon she will follow him. Both the merrymakers and an old gray-haired knight warn him of Orgeluse's treachery, but he leads the horse to her none the less. (503, 1—514, 30)

    The bands she'd been untying   515
That else round her chin were lying:[1]
These ribbands on her head she laid.
Battle-ready seems a maid
That any man should see so clad.
Methinks of amusement she'd be glad.
What other clothes were on her?
Think ye I should do honor
To all that made her look so nice?
I say she was fair, that should suffice.   10
When Gawan the lady neared,
Her pretty lips his spirit cheered:
Quoth she to him, "Welcome, goose!
Such folly ne'er a man let loose
As yours, in trying to serve me.
I think you'd better let that be!"
Said he, "If you're so quick to wrath,
Good will comes on the selfsame path.
Since you chide me so severely,

You'll repay me just as dearly;
Service I meantime will accord,
Till 'tis your will to grant reward.
Command, and I'll lift you on this horse."
Said she, "I asked for no such course.
Your hand, untried for such a rise,
May reach out for a lowlier prize."
With that, her limbs around she swang,
From the flowers on her horse she sprang.
Thereon she bade him ride ahead.
"Too bad if I should lose," she said,
"An escort so unhumble.
God grant you take a tumble!"

   Whoe'er with me would fain concur,
Let him not yet speak ill of her:
Let no one's tongue start moving,
Till he knows what he's reproving,
Till from my story learning
What in her heart was burning.
I too could be indignant
At this beauty so malignant;
But all that she to Gawan did
In wrath, misdeeds that were not hid,
Or what she yet will do, still worse,
For that she does not bear my curse.
This Orgeluse mighty,
Unsociable and flighty,
Toward Gawan she rode apace,
With so much anger in her face,
That for myself I'd ne'er believe
That cares of mine she would relieve.[2]
Forthwith the two went riding
To a heath, near by abiding.
He saw an herb upon the ground,
Whose root, he said, would cure a wound.
This man of worth uncounted
Upon the earth dismounted:
He dug it and rode his horse once more.
To speak, this lady ne'er forbore:
Quoth she, "If this escort of mine

Can be both knight and doctor fine,
To make good money he'll not fail 517
By peddling round his salves for sale."
Gawan straight to her replied,
" 'Tis to a wounded knight I ride.
A linden is his cover.
If the knight I rediscover,
I hope this root his wound will cure
And strength renewed to him assure."
She said, "Now that I'd like to see:
I'll profit too, if skill it be." 10
    Soon followed after them a squire:
To speed some news was his desire,
To him 'twas delegated.
Gawan for him waited.
The man looked like a fury;
Malcreätiure[3] he
Was named, this squire bold[4] and free.
Cundry la surzierë, she
Was his sister passing fair.
He had all her face and air, 20
Save that he was a man, forsooth.
On his face too—each side—a tooth
Like a wild boar's tusk protruded.
He seemed from mankind excluded.
The hair he had could not have swung
Like Cundry's, as on her mule it hung:[5]
Short, bristly, urchin-like it was.
Along the river called Ganjas,[6]
In that far land Tribalibot,[7]
Such sin-begotten folk we note.
    Our father Adam, it is thought,[8] 518
This skill by God the Lord was taught:
To every thing he gave a name,
Both to wild things and the tame.
Every species well he knew,
Likewise the paths the stars pursue,
Those of the planets seven
And all their powers in heaven.
He knew the power of every wort,

The force that each one could exert.   10
When his daughters reached the state
And age when they could procreate
And bore within them human seed,
He warned them to beware of greed.
Whene'er a daughter was with child,⁹
He gave her frequent counsel mild;
Quite oft his knowledge he employed,
And bade her many roots avoid
Which human fruit distorted
And human welfare thwarted,   20
"Not like the measure God did mete,
What time he fashioned me complete,"
Said he, "my dears, bear this in mind:
To your salvation be not blind."

   The daughters did as women do:
Some from frailty took their cue,
So they soon enacted
What heart's desire exacted.
Thus was malformed the human race.
Adam felt it as disgrace,
Yet ne'er he wavered in his will.   **519**
A certain queen named Secundill',¹⁰
Whom Feirefiz with knightly hand
Had won, her person and her land,
Had in her realm abounding—
I affirm this thing astounding—
Many men, from days of old
With heads set backward, we are told:
Wild were their looks; so runs the tale.
Someone told her of the Grail,   10
How naught on earth so splendid was,
And of its king, called Anfortas.
Such praise she'd never have believed.
From many streams her land received
Precious gems instead of sand;
Large mountains also claimed her land,
Of gold, and other substance naught.
The noble queen had this thought:
"How get tidings of that king

GAWAN AND ORGELUSE 241

To whom the Grail's an underling?" 20
She sent to him her treasured prize:
These persons twain of curious guise,
Cundry and her brother fair.
She also sent him gifts, so rare
No money could outweigh them,
No man for sale display them.
Then sent the kind king Anfortas,
Since he was very generous,
To Orgelusë de Logroys
As gift this squire so *curtoys*.[11]
Because his granddam showed such greed, 520
He differed from the human breed.
   This churl, to herbs and stars akin,[12]
Hailed Gawan with mighty din.
Gawan there was biding;
The other came a-riding
Upon a weak and sickly nag.
'Twas lame, all four legs seemed to drag,
And oftentimes it fell to earth.
Jeschutë, lady fair of worth, 10
A better horse she rode that day[13]
When Parzival in valiant fray
Her husband's pardon sought and won
For wrongs that she had never done.

Malcreätiure reviles and threatens Gawan for leading Orgelusë away, whereupon Gawan seizes the misshapen fellow by his bristly hair and drags him from his horse. The bristles cause the attacker's hands to bleed. Gawan now finds the wounded knight and applies the healing herb to his wound, whereupon the knight warns him against Orgelusë who, he says, has caused his downfall, too. He asks Gawan to untie his horse so that he and the lady may ride to a nearby hospital. But after Gawan has done so and helped the lady upon the horse, the wounded man nimbly leaps upon Gawan's steed and rides away with his lady. Orgelusë's mockery only elicits new assurances from Gawan that he will not renounce her. Soon the wounded knight returns and tells Gawan that he had merely intended to avenge the insult which Gawan had done him four weeks ago when he sent him as a prisoner to King Arthur, at whose court he was forced to eat with the dogs. Gawan recognizes him as Vrians and assures him that his unchivalrous treatment of a young lady should have merited much more severe punishment. Vrians rides off with Gawan's horse. In anger Gawan relates that Vrians would have suffered death by hanging, had not he, Gawan, interceded for him with King Arthur. Gawan now mounts Malcreätiure's miserable mare, while the owner follows on foot. Orgeluse again taunts him but he vows fidelity. He notices that the mare's back is about to break and dismounts, leaving only his shield upon the poor creature. Orgeluse now speaks. (520, 15—531, 11)

    Quoth she, "What, bear you huckster's trash
  Here in my land for vending?
  Who's so intent on lending
  Me doctor's help and a merchant's pack?
  Look out for tolls along your track![14]
  My men, toll from you taking,
  Will see you joy forsaking."
  Though thus she fain had teased him,
  Her salty speech so pleased him,   20
  He cared not what remark she made;
  Whene'er on her his eyes he laid,
  His pledge to sorrow was redeemed.
  To him a day in spring she seemed,
  Before his eyes a radiant flower,
  Sweet to his glance, to his spirit, sour.
  Since she was lost and found in one,
  Through whom sick joy to heal begun,
  In every hour that came around
  Both free he was and sorely bound.
  Many a master says 'tis so   532
  That Amor and Cupido,[15]
  And that couple's mother Venus
  Thus scatter love between us:
  With fire and with arrow.
  Such love can only harrow.
  A man of heartfelt loyalty
  Of *Minnë* never will be free.
  Though love bring joy or sorrow new,
  Minnë true is ever true.   10
  Cupido, thine arrow[16]

I miss by a margin narrow.
'Tis the same with Amor's spear.
If ye are ruling *Minnë* here,
And Venus with her torch so hot,
That is a woe I haven't got.
If true love ever sway my heart,
Fidelity must play its part.
If e'er my witty shoving
Could save a man from loving,   20
Gawan is so by me adored
I'd serve him well without reward.
'Twould not be right to blame him,
Though *Minnë* hold and tame him
If *Minnë* binds his senses,
Who shatters all defenses.
He was a staunch defender,
Who good defense could render,
Hence 'tis not meet that a man so brave
Should e'er be any woman's slave.
Come close to me, Sir Minnëstress.[17]   533
You rend our joy with such address
As to trample holes in joy's own ground
And break a trail for woe profound.
Thus tribulation lengthens out.
If she'd go traveling about
Elsewhere than into spirits high,
'Twere better for our joys, say I,
Would *Minnë* play the naughty brat?
Methinks she is too old for that.   10
Or does she blame her tender years[18]
For causing lovers bitter tears?
I'd rather say her youth's to blame
Than see her old age soiled with shame.
Many a prank has *Minnë* played:
Shall this to age or youth be laid?
If with youthful capers heady
In her old ways she's unsteady,
Her worth will soon be low in price.
She surely needs some good advice.   20
Love that's pure and true I prize,

> So do all men who are wise;
> Be you man or be you maid,
> The things I've said you have obeyed.
> If love to loving always knew
> Fidelity that's pure and true,
> So neither lover felt distress
> That *Minnë* did his heart possess
> With love that shuns inconstancy—
> Such love is the highest love there be.
> Fain as I'd be to save the man,   534
> Still, never can my lord Gawan
> Escape from *Minnë's* urging,
> His life of pleasure purging.
> What can my intervention do,
> Though all I think and say is true?
> Good men with love should have no strife:
> 'Tis she that helps them gain new life.
> Gawan ate love's bitter fruit:
> The lady rode, he walked afoot.[19]   10

On the opposite bank of a river Gawan and Orgelusë see a magnificent castle, from the windows of which about four hundred ladies look down upon them. In a spacious meadow facing the castle a knight accosts Gawan; the latter is scornfully urged by Orgelusë to fight bravely and told that only if he is victorious will he see her again. Then she departs for the castle. The knight turns out to be Lishoys Gwelljus. Before Gawan can decide whether to meet him on his wretched horse or afoot, Lishoys is upon him. A bitter fight ensues, in which Lishoys is finally forced to the ground. But he refuses to surrender, preferring death. Gawan, however, is unwilling to kill him, yet he appropriates the horse of Lishoys, which turns out to be his own steed, Gringuljetë, stolen by Vrians. A second encounter between Gawan and Lishoys turns out just like the first one, and again the latter refuses to surrender because he would rather die than renounce Orgelusë, for whose love he says he is fighting. Lishoys is turned over to an old ferryman, and by him and his daughter, Benë, Gawan is well treated and put up for the night. (534, 11—552, 30)

Book Eleven
Gawan and the Marvelous Bed

Book Eleven

GAWAN AND THE MARVELOUS BED

Gawan sleeps until just before daybreak, when he awakens and again sees the ladies at the windows of the castle. Surprised that they are not sleeping, he returns to his bed. Awakening again, he finds Benë and her maids ready to do his bidding. When he asks Benë the meaning of the ladies at the castle windows, she breaks out in loud lamentation. Her father hurries to the scene and after some hesitation informs Gawan that he is in the country of Terre Marveile (Marvelous Land), where the precious lit marveile (marvelous bed) is to be found in the Chastel Marveile (Marvelous Castle) on the opposite river bank. Terrible trials face Gawan there, but if he can withstand them and liberate the ladies (and their knights) who are enchanted in the castle, he will become lord of the entire domain. The host also tells of another knight whom he had ferried across to the castle only yesterday but who did not inquire about its mysteries. By his description Gawan realizes that it must have been Parzival. Gawan is now armed, given a new shield, and told to leave his horse with a merchant at the castle gate. He is also warned not to give up his shield and sword. Now he is ferried across the river by his host (whose name is Plippalinot), leaves his horse with the merchant, whose costly wares he inspects, and enters the castle. (553, 1—564, 26)

He found the castle strong and wide.
The battlements on every side
Were built for stubbornest defence.
Not a fig, at all events,
'Twould give for a siege of thirty years.   565
No storming could cause it any fears.
Within, a courtyard spacious:
Well, the Lechfeld's[1] more capacious.
Many towers o'er parapets were shown.
Our story clearly makes it known
That when Gawan this castle spied,
He found the roof on every side
Like a peacock's plumage gay,
Shining bright on every day.[2]   10

Truly, neither rain nor snow
Dimmed the roof's resplendent glow.
  The hall was decorated
And nicely variated;
The window-pillars were embossed,
Above, the vaulting arches crossed.
All around stood bed on bed,
Each one separately spread.
The silken quilts upon them laid
Were various and richly made.   20
The maids had there been sitting,
But soon, and not unwitting,
They all had taken to leaving:
No chance of their receiving
Their day of bliss, their joy that came,
Given to them with Gawan's name.
If him they only could have seen,
Could greater still their joy have been?
On him perforce no eye they laid,
Though he had come to bring them aid.
They couldn't help what then began.   566
So now my valiant lord Gawan
Walked across from wall to wall,
Taking in the spacious hall.
Then his eye discerning—
To right or left hand turning?—
Took in a door, opened wide,
Where he was to go inside,
The highest fame acquiring,
  Or in the attempt expiring.   10

He enters a room the floor of which consists of highly polished precious stones, and finds the costly and marvelous bed there, which at first eludes him with lightning-like rapidity but into which he finally leaps with his shield. Lying in it, he endures various trials—a volley of rocks shot from slings, five hundred arrows, a menacing peasant, and a hungry lion. After killing the lion, he swoons because of his many wounds and comes to rest upon the beast's body. Some of the enchanted maidens under instructions from old Queen Arnivë (Gawan's grandmother and King Arthur's mother), who is also present but not recognized

by him, he is well cared for and soon feels ready for further adventure. The other queens, who are also captives in the castle, are told that the unidentified champion is still alive.
(566, 11—578, 2)

> They shouted all, "Dieu merci[3]."
> The wise old queen[4] sagaciously
> A couch for resting ordered,
> All with a carpet bordered,
> Before a flaming fire.
> Salves rich beyond desire,
> With wisdom well compounded,
> Good for the bruised and wounded,   10
> Likewise by the queen were brought.
> Next, four maidens she besought
> With kindness to receive him
> And of armor to relieve him,
> This gently from him taking,
> Meantime all efforts making
> To save him from embarrassment.
> "Put silk around you like a tent,
> Disarm him then behind that screen.[5]
> If he to walk himself is keen,   20
> Let him, or carry him instead
> To where I'm standing by the bed.
> I'll wait where he's supposed to lie.
> Then, if he's not going to die,
> Was not dealt a fatal wound,
> I'll very shortly make him sound.
> But if some mortal wound he drew,
> Our happiness is cut in two:
> Then we also would be slain
> And, living, bear death's cruel pain."

The old Queen Arnivë treats Gawan's wounds with a salve that Cundry had procured from Munsalvaesche Castle. She also places a healing root in his mouth, and he sinks into a deep slumber. When he awakens he is offered sumptuous food and drink by the zealous ladies. Then he falls asleep again. (579, 1—582, 30)

Book Twelve
Gawan and Gramoflanz

Book Twelve

GAWAN AND GRAMOFLANZ

Who Gawan's rest were stealing, 583
When he needs rest for healing,
Would choose a base and sinful course.
According to the story's source
With labor never lightened,
He'd broadened and he'd heightened
His fame, nor found an easy lot.
Whatever noble Lancelot[1]
Upon the sword-bridge sorely wrought,
Or when with Meljacanz he fought, 10
Was naught compared with this dismay.
And say of Garel[2] what you may,
That king so proud and sightly,
When he in fashion knightly
The lion from the palace threw
At Nantes, where it the people slew.
(Garel, that knife securing,
Found it less alluring
Inside the marble post to dwell.)
If so many bolts on a mule's back fell, 20
It would break down beneath the load
Which Gawan, who endurance showed,
Allowed against himself to fly:
His proud heart bade him do or die.
Li gweiz prelljus[3] the ford,
And Erec winning Schoydelacord[4]
From terrible Mabonagrin,
To know such pain did not begin,
Nor did proud Iwein meet such ill,
What time the water he would spill
On the stone[5] of which Adventure told. 584
Were into one these woes all rolled,
By Gawan's woe they'd be surpassed,
Were both into the balance cast.
   Ye ask, what woe did he endure?
If ye'll not deem it premature,

The nature of it I will name.
Orgeluse 'twas, who came
Into Gawan's heart and mind,
A man to fear quite disinclined 10
And full of strength and warlike zeal.
How could so small a place conceal
Such a woman tall and great?
She walked upon a pathway strait
Onward into Gawan's heart;
His every other kind of smart
Before this torment fled his mind.
It was a chamber quite confined⁶
In which so tall a woman sat,
Whom never he, awake, forgat 20
To serve, before or after.
Let none burst into laughter,
Amused because a woman can
Defeat so powerful a man.
Alas, alas, how can that be?
Dame *Minnë* shows her enmity
To him who sought and won success.
Valorous and terrorless
In *Minnë's* ears he'd sounded.
Against the hero wounded
She shouldn't use such violence. 585
It ought to count in his defence,
That when he'd all his powers still
She conquered him against his will.
Minnë, if honor you'd not miss,
You'd better listen well to this:
No honor's gained in such a strife.
Gawan has acted all his life
As for your favor you'd require.
The same was done by Lot, his sire. 10
His mother's whole relation
Showed you veneration,
From days of Mazadanë,⁷
Who went to Famurganë,
There by Terdelaschoyë led,
Whom your power visited.

Of Mazadan' the progeny
We've often heard, and all agree:
None from your service sought release.
Take Ither, knight of Kahaviez, 20
He also bore your coat-of-arms.
When women heard praise of his charms,
None would ever feel ashamed,
If anywhere his name was named,
If she succumbed to *Minnë's* law.[8]
Think how each felt when him she *saw!*
She knew how *Minnë* can amaze.
His death deprived you of much praise.
Why not kill Gawan on the spot,
As fell his nephew, Ilinot,[9]
Who by your power was so subdued 586
That he, the winsome stripling, wooed,
And sought as his amië,
Of Kanadig[10] Florië.
As child his father's land he fled
And by this selfsame queen was bred.
He was in Brittany[11] a guest.
Love for the queen his heart oppressed
And drove him from her land renowned.
In her service he was found 10
Dead, as ye no doubt have heard.[12]
Gawan's kin have oft incurred
Minnë's deep, heart-searing flame.
Others of his line I'll name
Who also suffered *Minnë's* woe.
How came it that the blood-stained snow
Banned Parzival, of steadfast life?
The reason was the queen, his wife.[13]
Galoës[14] and Gahmuret,
Minnë, by you were so beset, 20
In death you caused them to be laid.
Itonjë,[15] the noble maid,
To Gramoflanz,[16] the famous king,
Her constant, loyal love did bring.
That was Gawan's sister fair.
Minnë, you made like woe to bear

Alexander's Surdamur.[17]
These and others, be ye sure,
Whom Gawan as kinsmen named,
Dame *Minnë*, you as vassals claimed.
All must needs obey your whim.   587
Now you want to conquer him.
If you'd but strive with the stronger,
Letting him live here longer,
Although so sick and wounded,
Quelling those who in strength abounded!
Many will sing of *Minnë's* bliss,
Whom she has never pressed like this.
I should perhaps be reticent,
And let fond lovers voice lament   10
For this Norwegian, brave and good,
Who, when this test had been withstood,
Attacked by a chilling shower,
Felt of *Minnë's* hail the power.

Gawan, awakening, yearns for Orgelusë and in his unrest brushes the bandages from his wounds. At dawn he arises and finds splendid clothing laid out for him which he dons. Then he inspects the castle. (587, 15—588, 27)

At no time had his eyes beheld
A hall such wealth declaring,
With what he saw comparing.
Upward rose along one side[18]   589
A winding staircase not too wide.
Above the roof 'twas seen to rise,
Winding its way up spiralwise.
On it a splendid column stood,
Fashioned not of rotten wood;
No, 'twas very strong and clear,
So big that Dame Camilla's[19] bier
Upon it had had room to stand.
Far, from Feirefiz's land   10
The wizard Clinschor[20] had it brought,
This column high, with magic fraught.
   Circular as a tent it was:
If the master Jeometras
Had been required this work to build,

He'd found his hand was not so skilled.
Its maker *magic* must enlist:
Adamas and amethyst
(So 'tis in the story said),[21]
Topaz yellow, garnet red,   20
Ruby crimson, chrysolite,
Emerald, carnelian bright—
These the windows had supplied.
They were high as they were wide.
Like the window-posts and frame,
All the roof was made the same.
Of all the window-posts seen there
None there was that could compare
With the pillar in the middle.
Adventure redes the riddle
Of miracles that it could do.   590
Gawan wished to get a view—
Upon the tower he climbed alone—
Of such a wealth of precious stone.
He saw there such a wondrous sight,
He could not tire of its delight.
It seemed to him that every land
On this column[22] could be scanned,
And that the countries went around;
The mountain peaks, he also found,   10
In orbits all collided.
The column a view provided
Of people walking and riding,
Some running, some abiding.
In one window a seat he took:
He wished to have a better look.

Arnive appears with her daughter Sangive (Gawan's own mother) and granddaughters Cundry and Itonje (Gawan's sisters—the former is *not* the sorceress). She explains that in the column of television one can see all that goes on within a radius of six miles. To his dismay he discovers in it his beloved Orgelusë riding with a strange knight. Arnive tells him that it is the redoubtable Turkoite. Gawan, still weak from bloodshed, decides to challenge him despite the warnings and protestations of the women. Armed by Plippalinot with a new spear, he rides out and wounds and unhorses the Turkoite, Florant, who up to now had been invincible. Again Orgeluse taunts him but finally accepts his offer of service to her. Riding beside her, he completely forgets his wounds. She demands that he secure for her a wreath from the foliage of a certain tree in the forest of Clinschor, which she points out to him. Then she rides away. He leaps from a high spot, fords Li gweiz prelljus (the perilous ford), where he almost loses his horse and his life, but finally finds the wreath. Immediately he is confronted by King Gramoflanz, the owner of the tree, who in vain demands the return of the wreath. Gramoflanz is not thinking of combat, for he is entirely unarmed. Moreover he explains that he never fights fewer than two men at a time and that he has offered his service to Orgeluse, whose lover Cidegast he has killed. He asks Gawan, whose name he has not yet learned but of whose conquest of the Terre Marveile he knows, to put in a good word for him with the fair Itonje. Gawan promises to do so, whereupon each reveals his identity to the other. They agree to meet for combat at Joflanze in sixteen days, each accompanied by a large retinue. Gramoflanz is happy over the prospect of jousting with Gawan, the only knight whom he would ever fight singly. Gawan returns as he had come. This time his horse is successful in hurdling the perilous ford. He hands the wreath to Orgeluse, who admits that she has suffered great anxiety for him. (590, 17—611, 30)

    "Lady, if it's true," said he,   612
"That in good faith you're greeting me,
Your own repute is heightened.
In this much I'm enlightened:
If honor by a shield is won,
Against the shield you had misdone.
True knightlihood ascends so high
That from mere scorn 'twould ever fly,
If a knight perform true chivalry.
Lady, if I may speak so free,   10
Whoe'er has seen me weapons wield
Must grant that well I bear my shield.
Another word you spelled me,
When first your eyes beheld me.
That I'll dismiss. This wreath accept.[23]
But, by the beauty you have kept,

On any knight of station
Bring no such degradation.
If scorn from you I must endure,
Henceforth all love I would abjure." 20
This beauty he loved so dearly
Said, weeping quite sincerely,
"Sir, if I confess the smart
I long since carry in my heart,
You'll see your woe is less than mine.
Whomsoe'er I might malign
Will please of blame relieve me.
Nothing more could grieve me
Than loss of joys that now are past
With my beloved Cidegast.
My dear and noble *bel ami*, 613
So glorious was his chivalry,
And so for merit did he sue,
That everyone—no matter who —
To whom a mother e'er gave birth
While he was living here on earth,
His supremacy conceded,
Which no man e'er exceeded.
Of virtue he a fountain-head
His youth with precious fruit bestead, 10
Preserved from evil slackness.
Toward light from out of blackness
He strove, to make his honor bright.
His goal he set so high in the light
That 'twas beyond attaining
If falseness strength was draining.
His fame could ever higher grow—
While others stayed perforce below—
Out of his spirit's kernel.
So o'er the star eternal 20
Doth course the speedy Saturnus![24]
Of faith a true Monicirus[25]—
Since now I dare to speak the truth—
Such was that exemplary youth.
Of that beast's death maids should complain:
Seeking their purity 'tis slain.

I was his heart, he was my life:
I lost him, loss-enduring wife.
Slain by Gramoflanz was he,
Whose wreath you won to give to me.
    Sir, if I used derision, 614
'Twas caused by this decision:
I thought I'd like to try you,
To see if I'd deny you
Or grant you love for merit due.
I know, sir, I was harsh to you,
But that was done to prove you.
Let kindness now behoove you.
Forgive, and cease your fretting,
Your wrath at me forgetting. 10
Your strength makes foemen tremble.
'Tis gold that you resemble,
Which men make pure in fire's glow:
You've purified your courage so.
He whom by you I've daunted,
As I want and ever wanted,
He's caused me everlasting pain."
Gawan to her replied again:
    "Lady, unless death should prevent,
I'll teach the king embitterment, 20
Whereby his pride is blighted.
My good faith I have plighted:
Against him I in joust will ride
Within a brief concerted tide:
Then stoutly will be striven.
You, lady, I've long forgiven.
If in your kindness you will take
Suggestions that I, foolish, make—
Be a woman, I'm beseeching,
Obey your virtue's teaching.
No one's present, only we: 615
Lady, favor show to me!"
Quoth she, "Within an armored arm
I never yet have gotten warm.
But still there is no reason
Why at other time or season

You may not claim my favor.
In sympathy I'll not waver
Until again you're wholly sound
In every place where you've a wound,   10
Till hurts are gone and you are well.
Away to Chastel Merveile
I will with you betake me."
"Great happiness you make me,"
Replied the hero amorous.
He lifted the lady beauteous,
Embracing her, upon her steed.
She'd not been worthy of such a deed
When at the well he saw her first[26]
And she into invective burst.   20

  As Gawan departs, Orgeluse with tears entreats him to avenge Cidegast's death. She tells him that she had already hired a host of knights for monetary or love's reward to represent her. Only one knight, Parzival, spurned her, she says, although she rode in mad pursuit of him. The rich treasures which Gawan saw at the gates of Chastel Marveile, she explains, were given to her by Anfortas, and with them she had hoped to lure Gramoflanz to destruction in the Chastel. Now Gawan and she ride to the Chastel, are ferried across the river by Plippalinot and enthusiastically welcomed by the inmates who had been enchanted there by Clinschor. Gawan sends a squire to King Arthur, inviting him to his joust with Gramoflanz at Joflanze, but enjoins the squire not to reveal to anyone that he, Gawan, is now lord of Chastel Marveile. When Arnivë, who does not know Gawan's identity, tries to worm this secret out of the squire, he refuses to reveal it. (615, 21—626, 30)

Book Thirteen
Clinschor

Book Thirteen

CLINSCHOR

Arnivë is angry at the squire, but to no avail. Gawan sleeps until late morning and when he awakens the servants dress him sumptuously. An elaborate feast is now prepared. Gawan's two prisoners, Lischoys and Florant, are set free. Without revealing his identity Gawan converses with his sister Itonjë and finds out that she really loves Gramoflanz. She eagerly takes the ring which Gramoflanz has sent her and confesses that she secretly dislikes Orgelusë because of her hatred for Gramoflanz. All those present at the feast are very happy because this is their first opportunity of conversing with each other since being enchanted by Clinschor. (627, 1—637, 30)

    Now approached the end of day: 638
Its light was passing fast away,
And through the clouds there came to sight
Many a harbinger of night—
The stars—and then once more they fled,
To find for Mother Night a bed.
No sooner had this vanguard passed,
When Night herself appeared at last.
Many a richly-candled crown,
Hanging high, shone brightly down   10
All around the palace hall,
Fully lit with candles tall.
Every single table
Bore candles as 'twas able.
On this the story touches:
So radiant was the duchess,[1]
Had no one brought a single light,
Around her naught had been in night.
Her eyes could sparkle bright as day.
Such was her beauty, people say.   20
You'd do a wrong if you should boast
You'd e'er seen anywhere a host[2]
So full of jubilation:
All there was exaltation.
Amorous joy was in the air:

Knights sitting here, the ladies there,
Each other viewed with eager eye.
Strangers who at first were shy
Gained confidence with every look.
I find it easy that to brook.
   Unless some glutton claimed more stuff, **639**
If you permit, they've had enough.
They bore away the tables all.
Then Gawan gaily began to call
For people good at fiddling:
Were there any more than middling?
The voice of many a squire rings
Out: he's learned to play the strings.
But none such mastery could unfold
As play a dance that wasn't old.[3]   10
Of modern dances knew they naught
Which from Thuringia to us are brought.
The host deserves your gratitude:
He sobered not their joyous mood,
And many a lady fair and trim
Stepped up to dance in front of him.
The dance seemed decorated
By being variated,
As knights among the ladies moved.
Foemen they of sorrow proved.   20
Between two ladies dancing
One often saw advancing
A handsome knight and debonair.[4]
One witnessed naught but pleasure there.
If a knight to serve so wanted
That love in turn be granted,
He found assent to his request.
Poor in cares, with pleasures blest,
In converse hours were speeded
As sweet lips coaxed and pleaded.
   Gawan and Sangivë, **640**
Sitting with Queen Arnivë,
Quietly watched the dancing.
Orgelus', entrancing,
Came beside Gawan to sit:

CLINSCHOR

She gave her hand, he welcomed it.
They had some conversation:
Her coming brought elation.
His grief grew small, his joy anew
Grew great: all sorrow from him flew.　　　10
If dancing made the others glad,
Gawan still greater pleasure had.
Queen Arnivë said, " 'Tis best,
Sir, that you should think of rest.
It's time you were retiring,
Such is your wound requiring.
Has the duchess here made up her mind
That she's to cover you inclined
Tonight, and keep you company?
A help and comfort she will be."　　　20
Said Gawan, "Pray you, question her:
To both your wishes I defer."
Unasked replied the duchess fair,
"I'll gladly take him in my care.
Let these people go to sleep.
O'er him tonight such watch I'll keep
As loving lady never gave.
Florand of Itolac,[5] the brave,
The noble duke of Gowerzin—
Let the knights be hosts and take them in."

　　Ended shortly was the dance:　　　641
Lovely maids of sparkling glance
Sat them here, sat them there.
Knights sat down among the fair.
He who pled for love's reward
And found his love in sweet accord,
His joy took vengeance on his woe.
The host said, since 'twas time to go,
"My night-drink now before me set!"
Wooers heard this with regret.[6]　　　10
The host, like the guests, was wooing:
Love was his heart pursuing.
For him, they'd sat there far too long:
His heart was gripped by *Minnë* strong.
The night-drink gave the sign to go.

Clustered candles all aglow
Preceded knights who left the hall.[7]
Gawan to knights and ladies all
His special guests commended:
These twain were not offended.   20
The guests, Lischoys and Florand,
Sought a bedroom there at hand.
The duchess followed ancient rite
As to the twain she bade good night.
And now the ladies all retired
To find the rest they much desired.
They bowed their heads politely:
They'd learned to do it rightly.
Sangivë and young Itonjë
Went away, as did Cundrie.

 With Benë's and Arnivë's aid   642
Preparations now were made
So that Gawan could comfort find.
Orgelusë was inclined
To show that she of help could be.
Gawan was guided by the three
To where he might be comforted.
He saw, into a chamber led,
Two beds separated stand.
But do not ask me to expand   10
Upon their decoration.
Expect a new sensation.
Arnivë to the duchess said,
"The knight who, seeking you, was led
Hither, you should assist to rest;
Should he help of you request,
'Twould honor you if granted.
Of me no more is wanted,
Save this to say: His every wound
Has by such skillful hands been bound,   20
That he could well bear arms again.
But his lover's woe should cause you pain.
If you his pangs can lighten,
His joy of living heighten,
We each will be the gainer.

So be not an abstainer."
Arnivë then begged to receive
The host's consent, and took her leave.
A light before her Benë bore.
Gawan himself then closed the door.
That these sweet creatures love could steal **643**
I am reluctant to conceal:
The truth I had fain related.
But men have e'er berated
All those who air such secret love.
Courtly folk still disapprove.
He who does, earns disrepute.
Where love exacts, discretion's mute.

Gawan cohabits with Orgelusë. The squire whom Gawan has sent to King Arthur's court arrives there and delivers the letter to Queen Guinevere. She is delighted to hear from Gawan and promises to come with her ladies, telling the squire that meanwhile Cunnewarë, Parzival, Jeschutë, and Ekuba have all left her. The squire, however, does not disclose Gawan's whereabouts to her nor to anyone else, revealing only that he has enjoyed good fortune. To none of the knights does the squire give any information concerning his mission. Now King Arthur is also shown the letter, and he has the queen read it aloud to the court. All those present agree to undertake the journey. The squire returns to Chastel Marveile, where Arnivë meets him at the bridge but again fails to elicit any news from him. Privately he tells Gawan his glad tidings. One morning while awaiting the coming of King Arthur, Gawan is sitting at a window with Arnivë, whom he thanks for all her help and asks to explain to him the wonders of the castle and its erstwhile lord, Clinschor. (643, 9—656, 5)

"Sir, the wonders he does here[8]
Seem tiny little wonderkins
Against the mighty ones he wins
In many lands outlying.
Whoso us is vilifying, **10**
Brings but sin upon his head.
Sir, I'll tell his habits dread.
To many a folk he's harsh and dour.
His land is called Terr' de Labuor.[9]
The man he claims as ancestor

Was himself a famous sorcerer,
In Napel born, Virgilius.
His descendant, Clinschor,[10] acted thus:
Caps was called his chiefest town.
He trod the pathway of renown   20
So well that fame he could not miss.
Of Duke Clinschor, in view of this,
Both sexes much narrated,
Till harm to him was fated.
In Sicilie upon the throne
A ruler sat, as Ibert known.
Iblis was his consort; she
Was loveliest by far to see
Of all that came from a mother's breast.
Into her service Clinschor pressed,
Till she his zeal rewarded.   657
The king took vengeance sordid.
  If I'm his secrets to reveal,
For your consent I must appeal,
But I must shun exposure
Of what brooks no disclosure:
How he took up a sorcerer's life.
Clinschor, crippled by a knife,[11]
Was impotent thereafter."
At this, uproarious laughter   10
Was uttered by my lord Gawan.
Again the queen to speak began:
" 'Twas there in Kalot Embolot[12]
That mockery became his lot:
That is a castle far renowned,
Where the king one day Duke Clinschor found
As he reclined in Iblis' arm.
If loving her he had grown warm,
For that he made full payment:
The king took off his raiment   20
And made his body smooth below.
He thought it his right to treat him so.
The king so operated
That Duke Clinschor was fated
To give no woman joy again.

But that brought many others pain.[18]
'Twas not in the land of Persia
But in a town named Persida:[14]
There sorcery was first devised.
He journeyed there and was apprized
Of how to carry out his will   658
With sorcery and magic skill.
Embittered by his body's shame,
Toward men and women he became
A creature full of hatefulness:
I mean to all folk of nobleness.
If their content he can destroy,
That gives his heart the fullest joy.

 A certain king, named Irot,
Feared to meet just such a lot: 10
In Roschë Sabinës, there dwelt he.
He offered of his property
Whatever Clinschor wanted,
Provided peace was granted.
Clinschor from his land received
This mount, impregnable believed,
And with the mountain all the ground
Extending for eight miles around.[15]
Clinschor on this mountain wrought
This wondrous work for which you fought.   20
Of all the riches on the earth,
Those here exceed them all in worth.
Were foes this fort attacking,
No supplies would here be lacking:
For thirty years there's ample food.
And Clinschor rules a multitude
Of *bea gent* and *mal gent*[16]
Who twixt the lofty firmament
Hover, and the solid ground,
Save God's protection they have found.

 Lord, seeing you such trials met   659
With valor, and are living yet,
The gift he got is in your hand,
The fort and its apportioned land.
Your ownership he'll not contest,

> And he will grant you peace and rest;
> For publicly he said it
> (And you his word may credit),
> Who this adventure can endure,
> May deem the castle his for sure.　　　　　　10
> Whatever folk of noble worth
> He saw upon the Christian earth,
> If maiden, wife, or man they be,
> All will bow to your decree,
> And men and women heathen born
> Must dwell among us here forlorn.
> Do let them homeward now return,
> Where friends for us must feel concern:
> Exile makes my heart feel cold.
> He who the countless stars has told　　　　　　20
> Must teach your heart assistance,
> Make glad our drear existence."

Arnivë adds that she herself was once a noble queen (the wife of Utepandragon), as was also her daughter(Sangivë, the wife of Lot). Finally Arthur and his retinue approach, but everyone except Gawan thinks they are hostile forces. At Logroys they engage in dreadful combat with Orgelusë's men. Now finally Gawan, still guarding his secret for a later happy surprise, prepares his forces for departure to meet King Arthur. Everyone but Gawan continues to expect a warlike encounter with a foe. But Arthur, not knowing Gawan's exact whereabouts, passes Chastel Marveile and pitches tent at Joflanze. Gawan, learnning of this, sends his marshal to prepare an encampment next to Arthur's. When this is ready Gawan follows with his entire retinue and surprises all those present. Arthur greets his own mother, Arnivë, Gawan's mother, Sangivë, and sister, Itonjë; the women too finally realize who Gawan himself is. Orgelusë's followers are also invited, arrive at night, and prepare another separate encampment. Arthur invites Gramoflanz to come for the encounter with Gawan, who inspects his armor and tries out his trusty steed, Gringuljetë, for the rigorous combat which he expects. At the river Sabins he meets a knight, unrecognized by him, whom Wolfram identifies as the real hero of his tale, Parzival. (659, 23—678, 30)

Book Fourteen
Parzival and Gawan

Book Fourteen

PARZIVAL AND GAWAN

If now our noble Gawan 679
Valiantly a joust began,
I ne'er found so affrighting
His faith in knightly fighting.
To fear for the other man[1] I ought,
But that I'll banish from my thought:
In strife with one he was a host.
From some far-distant heathen coast[2]
Was brought his splendid panoply.
A ruby ne'er so red could be 10
As the raiment of both man and horse.
The hero rode adventure's course:
His pierced shield was the token.
Likewise he had broken
Off the tree, where underneath
Gramoflanz stood guard, a wreath
So fair, that Gawan knew it.
He feared his fame would rue it,
Should the other vainly for him wait.[3]
If the king was come to try his fate, 20
Forthwith a jousting must be run,
Though ne'er a lady saw it done.
    From Munsalvaeschë were the two[4]
Chargers, that without ado
Nearer dashed and nearer,
Each with its valiant spearer:
Sharp spurring gave them such command.
Clover green, not dusty sand,
Stood dewy where the joust was wrought.
Grief to me has their battling brought.
With skill they did their thrusting, 680
For a race adept at jousting
Both these doughty knights had borne.
Little winning, much forlorn,
Will be he who wins this prize.
He'll regret it if he's wise.

Here constancy faced constancy;
Their faith, not now or previously,
Had e'er a hole or damage won.
But hearken how this joust was done.   10
    Dashingly it went, yet so
That neither one could triumph know.
Noble friendship, kinship true,
Angry at each other flew
In bitter strife with deadly thrust.
Whichever one may win the joust,
His joy will bring grief all the more.
Each hand its spear so stoutly bore,
That they, both friend and brother,
Must needs unseat each other;   20
Thus each charger took a fall.
Then they hammered, not at all
Lamed, as one would drive a wedge,
Till each man's sword became a sledge.
Splinters with the verdant grass
Mingled in a motley mass
Soon as their fighting started.
The wait till they were parted—
As yet 'twas early—took too long.
No intercessor came along.
    Besides them not a soul was near.   681
Will ye the further story hear,
How at this very hour
Arthur's scouting power
Found Gramoflanz with all his host
On a meadow near the coast?
On one side flowed the Sabins,[5]
Opposite, the Poynzaclins.
Here these rivers reached the sea.
The fourth side, there upon the lea,   10
Was fronted, with encircling wall,
By Rosch' Sabins, the capital;
Before it moats wide and deep,
Above it towers high and steep.
The camp for Gramoflanz's train,
Spread out a mile along the plain,

Filled a belt full half as wide.
Toward Arthur's vassals see them ride:
Knights a-many, strangers,
Men-at-arms, light rangers,
Mail-coated and with lances.
Behind them, see! there prances
Under many banners bright
Troop on troop in armored might.
  Now the trumpets' blare is heard.
All the mighty army stirred:
The host was just departing,
Toward Joflanzë starting;
The ladies' reins went tingaling.[6]
Gramoflanz's tented ring[7]
By ladies was surrounded.
If I know how a tale is grounded,
I'll mention to you many a name
Of those encamped, who hither came
To join his noble company.
If this to you is novelty,
Let me inform you as I'm wont.
From the water-fortress city Punt[8]
His uncle there escorted in—
His name was Brandelidelin—[9]
Six hundred maidens in a row,
Each of whom would like to know
If her lover armed for fight
In chivalry showed greatest might.
The noble men of Punturteis
Were happy in this enterprise.
If you'll believe me, there appears
The famous Bernous de Riviers.
His wealthy father Narant
To him bequeathed the Uckerlant.
He brought in ships across the brine
A host of ladies just as fine,
Whose radiant beauty one could prize,
Of whom no one spoke otherwise.
Of these, the prince had sundered
Maidens full two hundred;

Two hundred wives had brought their men,
If how to count I rightly ken.
Bernout fiz cons Narant,
Knights five hundred, all gallant,
Would at his call assemble.   683
They made all foemen tremble.
  Thus Gramoflanz upon the heath
Would avenge the stealing of his wreath,
So many eyes might witness
Who showed the greater fitness.
The princes[10] from his region
Brought knights, a valiant legion,
And many ladies passing fair:
Handsome people saw one there.   10
Arthur's envoys entered now
And found the king: I'll tell you how.
On a mattress thick of silk palmat[11]
Gramoflanz the ruler sat,
Cushioned by a quilt of silk.
Maidens fair of cheerful ilk
Were drawing greaves sedately
Upon his members stately.
As canopy a silken piece—
Fashioned in Ecidemonis[12]—   20
Wide and long it had been made—
Swung above him, giving shade.
On twelve poles it was fastened.
Up Arthur's envoys hastened.
To him, with pride all swelling,
They spoke, their message telling:
"Lord, King Arthur sent us here,
Known for this both far and near:
He has achieved some little fame,
And noble is his royal name.
Of fame him you're depriving.   684
How could you be conniving
At treating thus his sister's son,
That by your hand he'd be undone?
Had Sir Gawan, the noble knight,

Caused you an even sorrier plight,
Yet he would still, as foes have found,
Be shielded by the Table Round:
All those to him their friendship give
Who share the same prerogative."   10
   The king said, "This appointed joust
My hand so fearlessly will thrust
This day, that I will make Gawan
A famous or dishonored man.
They tell me it is really true
That Arthur's come with retinue
And with the noble queen his wife:
I bid her welcome to our strife.
And if the duchess,[13] still irate,
Against me stir up Arthur's hate,   20
Youngsters, you should intervene.
All the same, naught comes between
Us who have resolved to fight.
I've with me so much mounted might,
No threat of force can make me leave.
Whate'er a certain hand achieve
I'll bear without objection.
But I must shun defection
From what I have engaged to do,
Or cease henceforth for love to sue.
Love, into whose hand I've given   685
Joy and life, for whom I've striven,—
God knows what by her grace he's gained:[14]
For ne'er before would I have deigned
To fight against one single man.
But since the noble Gawan
With such distinction lives his life,
I'm pleased to join with him in strife.
Thus my virtue is debased:[15]
Such an easy fight I've never faced.   10
I have fought, so men admit
(If you desire, seek word of it),
Against men none of whom denies
That with my hand I won the prize.
Against *one* man I've never fought.

Nor should the ladies praise me in aught,
In case I win the prize today.
My heart with happiness is gay,
For I have heard that she[16] is free
For whom this fight is now to be.   20
King Arthur of lofty station
O'er many a foreign nation
In undisputed might holds sway.
Perhaps she's here with him today,
At whose command until my death
I'll proffer joy or anguished breath
In service unabated.
What greater joy were fated
Than if the happiness occur
That she behold me serving her?"

    Benë[17] sat close by the king.   686
The contest she was welcoming.
The fact that she'd so often seen
His prowess made her feel serene.
She was not anxious for the man.
But had she known that Sir Gawan
Was her own lady's brother,[18]
And the harsh words meant no other
Than him whom she as master served,
From joyfulness her heart had swerved.   10
This maid had brought a finger-ring
Which young Itonjë sent the king
To show how love her spirit claimed.
This very ring her brother famed[19]
Had fetched across the Sabins.
Benë upon the Poynzaclins
Had sailed down in a little boat.
She brought a word for him to note:
"My lady from Chastel Merveile
Is here, nor do her ladies fail."   20
Requests for faith and truth she bore
From Itonjë, whose plea was more
Than e'er from maid came to a man.
Remember her distress, it ran,
Since, shunning joys she could obtain,

She'd serve but him, his love to gain.
This gave the king new hope and trust,
But toward Gawan he stayed unjust.
(If a sister cost me such distress,[20]
I'd wish that I were sisterless.)
   They brought his harness rich and rare, 687
So costly, 'twas beyond compare.
And ne'er a knight that *Minnë* drove
To seek a lady's gift of love,
Not Gahmuret or Galoës,[21]
Nor yet the king Kyllicrates,[22]
Could achieve such decoration
For his lady's admiration.
Not from Ipopotiticon,[23]
Nor from far-distant Acroton,   10
Nor from Kalomidentë,
Nor from Agatyrsjentë,[24]
No better silk was ever brought
Than that for *this* apparel wrought.
Then he kissed the finger-ring
That by Itonjë to the king
Was sent as loving token.
Whene'er his joy was broken,
Her faith this ring so well revealed
That her love to him was like a shield.   20
   Armed was now King Gramoflanz.
Twelve young maids began to prance,
Each upon a handsome mare.
Zeal they did not wish to spare:
This company of winsome look,
Each a shaft in hand they took
And thus the awning carried
Neath which the ruler tarried.
In motion they would shade the king
All eager for his tourneying.
Two other maidens not too weak   688
(The fairest there that you could seek),
Under his mail-clad arms they rode.
No more the envoys there abode:
Arthur's men forthwith returned,

And on their homeward way discerned
Gawan amid a battle-scene.
So alarmed these squires had never been.
They shrieked to see him in his need:
This was to them a loyal deed.

   The fight almost so far had run
That he[25] the victory had won
Whom Gawan had engaged in war,
Whose strength exceeded his so far
That Gawan, the valiant knight,
Almost gave up as lost the fight.
But they, his need perceiving,
Named him in their grieving.
He who till now the fight had pressed
Lost forthwith his battle-zest.
Far from him his sword he tossed:
"Woe to me, I'm cursed and lost!"
Cried the weeping stranger.
"My fortune is in danger,
Since my dishonored hand has found
This battle on the present ground.
Unseemly was this knightly tilt.
I must confess my horrid guilt:
Misfortune came before me
And from salvation tore me.
The coat-of-arms, which long I feared[26]
As ever now has reappeared.
To think that I against Gawan
In battle here as foeman ran!
Myself I have defeated,
Misfortune thus entreated.
No sooner was this fray begun
Than my salvation off had run."

   Gawan heard and saw this cry.
To his battle-mate he made reply:
"Sir, whoever you may be,
You speak so graciously to me.
Had you but sooner spoken,
While my strength was still unbroken!
In that case I'd have kept the fame

Which you have taken from my name.
Pray you your name to tell me.
Then, if the wish befell me,
I'd know where I my fame could seek.
The while my fortune was not weak, 20
No one man e'er had laid me low."
"Cousin, thou my name shalt know:
Thee will I serve whate'er befall.
I am thy cousin Parzival."[27]
Quoth Gawan, "So 'twas bound to be:
That rectifies fatuity.
Two simple hearts devoid of sense
Have shown with hate their violence.
Thy hand has conquered thee and me:[28]
For both of us feel sympathy!
Thine own hand thou hast thwarted, **690**
If thou are loyal-hearted."
   When Gawan had spoken this,
Strength his frame began to miss,
Till, utter weakness feeling,
His body took to reeling,
Because his head was filled with sound,
And down he fell upon the ground.
One of Arthur's squires sped
To him and lifted up his head. 10
The sweet lad seemed to understand:
He doffed his helm, his face he fanned
For him with a white hat, peacock-plumed.
The labors that the youth assumed
Brought back again his vanished strength.
From either army[29] came at length
Comrades with their troops apace
Each to its appointed place,
Where painted posts were driven
And thus the limits given. 20

   Thus the hosts of King Arthur and King Gramoflanz take their positions, eager to witness the contest between Gawan and Gramoflanz. The latter approaches and realizes that a terrific battle has already taken place between two knights who should never have fought each other. He pities them. Despite his exhaustion Gawan leaps to his feet when he sees Gramoflanz. Benë weeps when she realizes Gawan's plight, and seeks to make him comfortable. Now Gramoflanz condescendingly volunteers to postpone the fight for one day, to give Gawan a brief respite. Parzival offers to take up the battle in Gawan's place, but Gramoflanz rejects this. Benë curses him and now at last learns to her surprise who Gawan really is. Gramoflanz departs. (690, 21—694, 18)

The king rode off, and all his men.
Arthur's youthful squires then   20
Caught the steeds[30] that ran away:
They too bore signs of a savage fray.
But Sir Gawan and Parzival,
And Benë fair, the maid in thrall,
Rode away to join their host.[31]
Parzival could fairly boast
His fighting force had gone so high
They all were glad when he came nigh.
Those that saw him nearing
Saluted him with cheering.
  I'll tell you more as best I can.   695
Talk turned alone upon this man.
The knowing ones on either side
Said with praise that none denied
How great was his achievement
That wrought his foe bereavement.
If ye agree, 'twas Parzival.
He was so strong, and fair withal,
No knight had e'er with him compared.
This men and women all declared,   10
When Sir Gawan brought him,
Who promptly then bethought him
That Parzival be freshly clad.
For both of them his vassals had
Brought like clothes of value great.
Everyone was quick to state
That Parzival had hither fared,
Of whom so oft it was declared
That he deserved all praises:
'Twas affirmed in many phrases.   20

Gawan asked him, "Wilt thou see
Here four ladies kin to thee,[32]
And many other ladies fair?
Then I'll gladly take thee there."
Said the son of Gahmuret,
"If noble ladies here are met,
Spare them my aspect chilling.
To see me each is unwilling
Who by the Plimizoel has heard
It said I speak a lying word.[33]
With God may women's honor rest! 696
I wish for women e'er the best.
My shame is still so searing,
I'd hate to be appearing."
"Yet it must me," was Gawan's say.
He led poor Parzival away.
'Twas there that four queens kissed the knight.
The duchess was in sorry plight,[34]
With a kiss this hero meeting
Who had declined her greeting,   10
What time she offered love and land
(For shame she knew not how to stand),
As he at Logroys joined in fray
And she'd pursued him far away.
Now Parzival, the man of worth,
By guileless talking back and forth
Was presently persuaded,
That thus all shame soon faded
Out of his heart, and diffidence,
So joy replaced his reticence.   20

   Sir Gawan for reasons good
Begged that Benë's sweet lips should
(If his favor still she sought)
To Itonjë mention naught,
"How King Gramoflanz's hate
Over his wreath does not abate,
So next day another fight
We'll essay when the time is right.
Toward my sister hold thy peace,
And prithee, let thy weeping cease."

Said she, "I've cause for weeping,   697
My heart lament is keeping.
Whichever is defeated,
Of joy my lady's cheated.
With each of you my lady's slain.
For her and me I must complain.
What good that you her brother are?
Upon her heart you're making war."
Meantime the host had all marched in.
For Gawan and his friends and kin   10
Food was all made ready there.
With the duchess gay and fair
Parzival was sitting.
Gawan thought it fitting
To recommend him to her grace.
Said she, "You're seating by my place
One who to women shows despite.
How shall I care for such a wight?
But since you ask, I'll treat him well,
Though he may think in scorn I fell."   20
Said the son of Gahmuret,
"Your heart's upon injustice set.
My nature I can recognize:
In me no scorn of women lies."
   If food there was, enough they served,[35]
Nor ever from good manners swerved.
Maid, wife, and man with pleasure ate.
Itonjë saw, as there she sate,
Watch o'er Benë keeping,
In secret she was weeping.
She too revealed an anguished look;   698
No more of food her sweet mouth took.
Thought she, "What's Benë doing here?
I sent her out that she should near
Him who my heart possesses—
This throbbing, how it oppresses!
What have I neglected?
Has Gramoflanz rejected
The service and the love I sent?
His true and manly sentiment   10

Naught other here accomplisheth
Than that my poor life suffers death,
While yearning I'm expending,
An agony heart-rending."
When the eating had been done
Past midday had gone the sun.
King Arthur and his noble queen,
Guinevere, forthwith were seen
To ride with knights and ladies fair
To join the knight beyond compare,   20
Amid the ladies seated.
Thus Parzival was greeted:
From many a lovely dame and miss
He saw himself receive a kiss.
Respect King Arthur showed him
For gratitude he owed him,
Because his fame well justified
Was both so long and so wide
That he, as judged by all who ken,
Was praised above all other men.
 To Arthur Parzival replied,   699
"Sire, when I last was by your side,
My honor was a target made.[36]
So high a forfeit then I paid,
I well nigh lost all my good name.
But, sire, today I hear you claim—
If you to candidness incline—
That still some share of praise is mine.
Although 'tis hard to credit,
I'd trust it since you said it.   10
Would that those others might believe
Who saw me go in shame and grieve."
Those sitting there declared: His hand
Had won the prize through many a land,
Triumphing with such high acclaim
That all unblemished was his name.
 The riders of the duchess all
Came where the handsome Parzival
By renowned King Arthur sat.
The noble ruler saw to that: 20

He welcomed them in Gawan's place.
King Arthur, wise in courtly grace,
Though Gawan's tents were surely great,
On the field before them sate.[37]
They took their place around the king,
Strangers faced them in the ring.
To name each category
Would make a lengthy story,
Should Christian men and Saracen
Be singly brought to people's ken.
Who belonged to Clinschor's host,   700
Who had ridden with martial boast
From Logroys, often seeking fame
In Duchess Orgeluse name?
Whom had Arthur hither led?
If we all lands and houses said,
Naming every neighbor,
'Twould cause us heavy labor.
Those present all conceded
That Parzival exceeded   10
In beauty every man above.
All women fain would grant him love.
They said that this man's excellence
Met all high requirements.
   The son of Gahmuret arose
And said, "To all I would propose:
Keep seated and give me aid in this,
To win what I so sorely miss.
What banned me from the Table Round
Was to me a mystery profound.   20
Will those who one time took me in
Not help me again a place to win
With you?" The boon he wanted
King Arthur kindly granted.
He had another plea at heart
(With some few knights he went apart):
That Gawan to him should cede the fight
Wherein, as soon as the time was right,
Tomorrow he'd subrogate him.
"With pleasure I'll await him,

King Gramoflanz, for it is he. 701
I broke a garland off his tree[38]
This morning, at the break of day,
To make him challenge me straightway.
I only wished to try his hand:
To joust with him I sought his land.
Thee, cousin, I could not expect:
Such grief I cannot recollect.
I thought the king came at me,
Determined to combat me. 10
Cousin, let me fight him still:
If ever he's to suffer ill,
My hand will give him treatment rough,
For once he shall have had enough.
My rights have been restored to me,
I can again thy comrade be,
As I before was rated.
Reflect that we're related,
And let tomorrow's fray be mine:
In manly power I shall shine." 20
Response was made by Gawan:
"Kinsmen, brother, many a man[39]
I have here serving the Breton king:
To none of them I'd grant this thing,
That he for me be jousting.
In my good cause I'm trusting,
And if good fortune favor,
I'll keep the prize forever.
God bless thee that thou'dst take the fight;
My day has not yet turned to night."

Arthur had heard, and curbed it: 702
This talk, he now disturbed it.
Into the ring he brought them back.
Gawan's steward saw a lack:
Youthful squires of his were told
To take to all fine cups of gold
Set with many a precious stone.
This steward did not go alone.
When this parting drink they'd shared,
Each to his privacy repaired. 10

Once more the night gan to return.
Parzival showed this concern:
He scrutinized his harness first,
To see if any strap had burst,
And ordered reparation,
With handsome decoration.
He bade them a new shield provide,
For the old one, outside and inside,
Great holes and jagged rents had won.
They had to bring a sturdy one. 20
This service was by sarjants shown,
Most of whom he'd never known.
Some of these hailed from France.
The steed that by strange circumstance
He from a templar could acquire
Was cared for by a willing squire.
So well the horse had ne'er been groomed.
Night and time for sleeping loomed.
Parzival retired to bed,
His harness all before him spread.
   Gramoflanz with anger boiled: 703
For his wreath in strife had toiled
Some man,[40] his place pre-empted.
His men had not attempted
Or dared to circumvent it.
He must perforce lament it,
That he had been belated.
Think ye the hero waited?
Since he'd always won the prize,
The king, ere yet the sun could rise, 10
Was fully armed, as was his horse.
Had wealthy ladies been a source
Of richness for his trappings fine?
E'en so these must resplendent shine.
He decked himself to please a maid
And gave her service unafraid.
Alone he rode with clangor.
It caused the king much anger
That Sir Gawan, the worthy knight,
Did not betimes appear in sight. 20

PARZIVAL AND GAWAN

But now with utmost secrecy
Parzival sought out the lea.
From a bundle he took out,[41]
In Angram made, a lance right stout.
He also put his armor on.
Alone the knight advanced anon
Toward the painted posts apace,
Where the fighting should take place.
He saw the king, who had not stirred.
Ere either one had said a word,
The other man addressing,   704
Each spear was fiercely pressing
The other's shield, to pierce it through,
Till from both shields the splinters flew
And through the air were thrusting.
Both men were skilled in jousting,
Likewise in other fighting.
Over the mead inciting
The drops of dew were scattered,
While both their helms were battered   10
By force of keen and cutting blade.
Both were battling undismayed.
Trodden was the verdant mead,
And dew was trampled by each steed.
I've pity for the flowers red,
More for the men who toiled and bled,
Lacking any cowardice.
Would anyone rejoice in this,
Save he'd been harmed by either man?
Now see, my lord Sir Gawan   20
Took heed of battle's warning.
'Twas come to the mid of morning,
Ere the tidings went around
That nowhere anyone had found
Parzival, the undaunted.
Was it a truce he wanted?[42]
Such was not his doing:
A fight he was pursuing
With him who fought an equal fray.
Now they had reached the height of day.

For Gawan a bishop sang the mass: 705
Throngs of fighters crossed the grass.
Knights and ladies, seated
On horses, there were greeted.
In Arthur's ring was their station.
Before the celebration,
Arthur came himself to share
In the mass conducted there.
With the benediction done,
Gawan to arm himself begun. 10
All had witnessed, e'en before:
On shapely legs that his body bore
The proud knight greaves was keeping.
The ladies started weeping.
The host marched out with one accord
To where one heard the clash of sword,
Where helmets fire were flinging
And foes with strength were swinging.
King Gramoflanz had else been wont
To think a duel an affront: 20
One man he scorned. But now he felt
That he with six good fighters dealt.
And yet 'twas Parzival alone
Whose fighting valor here was shown.
He gave to the other's breeding
A rule men still are heeding:
No more King Gramoflanz would claim
This special honor for his name,
That he would only fight with two.
One man gave him too much to do.

   The troops[43] had moved on either side 706
Onto the meadow green and wide,
There at the barriers staying.
They watched the game now playing.
The fighters, nimbly landing,
Had left their chargers standing.
Now these valiant knights renowned
Went on fighting on the ground
As hard a fight as e'er was manned.
On high their sword from hand to hand 10

They flung, and did not falter
The cutting blade to alter.
For his wreath King Gramoflanz
Got his interest in advance.
But Itonjë's kin[44] no less
Got from him scant happiness.
Parzival must damage take
For the fair Itonjë's sake,
Who should have given enjoyment,[45]
If right found right employment.
They oft for glory faring
With strife hard toil were sharing:
One fought to aid a friend in need,
The other love's command must heed,
For of love he was a serving man.
Now came as well my lord Gawan,
What time the fight so far was done
That almost victory had been won
By the proud and valorous Waleis.[46]
Brandelidelin of Punturteis[47]
And Bernous de Riviers
And Affinamus de Clitiers,
These three, with their heads all bare,
Rode up to the fighting pair.
Arthur and Gawan were seen to ride
Forward from the other side
Toward the battle-weary two.
These five men[48] agreed to sue
For a speedy ending of the fight.
Gramoflanz thought that quite right,
And added, he'd cede victory
To the opponent they could see
There against him pitted.
By others too 'twas admitted.

Now the fight between Gramoflanz and Gawan is again postponed for a day, but this time it is Gawan who condescends to suggest the postponement. Parzival is gently chided by Arthur for having joined battle with Gramoflanz contrary to agreement. Gramoflanz dispatches messengers to Arthur, again demanding the right to joust with Gawan, and with him alone. He also sends a letter to Itonjë, who beseeches Arthur to use his good offices in effecting a reconciliation between her brother Gawan and her lover Gramoflanz. He agrees and invites Gramoflanz to come to his court. Beakurs, the brother of Gawan and Itonjë, fares forth to meet him. Through her resemblance to Beakurs Gramoflanz immediately recognizes his beloved Itonjë, whom he had never yet seen. Now he and Gawan are formally reconciled. The hostility between Gramoflanz and Orgelusë is also ended. The couples are wed simultaneously, Gramoflanz and Itonjë, Lischoys and Cundrie, Sangive and Florant. Moreover Gawan and Orgelusë celebrate their wedding feast. Gramoflanz orders his entire court retinue to join him in the greatest splendor. Amid this general merry-making only one man feels sad. It is Parzival. (707, 15—731, 30)

    Once again Sir Parzival   732
His fair wife could not but recall,
Her chasteness and her sweetness.
Could he with any meetness,
Another lady wooing,
Fall into faithless doing?
No, such love he'd ever shun.
Great constancy for him had won
A manly heart, a body strong,
Till to no other could belong   10
His love and his endeavor,
Save but his queen forever,
Condwiramurs,
The fairest flowering *bea curs*.[49]
He thought, "Since *Minnë* I can show,
Why has love abused me so?
Of *Minnë* surely I was born,
Then why through *Minnë* am I lorn?
If toward the Grail I am to strive,
My heart must ever feel the drive   20
Toward the pure embrace and kiss
Which I gave up, too long to miss.
The while my eyes see happiness,
My heart knows nothing but distress—
Unlike are those positions.
Ah, under such conditions

I can't as happy know me.
May my good fortune show me
The way on which I best were led."
His armor lay before him spread.
   He pondered, "Since I have to miss   733
What they command who live in bliss,
(*Minnë* is she of whom I think,
Who many a man on sorrow's brink
With new delights has greeted)—
Since I of this am cheated,
I care not what becomes of me.
God does not wish my joy to see.
She who for love makes me to pine,
My wife, were our love, hers and mine,   10
So made as us to sever,
That we in love could waver,
Another love perhaps I'd gain.
But love for her from me has ta'en
All other love and joy I dreamed.
Of sadness I am unredeemed.
May fortune grant her pleasure
To those who seek full measure.
God, joy on all these throngs bestow!
From all these joys away I'll go."   20
He seized the harness, near him laid,
Which oft he'd donned without men's aid,
And soon he had it on again.
He'll go in search of further pain.
When now the man who pleasure fled
Had armed himself from foot to head,
He saddled, all alone, his horse.
Shield and spear he took perforce.
They wept that he'd departed:
The sun rose when he'd started.

Book Fifteen
Parzival and Feirefiz

Book Fifteen

PARZIVAL AND FEIREFIZ

Impatience men have not concealed 734
To find the ending unrevealed:
Many thought it should be told.
This thing no longer I'll withhold.
With me the truth be sharing,
For in my mouth I'm bearing
The lock that makes the tale complete:
How that beloved man and sweet,
Anfortas, at last was cured.
Adventure tells, we are assured, 10
How the queen of Belrapeir'
Her purity did not impair,
Till just reward was hers to claim[1]
And into highest bliss she came.
Parzival will retrieve it.
If my skill can but achieve it,
I'll tell you first the toil he sought.
Howe'er before his hand had wrought,
A child's game, seemingly, he'd played.
If I this telling could evade! 20
I risk his life reluctantly.
That even causes pain to me.
I can but to his heart commend
His fortune, bliss's course and end,
Where rashness e'er by virtue lay,
Since diffidence he'd ne'er display.
May this give strength to him in strife
And help him to preserve his life.
For now the tale has gone so far
That he must face a master of war
On his intrepid journey. 735
This chief at joust or tourney,
From heathen lands he hither came
And ne'er had had baptismal name.
   Proceeding, Parzival could ride
Into a forest deep and wide,

Where in a sunlit clearing
A stranger he saw appearing.
I hardly think that I, poor wight,
Can tell you all the wealth aright   10
That on his gear the heathen bore.
If I should tell enough and more,
More detail I must tender,
Full justice here to render.
Whatever served King Arthur's hand
In Brittany and Engelland
Could not for all the jewels pay
That on the hero's surcoat lay,
Richly sewed on hem and sleeve.
'Twas costly, that you may believe!   20
Your rubies and chalcedonies
Would not make up the worth of these.
His mantle showed a brilliant sheen:
In the famous mount Agremuntin[2]
The snakes called salamander[3]
Had wrought it for this commander
All in the flaming fire.
All over his attire
Lay precious stones both dark and light.
The names of all I can't recite.
For *Minnë* he was yearning,   736
Toward fame his heart was turning.
His raiment mostly had been given
To him by ladies who had striven
To see him well provided.
Love herself had guided
Into his heart a courage high,
As to her servants she'll supply.
A guerdon on his helmet shone
A trophy, called ecidemon.[4]   10
All snakes that venom may secrete,
When this ecidemon they meet,
A mortal blow to them is dealt
When they its close approach have smelt.

Wolfram continues his description of Feirefiz in the same vein. Feirefiz had landed at a wooded point with a fleet containing members of his twenty-five armies, representing the various nations and tribes over which he rules. They had remained behind on the ships, while he sallied forth alone in search of chivalrous adventure. But Parzival, Wolfram adds, is not alone either, for he has brought his manly valor along. Wolfram regrets that these two so closely related and noble champions are now destined to engage in combat. He fears for his hero Parzival but is reassured that the power of the Grail and of *Minnë* will stand him in good stead. (736, 15—737, 30)

     My skill does not give me the wit   738
To tell you every single bit
Of fighting, just as it took place.
Joy lit up each fighter's face
To see the other coming nigh.
But though with joy each heart beat high,
Sorrow was not far away.
In them, both pure in heart and gay,
Since each one bore the other's heart,[5]
Though strangers, kinship played its part.   10
These twain I cannot sunder,
This pagan and Christian wonder,
Without a hateful clashing.
The joy this must be dashing
Of all those known as women good,
Since for a woman's gratitude
Each stakes in fight his living breath.
May fortune part them without death!
     The dead cubs that the lioness bore[6]
Are brought to life by the lion's roar.   20
These two were aroused by battle-crash,[7]
And famed for many a jousting clash.
High skill they had at jousting,
Which shattered spears in thrusting.
The tightened reins now dropping,
They dashed up without stopping,
The foe kept well in vision,
Each striking with precision,
This detail not omitting:
Firm in the saddle sitting.
     They whirled for the gallop, stirring   739

Their steeds with eager spurring.
So grimly in the joust they clashed,
Both collars were wide open slashed
By sturdy spears that never bent,
Till splinters in all directions went.
In wrath the heathen further coursed,
Seeing yon man was not unhorsed:
No other man had kept his seat
Whom he had met in battle's heat.   10
Did they have swords for smiting,
As they drew near for fighting?
Yes, they were sharp and broad of blade.
Skill and manhood were displayed
As each man's special feature.
Ecidemon the creature
Suffered now and then a wound.
At that the helm below it frowned.
The steeds with weariness grew hot:
Oft they tried a different spot.   20
Now both from the horses springing
Set swords to really ringing.

    The heathen inflicted injury.
His battle-cry, it was Thasmê.[8]
When "Thabronit"[9] resounded,
One step he forward bounded.
Equally the Christian man,
As oft they at each other ran,
His life and limb defended.
So far their strife had wended,
That this to say I will not fail: 740
I must with truth their strife bewail,
Since men of the selfsame blood and strain
Gave each other cruel pain.
Each called the selfsame sire his own,
Pure loyalty's foundation-stone.
To love the heathen was dedicate,
Hence in strife his heart was great.
The prize of honor he could take
For Queen Secundillë's sake,   10
Who Tribalibot had yielded:

In need by her he was shielded.
The heathen's battling power grew.
What can I for the Christian do?
Unless he give attention
To love, I've no prevention
That he, in battle vieing,
By heathen hand will be dying.
Grail, avert it, virtue's rest!
Condwiramur, with beauty blessed, 20
Here stands the man who serves you two
In the greatest need he ever knew.
The heathen's blade high up was flung.
Many a time so hard he swung
That Parzival fell on his knees.
It may be said: So battled these,
If one will speak of them as twain.
They are but one, and one remain.
My brother and I, that is one life,
As a good man and his good wife.

 The heathen inflicted injury. 741
His shield was of wood called aspindë,
Which stands decay or burning.
In love to him was turning
The heart of her who gave him this.
Turquoise and crisopassis,[10]
Rubies red and emeralds green,
And many special gems were seen
Inlaid, to make a higher cost,
Around the hub where 'twas embossed. 10
Upon the central boss you'd view
A gem that I will name to you:
As anthrax[11] there they show it,
We as carbuncle know it.
That *Minnë* lend him escort sure,
Ecidemon, the creature pure,
To him as weapon she did give
In whose affection he would live:
His queen and wife, Secundill'.
This weapon showed and was her will. 20
Pure faith in conflict here we see:

Loyalty fought with loyalty.
Each had placed, for *Minnë's* sake,
In strife fore God his life at stake.
Each fighter's hand was pledge and seal.
The Christian's trust in God was real,
Since leaving pious Trevrizent,
Who urged him, with heartfelt intent,
That he to God for help should pray,
Who sends us joy e'en in dismay.

   The heathen's limbs were strong and fit, 742
And when he shouted "Thabronit"—
The place where Secundillë was,
Before the mountain Kaukasas—
With courage new the fight he braved
Gainst him who had so far been saved
From such a battle's overweight.
He was unknown to conquering fate:
He never had endured it;
From him foes had secured it.   10
With skill their arms were swinging,
Bright sparks from helmets flinging.
Their swords set up a tempest wild.
God save Gahmuret's brave child!
To save them both were righter,
The Christian and heathen fighter.
I said they were one being.
With this they'd be agreeing,
If each the other better knew.
Then a lower stake would do.   20
The fight they found involved no less
Than honor, health, and happiness.
Whichever one takes over,
If he's of faith a lover,
Will gain but sorrow, to his cost,
All worldly joy he will have lost.

   Why art delaying, Parzival,
That on that fair one not at all
Thou thinkest (aye, I mean thy wife)?
How else wilt thou preserve thy life?
The heathen had two special friends: 743

On these most of his strength depends.
One was, that love he'd fain obey,
Which in his heart forever lay.
One was his jewel's splendor,
Whose purity could tender
Him confidence unceasing,
The while his strength increasing.
The Christian makes me worry,
Since battle's strain and hurry   10
Are weakening him with heavy blows.
If neither to him succor shows,
Condwiramur nor yet the Grail,
Parzival, thou shouldst not fail
To take new courage from the joys
Thou hast in those two darling boys.
Let them not, orphaned, life begin:
Kardeis and Loherangrin,
The fruit his consort living bare
When last he embraced her body fair.   20
Children born in wedlock pure,
I ween, man's happiness assure.[12]

   The Christian now increased his strength.
He thought ('twas time he did at length!)
About the queen he'd married,
Her love that ne'er miscarried,
Which he that time with sword-play won
When flashing sparks from helmets spun
At Belrapeir' gainst Clamidê.
"Thabronit" and "Thasmê"—
Now they found a counter-cry.   744
Parzival made this reply:
He shouted stoutly: "Belrapeir'."
Condwiramur (was time to spare?)
Four extensive kingdoms through
Sent with love great strength anew.
From the heathen's shield went springing,
I ween, many splinters winging:
A hundred marks for each were paid.
Of Gahaviez[13] the sturdy blade   10
Smote the heathen's[14] helm, then broke!

The brave man, though, beneath the stroke
Fell as in prayer upon his knees.[15]
The Lord no longer did it please
That Parzival's theft from the dead
Should further stand him in good stead:
This sword he had from Ither won
While acting as a simpleton.
He, ne'er yet felled by swordsman's swing,
Upon his feet did nimbly spring.   20
The outcome is yet uncertainty;
For both the judgment still must be
In the hands of the Highest lying.
May He avert their dying!
   The heathen brave and gifted
A courteous voice uplifted
In French, which he had come to know
(He spoke it like a heathen, though):
"I see, courageous man of might,
That swordless thou henceforth must fight.
What honor then to conquer thee?   745
Stand thy ground and answer me,
Valiant man, what is thy name?
In truth thou wouldst have ta'en my fame,
Which long I've held as token,
Had thy good sword not broken.
A truce for now is my request,
Until our limbs have time to rest."
They sat them down upon the grass,
Both well-bred men of noble class,   10
And both of proper years were they,
Not old, not young for sword and fray.
The heathen addressed the Christian knight:
"Believe me, I have ne'er caught sight
In life of a man so battle-wise
Who better would deserve the prize
That one in battle should obtain.
Hero, wilt thou kindly deign:
Tell me both thy name and race.
Then to some good I've sought this place."   20
Answered Herzeloyde's son,

PARZIVAL AND FEIREFIZ

"My name because I'd danger shun?[16]
This is a wish I'll not fulfill
If I must speak against my will."
Said he who from Thasmê came,
"I'll be the first to name my name.
Let any odium be mine.
I'm Feirefiz Anshevine.
Such power is mine that many a land
Pays tribute to my royal hand."
   Hearing the heathen thus confide,   **746**
Parzival turned and replied,
"By what right are you Anshevine?
Anjou by heritage is mine,
Castles, towns, and all the land.
Sir, I beg you'll understand:
Choose yourself another name.
If I'm to lose the land I claim,
And the noble town of Bealzenan,
Violence will to me be done.   **10**
If either of us is Anshevin,
'Tis I, for Anjou is my kin.
Yet, word to me has been conveyed
That there's a hero unafraid
In heathendom residing,
In knightly strength abiding,
Who in love and fame progressing
These twain is now possessing.
As brother he to me is named.
There they think him highly famed."   **20**
Then continued Parzival,
"Sir, if I could see at all
Your features, and their aspect knew,
I would quickly tell you true
If you're the one of whom they tell.
Sir, if you will trust me well,
Take the helmet from your head.
If you'll believe what I have said,
My hand from fighting will refrain
Until your head is armed again."
   The heathen man this answer made: **747**

"Of thine assault I'm not afraid,
Though bare my head, since I've a sword.
Defeat of you I'd soon have scored,
Seeing thy blade is broken.
No skill would for thee betoken
Release from death in strife unfair,
Did I not choose thy life to spare.
Ere a wrestle thou wert trying,
My good sword would be flying   10
Through thy armor and thy hide."
The heathen marked by power and pride
Now showed his spirit virtuous:
"This sword shall be for neither of us!"
His sword the fighter bold and good
Hurled far from him into the wood.
"If fighting here take place," quoth he,
"Then equal must the chances be."
Continued then rich Feirefiz,
"Hero, let courtesy not cease.   20
Since thou dost claim a brother, knight,
Describe him now to me aright
And limn his countenance for me,
What men say his complexion be."
Parzival replied to this,
"Like parchment manuscript, I wis:
Black and white parts alternate.
So much did Ekuba[17] relate."
The heathen answered, "I am he."
Then both of them, and speedily,
Began their heads as bared to show   748
Of helmets and the coifs below,
So each the other's face could see.
Parzival's discovery
Was such that none he more had prized.
The heathen man he recognized,
For he looked like the magpies all.
Feirefiz and Parzival
Kissed to put an end to hate.
Friendship was a fitter state   10
For them than enmity of heart.

Thus faith and love their strife could part.
  The heathen then exclaimed with joy,
"Well for me that Gahmuret's boy
I'm privileged in life to see.
By this my gods will honored be.
My glorious goddess Juno[18]
Through this new happiness will know.
My mighty god, great Jupiter,
On me this blessing could confer.   20
Gods and goddesses above,
Your power I shall ever love.
So the planet I shall laud,
Beneath whose light I fared abroad,
Seeking for adventurous fight
Against thee, dreadful precious wight,
Which almost cost me endless rue.
Honored be the air, the dew,
Which this day laved me from above.
Thou key to sweet and chivalrous love!'
Well for the wives who thee will see!   749
What bliss awaits their eyes through thee!"
"You say well; better I would do
If I but could, and kindly too.
Alas, I'm not in speech so wise
That your great glory I could prize
In words, to make it higher.
God knows my high desire.
My powers of heart and eyes and sense
Are guided by your excellence: 10
They follow as you point the way.
No knight e'er gave me such a fray,
And held me so in travail's vise,
As you," said he of Kanvoleiz.
The mighty Feirefiz replied,
"Noble hero, Jove has tried
Out his zeal and skill in thee.
Say no longer 'you' to me:[19]
See, one father had we both."
He begged him with fraternal troth   20
No more in speech to call him 'you,'

But 'thou,' as brothers always do.
Yet Parzival would not say yes.
"Your wealth, my brother, is hardly less
Than what the Baruk's is said to be.
Besides, you're earlier born than me.
My youth and poverty preclude
Such loose and flippant attitude
That 'thou' and 'thee' I'd dare to say,
So long as courtesy I obey."
    The man from Tribalibot   750
Jove, the highest god he wot,
Praised with words in numerous ways.
Then he also spoke the praise
Of Juno, goddess vaunted,
That favoring wind she'd granted,
Permitting him and all his host
To reach the land along the coast,
Where on the ground his foot he set
And so his brother he had met.   10
Again they fell to sitting,
Good manners not omitting:
Respect they showed each other.
The heathen addressed his brother:
"To thee I'll cede two wealthy lands,
Forevermore to serve thy hands,
Which once our father had acquired
What time King Isenhart expired:
Zazamanc and Azagouc.[20]
He cheated none, from none he took,   20
But me, poor abandoned child, he left.
That thus my father me bereft
Has never been avenged by me.
His wife, whose son I'm proud to be,
Yearning for him, ne'er survived
When of his love she'd been deprived.
I'd like to see my sire some day,
For I have heard the people say
No better knight lives far or near.
He prompted my costly journey here."
    Parzival to this replied,   751

"I too my father never eyed.
Of goodly deeds by him I've heard
(In many spots that has occurred),
And that, battle-skill commanding,
His fame he kept expanding
And raised his glory high o'erhead.
All graceless doing from him fled.
He gave to women service true;
If they were loyal to him too, 10
In ample wise they would repay.
What honors Christians to this day
He showed: unswerving faithfulness,
And he could in himself suppress
Every trace of falsity,
Impelled by true heart's constancy.
Such things as this those men could tell
Who'd seen the man, and knew him well,
Whom gladly you'd be seeing.
In his praise you'd be agreeing, 20
Were he alive and thriving.
For fame he went on striving.
Love-service drove this paragon,[21]
So that King Ipomidon[22]
In jousting met him face to face:
Before Baldac the fray took place.
Thus his glorious life and breath
For *Minnë's* sake were done to death.
In noble jousting we have lorn
The man from whom we both were born."

"O loss irreparable!" said **752**
The heathen, "Is my father dead?
A loss of joy I have sustained,
A find of joy I've also gained.
E'en while the selfsame moment passed,
I lost joy, found some more to last.
If I am right, I must avow
That both my father dead and thou
And I were all a unity,
Although in numbers we were three. 10
Where'er one sees a man that's wise,

He never speaks of family ties
Twixt children and their father,[23]
If he pure truth would gather.
Against thyself thou'st battled, knight,
Against myself I came in fight.
Myself I gladly would have slain,
But thou courageously must strain
Death from *my* body to repel.
Jove, record this miracle! 20
To us thy power succor sent,
Our death in battle to prevent."
With laughter and furtive weeping
From heathen eyes were creeping
Tears of true emotion
In Christianlike devotion.
Our Faith true faith is teaching,
Since our New Testament's preaching
Derives from Christ as savior:
Faith was in Christ's behavior.

    The heathen spoke, I'll tell you how: 753
"No longer let us tarry now.
Ride with me, 'tis close at hand,
And I will presently command
To meet thee, landing from the sea,
The mightiest host that e'er could be,
With Juno's favor sailing.
In truthfulness unfailing
I'll show thee many a noble man
Who serves me as he must and can. 10
I beg thee, thither with me ride."
"Do you, then," Parzival replied,
"Have over them such mighty sway
That they will wait for you today
And all the while that you are out?"
The heathen said, "Without a doubt!
If I were gone for half a year,
Both rich and poor would await me here.
They wouldn't dare go anywhere.
Provided well with goodly fare 20
Their ships lie anchored in the bay.

Nor horse nor man dare go away,
Except to seek fresh water there
Or else to breathe the balmy air."
　Parzival said cordially,
"Brother, ride along with me,
See ladies fair and pleasant sights,
And of your great race many knights
Of proud and courtly bearing.
Arthur came hither faring,
The Breton, with a noble train.　　　754
Today I quitted him again.
Of beauteous folk he has a throng:
We'll see fair ladies there ere long."
When the heathen heard him 'ladies' say
(His very life and breath were they),
He clamored, "Take me there with thee.
And I would beg thee, give to me
Some long-sought information.
What folk of our relation　　　　　　10
Shall we meet at Arthur's court?
Of him I've often heard report
That he in fame and name is great
And moves about in royal state."
Parzival replied again,
"We'll see fair ladies in his train.
Our journey cannot but succeed.
We'll find men of our selfsame breed,
From whom we get our lineage sound,
And some whose heads may yet be crowned."　20
Neither one would longer sit.
Parzival did not omit
To fetch again his brother's sword,
Which to its sheath he then restored
For his deserving brother.
All hate for one another
Was gone, all strife and violence.
Companion-like they trotted thence.

　Now Parzival and Feirefiz set out for King Arthur and his retinue, who have meanwhile already been apprized by a messenger from Chastel Marveile that the wonderful column there revealed two knights engaged in the fiercest combat ever witnessed. Although both Parzival and his brother show signs of their deadly encounter, everyone admires the splendor of Feirefiz. They stop at Gawan's tent, whither King Arthur comes to bid them welcome. At Arthur's request both Parzival and Feirefiz now catalogue the numerous princes and other rulers whom each has defeated in joust. On the next day Feirefiz is accepted as a knight of the Round Table amid much pomp and ceremony. In depicting the event, Wolfram tells us that he is following the description of Kyot, his source. (754, 29—778, 12)

  The day of her coming I would sing:
Hail the sweet word she doth bring,
Which soon they all were hearing!
One saw a damsel nearing.
Her clothes were dear, well cut and sewed,
And precious, like the Gallic mode.
Her cape was satin, rich indeed
And blacker than a Turkish steed.   20
In rare Arabian golden braid
Were turtle-doves[24] on it displayed,
The Grail's insignia bearing.
One saw the people staring
At her in utmost wonderment.
She'll come apace, with your consent.
A headdress high and bright she wore,
And many a covering thick she bore,
Her features all concealing,
To none her face revealing.
Gently, but at an ambling trot   779
She rode across the grassy plot.
Her bridle, saddle, pony small
Were rich, as could be seen by all.
They let her, there abiding,
Into the ring come riding.
This wise one, shrewd and knowing,
Around the ring kept going.
They pointed out King Arthur's seat,
And him she did not fail to greet.   10
In French she did her speaking.
She begged that none be wreaking

Vengeance on her for her deed,[25]
But everyone her message heed.
To king and queen she made a plea
That all her words accepted be.
She turned away from them at that
And went to where our hero sat:
Near Arthur he was sitting.
Her pony's saddle quitting,   20
She sprang upon the turf at hand.
With all the grace she could command
She fell before him seated
And, weeping, begged to be greeted,
So that his wrath he would dismiss
And pardon, if without a kiss.[26]
Arthur and brother Feirefiz
Gave her their support in this.
Parzival, though still irate,
Was by his friends brought to the state
Of pardoning as his duty.   780
Noble, not a beauty,
She sprang up and before them stood.
She bowed and spoke her gratitude[27]
That though she'd sinned unduly,
They'd given her pardon truly.

   And now, no longer quailing,
Her hands unbound her veiling:
The hood and hands—her face they bound—,
She threw them down upon the ground.   10
The sorceress, the feared Cundry,
Was recognized immediately.
The Grail's insignia she wore,[28]
To view it nobody forbore.
Her face and form were still the same
As those had witnessed when she came
To the Plimizoel upon the sward.
Ye heard me once her looks record.
She had the same eyes in her head:
Yellow as topaz, be it said.   20
Her teeth were long, her mouth was blue
As violets of purple hue.

Had she of her looks not taken thought,
The costly hat she'd not have brought
That by the Plimizoel she wore.[29]
The sun could harm her nevermore:
Through *such* hair its brightest beam
Tanned not her skin, for all its gleam.
She stood composedly, and voiced
Good news o'er which they all rejoiced.
No longer now delaying,   781
Thus she began her saying:
"Thou'rt blest, of Gahmuret the son,
God's gracious favor thou hast won.
Thou child of Herzeloydë true!
Yon Feirefiz of dappled hue
I also welcome here by name
For Secundillë's sake, my dame,[30]
Likewise because of noble ways
Which since his youth have won him praise."   10
    To Parzival she spoke again:
"Be joyful, yet thy joy restrain.
Blest thy high destination,
Thou crown of divine salvation!
The inscription has been read. All hail!
Thou'lt be the ruler o'er the Grail!
Condwiramur, she who has been
Thy wife, thy son Loherangrin,
Are summoned by the Grail's command.
When thou wentst from Brobarz, thy land,   20
Two sons she in her body bore;
There Kardeiz, too, has enough and more.
Knewst thou no further joy than this,
That thy truth-speaking lips in bliss
That dear king will be greeting
And him of torment cheating—
For King Anfortas soon will hear
Thy question asked, to bring him cheer
And end his grievous suffering now—
Who could be blissfuller than thou?"
Seven stars she went on naming   782
In heathen tongue;[31] of them claiming

Lore was Feirefiz, the knight,
Who faced her in his black and white.
Said she, "Note this, Parzival!
The highest planet, known as Zval,
And the rapid Almustri,
Almaret, the bright Samsi,
Proclaim thy future bliss and cheer.
The fifth one is Azofir,
The sixth is known as Alkiter,
The closest to us Alkamer.[32]
No dream is what I represent:
These seven brake the firmament,
They check its speed and hold it back,
And they resist it in its track.
An orphan thou hast made of woe.
As far as all those planets go,
Far as their light's extending,
So far, without an ending,
Thou mayst reach out and spread thy sway.
Henceforth thy grief must fade away.
But all immoderation
Will spoil thy high vocation.
The Grail forbids with all its force
That false companions thou endorse.
Thy youth deep sorrows bore and reared,
At sight of joy they've disappeared.
Peace of soul thou'st won in strife,
Awaiting in sorrow the joys of life."
  At this our hero was not annoyed.
From out his eyes flowed, overjoyed,
Water from the heart's well-spring.
He answered, "Mistress, if the thing
Of which you have apprized me,
That God has recognized me,
So that despite my sinful life
I and my children and my wife
Can have such honors come to us,
God has to me been bounteous.
The nature of your recompense[33]
To me reveals your loyal sense.

And yet, had I myself not erred,[34]
I had been spared your wrathful word.
Salvation's time had not yet come.
Of that you give me such a sum
That all my sorrow has an end.
Your doves full confirmation lend.
When there at Munsalvaesch' I was
With the unhappy Anfortas,   20
The shields that I found hanging there
Bore the same emblem which you wear.
Many the doves your robes allow.
Mistress, tell me when or how
To all my joys I'll find my way,
And let me not too long delay."
"Dear my lord," responded she,
"But *one* man may go with thee.
Choose him. I will be your guide.
Help is needed, haste!" she cried.

   To everyone it was made clear: 784
"Cundry la surziere is here!"
And what that was implying.
Orgeluse for joy was crying[35]
That Parzival with questioning
To Anfortas relief would bring
And end his sad condition.
Arthur of high ambition
Politely Cundry now addressed:
"Lady, ride to seek your rest   10
And tell them how to care for you."
"Is Arnivë here?" she spoke anew.
"Whatever room she may assign,
I'll be content to call it mine
Until my master ride away.
If she no more in prison stay,
Pray give me leave on her to call,
And with her other ladies all
Whom Clinschor's treachery reft of cheer
In prison now this many a year."   20
Two knights now placed her on her horse,
She to Arnivë took her course.
   Now 'twas mealtime for them all.

PARZIVAL AND FEIREFIZ

With Feirefiz sat Parzival,
Who begged him, "Come and sit with me!"
Feirefiz was quick to agree
That he to Munsalvaesch' would ride.
Forthwith one saw on every side
People rising, maid and man.
The heathen broached a noble plan:
He asked of Gramoflanz the king,   785
If love were now a settled thing
Between him and the speaker's niece,[36]
He should show love for Feirefiz:
"You and my cousin, Sir Gawan,
Tell princes, kings, and every man,
Barons and also any knight,
That none of them should take to flight
Ere they my precious gifts have seen.
Methinks I'd show a paltry mien   10
If off I went and gave them naught.
All vagrants that have here been brought
Should now await a gift from me.
King Arthur, let me beg of thee,
Lest lords my gifts be scorning,
Show that it's them adorning:
My gifts won't have disgraced them.
No richer man e'er faced them.
Have envoys tell them in the bay
To send the presents right away."   20
They answered, promise giving
That four more days of living
They'd spend there ere away they sped.
The heathen was glad: so I've heard said.
Clever envoys Arthur lent
Who straightway to the port were sent.
Feirefiz son of Gahmuret
His will with ink on parchment set;
In his distinctive signs he wrote:
So much has ne'er been done by note.[37]

   Forthwith away the envoys sped.   786
But Parzival explained and said
In French what Trevrizent had told

To him as true since days of old:
The Grail no man had ever
Acquired by forced endeavor,
Save he whom God gave its command.
This word went out to every land:
By force the Grail one cannot win.
This taught men never to begin   10
The holy Grail by force to get.
That's why the Grail is hidden yet.
Parzival and Feirefiz
Made the ladies' woe increase.[38]
No other purpose in them glowed:
To each of the four hosts they rode[39]
And bade the people all good-bye.
They were in spirits blithe and high,
Armed for any kind of fray.
Thereafter came, on the third day,   20
The heathen's gifts, to Joflanz' brought.
Such gifts as these were never thought.
The gifts each ruler took away
Would surely help his land for aye.
No man had e'er received, to fit
His rank, such bounties exquisite.
To all the ladies did he present
Gifts from Triand or Nourient.
I know not how the hosts departed;
The twain and Cundry, away they started.

Book Sixteen
Parzival Becomes King of the Grail

Book Sixteen

PARZIVAL BECOMES KING OF THE GRAIL

Anfortas and his retinue   787
Suffered woe forever new.
Their love for him prolonged his pain,[1]
And oft for death he begged in vain.
He would have perished speedily,
Had they not always let him see
The Grail in all its power great.
He said to those who formed his state,
"I know, if ye were faithful,
Ye'd deplore my fortune scatheful.   10
How long must I this fate endure?
If ye your own rights will secure,
To God for this ye'll have to pay.
I've served you well in every way
Since first a fighter's arms I bore.
Enough I've suffered evermore
For things unlovely I have done
Whereof your eyes have knowledge won.
If ye of faithfulness partake,
Free me for the helmet's sake   20
And for the shield's deserving.
Ye must have been observing,
If it is not beneath your thought,
How I both shield and helmet brought
Unweariedly to knightly rank.
O'er dales and hills that rose and sank
I've taken part in many a joust
And with my sword I've cut and thrust
Till every foeman was dismayed—
Though from you little has been my aid.
I, far from joy who wander,   788
On Judgment Day up yonder
Your names I shall be calling,
So ye to hell are falling—
Unless ye speed my parting.
My woe should cause you smarting.
For ye have seen and ye have heard

How my discomfiture occurred.
Why keep me as your ruler now?
Too soon ye will discover how   10
Ye've lost your souls because of me.[2]
What kind of treatment may this be?"
   They would have freed their king of grief,
Had not the words vouchsafed relief
That Trevrizent—so he had said—
Upon the Grail had seen and read.
Again he is awaited
Whose joy had once abated,
And the hour of blest assistance,
His questioning insistence.   20
The king would choose quite frequently
To close his eyes, refuse to see,
Sometimes for nearly four whole days.
Then, would he or no, his form they'd raise
And take him to the Grail. His eyes
His sickness forced to visualize:
So he would open them again.
Thus, though to live he was not fain,
He had to live and never died.
This went on so, till from outside
Parzival came riding in,   789
And Feirefiz of dappled skin.
To Munsalvaesch' they rode with cheer.
But now the appointed time was near
When Mars and Jupiter with force
Had ended once again their course[3]
In angriest rotation
(This was his ruination),
And came to whence they'd started.
His wound then fiercely smarted.   10
King Anfortas made such moan
That maids and knights could hear him groan,
Often loudly screaming;
And glances pitiful seeming
Expressed the pain he must endure.
No remedy his wound could cure.
No pains could they alleviate.

PARZIVAL BECOMES KING OF THE GRAIL

  And yet the story does relate
That help was nearing, real and true.
Sadly, they did what they could do.   20

The atmosphere of the sick-room was often sweetened with aromatic herbs and other devices. A detailed description of the ornate bed then follows: this ends with a catalogue of about sixty various kinds of gems with which it is studded, influenced directly or indirectly by some version of the Lapidary of Marbode of Rennes (late eleventh century). These gems possessed mysterious power over the invalid. (789, 21—791, 30)

  One brought to him a cheerful mood,   792
And some for joy and cure were good,
As each one had the quality.
In them vast power one could see
Whose skill his wit can strengthen.
In this way they must lengthen
Anfortas' life—their heart he bore.
His fate brought on them grieving sore.
But joy is reaching him afresh,
For *he* has reached Terr' de Salvaesch'   10
From Joflanz' in a hurry
Who's lost his former worry:[4]
Parzival with brother and a maid.
To me the tale has not conveyed
The measure of that distance.[5]
Without Cundry's assistance
There had been fighting. She as guide
Saw that strife was laid aside.
Nearing an outpost tower,
They saw approach with power   20
A troop of templars mounted well
And armed—so courtly, they could tell
By the guide who sought to near them
That joy would soon endear them.
The leader of the outpost cried,
When all the turtle-doves he spied
On Cundry's garb expended,
"Now our cares are ended!
The Grail's insignia guarantee
What we have longed for ardently

Since first we donned this mourning band. 793
Stand still, for joy is close at hand!"
   Feirefiz, the Anshevin,
Urged Parzival, his nearest kin,
At once with words inciting,
And forward moved for fighting.
Cundry, his charger reining,
Saw him from joust abstaining.
The shaggy maid was moved to call
Upon her master Parzival,   10
"These shields and banners, if you're wise
Speedily you'll recognize:
These knights are sworn the Grail to serve,
From your command they'll never swerve."
Said the heathen noble-hearted,
"Then let no strife be started."
Parzival bade Cundry then
To ride ahead and meet these men.
She advanced with message cheering
Of the joy that now was nearing.   20
All the templars, hearing that,
Dismounted; on the grass they sat.
And now, such comfort finding,
Their helmets they're unbinding.
Parzival they met on foot:
A blessing they felt in his first salute.
And Feirefiz they greeted,
To whom black and white was meted.
Onward they rode to Munsalvaesch',
Weeping and yet with rapture fresh.
   They found there populace untold   794
And many a handsome warrior old,
Sarjants, many a noble page.
The whole unhappy appanage
Might well be glad when they came in.
To Feirefiz, the Anshevin,
And with him brother Parzival
Before the stairs that meet the hall
Warm greetings were extended;
To the palace then they wended.   10

Here men had placed, by custom bound,
A hundred circular rugs around,
On each a downy pillow laid,
With covers long, of satin made.
If these two guests were witting,
Right here they would be sitting
Until their gear from them was ta'en.
There came to them a chamberlain.
Rich clothes by him were offered,
To both the same he proffered, 20
They sit—all who for knights can pass—
And cups of gold (not made of glass)
Are duly brought to each and all.
Feirefiz and Parzival,
After drinking, go from there
To see Anfortas in despair.

   Ere now from me you've heard all that:
How he must lean and seldom sat,
And of his bed, how fine it was.
The two were hailed by Anfortas
With joy, though racked by misery: 795
"I've waited long and painfully
To have you come and end my woe.
Last time you parted from me so
That if with help you would be true
One needs must see you suffer rue.
If honor to you was ever paid,
Prevail upon them, knight or maid,
To let expire my failing breath
And grant an end to woe in death. 10
If you are Parzival, all hail!
Prevent my looking at the Grail
For seven nights and eight days:
Complaint no longer then I'll raise.[6]
Naught else am I allowed to say:[7]
You're blest if you give help this day.
Your friend's a stranger here: 'tis meet
That I should offer him a seat.
Why not let him rest his head?"
Parzival wept as he said, 20

"Tell me where the Grail is found!
If the grace of God in me abound,
Of this your folk will grow aware."
Thrice kneeling toward the Grail in prayer
To reverence the Trinity,
He prayed that this poor man should be
Relieved of woe that plagued him sore
He then arose and added more:
"What afflicts thee, uncle dear?"[8]
Who through Sylvester caused a steer,[9]
Already dead, to turn alive;   796
He who bade Lazarus revive;
'Twas he who helped Anfortas find
Once more his health and peace of mind.
The bloom that Frenchmen call 'flori'
Suffused his skin immediately.
Parzival's beauty was forlorn,
And Absalon to David born,[10]
And Vergulaht of Ascalun,
All who by birth great beauty won,   10
The beauty ascribed to Gahmuret
Upon the day when forth he set
At Kanvoleis in glamor rare—
Not one in beauty could compare
With Anfortas no longer ill.
Aye, God is versed in many a skill.
  That man was now elected
By Grail inscription directed
To be the ruler o'er the Grail:
Parzival must now prevail   20
As ruler and as master there.
I ween that no one anywhere
Could find two men as rich as they
(If wealthiness I can assay):
Parzival and Feirefiz.
It seemed that no one wished to cease
To serve the ruler and his guest.
I know not through how many a rest[11]
Condwiramur was riding
To the Grail in joy abiding.

The truth ere this had come to her, 797
And such a word by messenger
As ended all her wailing mood.
Duke Kyot her uncle good
And many another noble man
Went with her, as her ride began
To Terrë de Salvaeschë, where
Segramors in jousting fair
Was felled, and where blood on the snow,[12]
Resembling her, wrought cruel woe.[13] 10
There Parzival should meet her:
No journey could be sweeter.
   A templar brought him the report:
"Many knights your queen escort,
In courtly cavalcade they ride."
This made Parzival decide:
Some Grail-knights taking thence, he rode
To hermit Trevrizent's abode.
His heart rejoiced, and glad he was,
That it was thus with Anfortas: 20
Death had now reprieved him,
The question had relieved him.
"To us, God's mysteries are dim:[14]
Who sits at a council board with Him?
Who knows if His power will e'er expire?
All the angels of the heavenly choir
The end of this will ne'er have heard.
God is man and his father's word.[15]
God is father, God is son,
Great help is from His spirit won."
   Said Trevrizent to Parzival, 798
"No greater wonder could befall:
Stirred by your wrath, God did decree
That His eternal Trinity
Your valiant will should hear and heed.
I lied, your spirit to mislead,
Of the Grail and its condition.
Grant me the sin's remission.
Obedience now I must accord
To you, my nephew and my lord.[16] 10

The angels God had driven,
As lukewarm, out of heaven,
Here with the Grail were staying —
That's what I once was saying—
Here to await His favor.
But God can never waver:
From those He'll always turn His face
Who, I told you, had come to grace.
Whoso God's favor would expect
These fallen angels must reject.   20
They are eternally forlorn,
Causing themselves the loss they mourn.
I grieved o'er your endeavor,
For it had happened never
That a man at any hour
Had won the Grail by power.
I'd have kept you from that enterprise,
But now it's turned out otherwise.
You attained a great success.
Now turn your mind to humbleness."[17]

   Parzival to his uncle said,   799
"I wish to see her whom I fled
And through five years saw not again.
What time we lived as one, we twain,
I loved her, and I love her still.
Advise me, if it be thy will,
As long as death still lets us live.
In need thou didst thy counsel give.[18]
I fain would go my wife to greet:
I hear she's come, myself to meet,   10
To the Plimizoel, a place I know."[19]
He asked the hermit's leave to go.
The good man gave him to God's might.
Parzival rode through the night:
His comrades well the forest knew.
At dawn he found his rapture true:
There many a tent he saw ahead.
From Brobarz, so I've heard it said,
Banners were up and flying,
Behind them shields came hieing.[20]   20

The princes of his land were there.
Parzival inquired where
The queen's own tent was planted,
If a special ring she wanted.[21]
They showed him where his consort chose
To have her tents a ring enclose,
Adorned with taste on every side.
Catalonia's duke they spied,
Kyot, who'd early left his bed.
To join this duke they rode ahead.
   As yet the light of dawn was gray,   800
But Kyot recognized straightway
The Grail's insignia they bore,
For turtle-doves each fighter wore.
Sadly sighed the gray old man,
For that his dear wife Schoysian'
At Munsalvaesch' he'd loved as bride,[22]
But when Sigun' was born she died.
Kyot went to Parzival
And welcomed him and escort all.   10
He sent a youth of noble mien
To seek the marshal of the queen
And bid him furnish ease and rest
For every new-arriving guest.
Together hand in hand they went
Into a royal dressing-tent,[23]
A little one, of buckram made.
Aside his harness there he laid.
Of this no knowledge had the queen.
Kardeis and Loherangrin   20
Asleep in bed with her he found
(Joy his heart with rapture bound):
A high, wide tent they occupied,
And all about on every side
Lay beauteous ladies, not remote.
Kyot on the cover smote
And bade the queen awaken
And smile, by joy o'ertaken.
She waked and saw her spouse, long gone.
A shirt was all that she had on.

The sheet around her form she flung, 801
From bed upon the rug she sprung,
Condwiramur of beauteous face,
And into Parzival's embrace.
They kissed—or so my sources say.
"Good fortune sent thee here today,"
Said she, "my love, my heart's delight."
Then she welcomed him aright.
"I can't be angry, though I should.
I bless this hour and day so good 10
Which brought this sweet embrace to me.
Henceforth my sadness sick will be.
My heart's desire is now my gain.
From *me* Care nothing can obtain."

Now the boys to wake begin,
Kardeis and Loherangrin;
Naked they lay upon the bed.
Parzival bent down his head
And kissed them both right tenderly.
Kyot, with due propriety, 20
Had the children borne away,
And told the ladies not to stay;
Soon the tent they quitted.
No welcome they omitted
To him on his returning.
Kyot, wise, discerning,
Bade the queen her husband to content;
With all the maids away he went.
As yet the day was young and new.
Stewards pulled the tent-flaps to.

If e'er those blood-drops and the snow 802
Had caused his wits from him to go
(He'd seen them on this very ground),
For all that woe reward he found:
Condwiramur had such to grant.
Nor from another did he want[24]
Love's help for love's great need to take,
Though oft 'twas offered for his sweet sake.
I ween his pleasuring did last
Till fully half the morn was past. 10

PARZIVAL BECOMES KING OF THE GRAIL

The entire army from Brobarz comes and admires the templars of the Grail. The king and queen, Parzival and Condwiramur, finally appear, and mass is celebrated. Then little five-year-old Kardeis is declared by his father to be king of Waleis, Norgals, Kanvoleis, Anshouwe, and Bealzenan. The lords all pledge him fealty; he is crowned and leaves with his subjects. On his way back to Munsalvaeschë, Parzival with his wife finds Sigunë's hut and discovers that she had died. In deep sorrow they bury her with her lover Schionatulander, to whom she had remained true to the end. Arriving in Munsalvaeschë, Parzival, Condwiramur, and their son Loherangrin are cordially received. Loherangrin, however, is at first repelled by his uncle, Feirefiz, whom he refuses to kiss. Feirefiz merely smiles. (802, 11—806, 3)

  At court they separated,
Soon as the queen got off her horse.
With her they gained a fresh new source
Of joy and bliss, a welcome troop.
They led her off to where a group
Of beauteous ladies stood on the grass.
Feirefiz and Anfortas   10
Were standing with a courtly air
With them beside the open stair.
Repanse de Schoyë
From Greenland Garciloyë,[25]
Florië fair de Lunel,[26]
Bright-eyed, with skin pink as a shell,
Virgins they, all praise beyond.
With them, slender as a wand,
Known as fair and good and mild,
The maid acknowledged as the child   20
Of him of Ril, Jernisë.
This maid was named Amphlisë.
Clarischanzë, a darling miss,
Came from Tenabroc,[27] I wis:
With radiant beauty was she graced,
Shaped like an ant around the waist.
  Toward the queen came Feirefiz:
She asked of him her cheek to kiss.
Anfortas too a kiss received:
She rejoiced that he had been relieved.

She led the heathen through the hall 807
To seek the aunt[28] of Parzival:
Repanse de Schoyë, it was she.
Kisses were given abundantly:
Her lips had been so red before,
From kissing they became so sore
That with regret my heart must stir
To think I cannot kiss for her,
For she was quite fatigued that day.
Maidens led their queen[29] away. 10
Within the hall remained the knights,
Where brightly shone the candle lights
In gay illumination.
Now ritual preparation
To greet the holy Grail was made.
For never might it be displayed[30]
As spectacle, the folk to please,
Only for high festivities.
When help they were expecting,
Since joy was them neglecting 20
That eve because of the bloody spear,
That time they'd had the Grail appear,
Desiring aid from Parzival.
Since then in grief he'd left them all.
Today the Grail is shown in joy,
Its power their sorrow can destroy.

   When the queen had laid aside
Her travel-dress, her hair had tied,[31]
She came out, proper garb she wore.
The heathen met her at a door.
Well, this could never be denied: 808
None heard or spoke at any tide
Of any woman quite as fair.
It helped her looks that she could wear
Fine silks that some artistic hand
Had wrought, like silk that once Sarand[32]
Had woven very skillfully
In that far city called Thasmê.
Feirefiz, the Anshevin,
Led her, radiant out and in, 10

Midway through the palace bright.
Three great fires were alight,
Smelling of lignum aloê.
Forty rugs and more seats you'd see
Than at the time when Parzival
Viewed the Grail in that same hall.
One seat of special pomp there was,
Where Feirefiz and Anfortas
Were given places beside the host.
Of courtly training he must boast
Who there to serve elected
When the Grail was expected.

   Enough ye have been told before
How the Grail they to Anfortas bore;
Now they see this service done
For Gahmuret's deserving son
And Tampenteirë's daughter fair.[33]
Maids now haste to do their share:
In proper order they arrive,
In number there are twenty-five.
The heathen deems the foremost girl's
Looks attractive, and her curls;
He thinks the others fairer still,
As swiftly they their places fill,
And costly looks their every dress.
Sweet and charming loveliness
Revealed each maiden's face and form.
Last, she who every heart could warm,
Repanse de Schoyë came, a maid.
I've heard, the holy Grail obeyed
This maid, was borne by her alone:
To no one else this grace was shown.
Her heart was chaste and free of sin;
Bright and flourishing was her skin.

   The tale of how they served and wrought,
How many stewards water brought,
How many tables there were laid
(A greater count than erst I made),[34]
How crudity was put to rout,
How many carts were drawn about

With cups of gold, as fitting,
Just how the knights were sitting—
Too long would be that narrative;
In haste a brief account I'll give.
In proper form they took what came
From the Grail, meat wild and tame.
To one his wine, to one his mead,
To satisfy each wont and need:
Mulberry, red wine,[35] or claret.
The scion of King Gahmuret
Found Belrapeir quite different   810
When first into that town he went.

   The heathen asked that he be told
How 'twas that empty cups of gold
Filled upon the tables stood:
This miracle, he deemed it good.
Said the handsome Anfortas,
Whose table-mate the heathen was,
"Sir, do you see right here the Grail?"
Replied the heathen black and pale,   10
"A green silk scarf[36] I see, no more,
The one my maiden[37] past me bore
Who with the crown stands there apart.
Her eyes go straight into my heart.
So vigorous my body seemed,
That maid or woman ne'er, I deemed,
Could rob me of joyance.
But now I feel annoyance
To think of any love I've won.[38]
Ill-bred it is, breeding to shun,[39]   20
To speak of love's distress to you,
Whom I've not offered service due.
Of what avail the wealth I take,
Or all my fights for ladies' sake,
Of what avail the gifts I give,
If so afflicted I must live?
O Jupiter, great deity,
Why bring me here for misery?"
The power of love and rapture's blight
Made him pale where he was white.

Condwiramur, as fair renowned, 811
In her almost a rival found,
This lovely maid with rapture fraught.
Netted by love of her was caught
Feirefiz, the noble guest.
His erstwhile love was now suppressed
On purpose by a forgetful will.
Of what avail to Secundill'
Her love, her land Tribalibot?[40]
A maid[41] caused him so fierce a lot. 10
Olimpia, Clauditte fair,
Secundille, others here and there,
All who their love accorded
And kept his honor guarded
To Gahmuret's son of Zazamanc—
Their love in value sank and sank.
   Anfortas could see right well
The pain that on his neighbor fell
(His spots of white turned ashy pale,
His cheerful mood began to fail): 20
"Sir," said he, "that sister of mine,
I'm sorry if she makes you pine.
No man e'er suffered *that* for her,
No knight to serve her touched a spur,
So her reward no one has ta'en.
She always shared my grievous pain:
I think her looks it has impaired
That little joy she ever shared.
Your brother is her sister's son,
Ask him to see what can be done."
"If that maid is your nearest kin," 812
Said Feirefiz the Anshevin,
"With crown upon uncovered hair,
Help me to win this creature fair.
O, she is all my heart's desire!
If aught with my spear I could acquire,
Would I had won it in her name
And she'd reward me for my fame."

  Feirefiz feels that all his power, knightly prowess, and wealth are in vain if he cannot have Repanse de Schoyë as his wife. But he is a heathen, and, as old Tyturel explains, is therefore blind to the Grail. Assured that, once a Christian, he would be eligible for her hand, he agrees to renounce his heathen beliefs and his heathen love for Secundille, and is baptized the next day. Now he is married to Repanse and sets out with her to his home in India, learning on the way of the death of Secundille. Repanse bears him a son, John, who later, as Priest John,[42] becomes a powerful Christian ruler in eastern Asia. In a brief excursus after the baptism of Feirefiz, Wolfram relates that an inscription appeared upon the Grail commanding any Grail knight sent out as ruler over a foreign land to leave the land immediately upon being asked his name and family. The reason for this, Wolfram explains, is an aversion to questions on the part of the Grail knights, who had had to wait so long for the question which redeemed Anfortas. This digression prepares the reader for the famous incident which now follows, involving Loherangrin, the son of Parzival and heir apparent to the Grail kingdom. (812, 9 —823, 26)

> Loherangrin waxed stout and strong:
> No fear could to his heart belong.
> When he'd arrived at knighthood's state
> He served the Grail with valor great.
>   Would ye hear yet more today?   824
> There lived a lady far away,
> Who was of all false doing free.
> Wealth and high nobility,
> These twain she did inherit.
> Her life showed signal merit,
> Since to be pure she must aspire,
> Shunning any base desire.
> There wooed her nobles of great renown,
> Some who even wore a crown.   10
> And many a prince like her in breed.
> To humbleness she gave such heed
> That all these suitors she ignored.
> Throughout her country many a lord
> Was angered, without feigning,
> That she was e'er refraining
> From taking as her wedded mate
> A man well fit for such a state.

PARZIVAL BECOMES KING OF THE GRAIL

To God alone she looked for aid,
Whatever anger they displayed. 20
Her innocence was spited.
Her lords to court she cited,
And from far countries suitors came.
To all, her answer was the same:
The man whom God should send her,
To *his* love she'd surrender.
 In far Brabant she wore the crown.
Just then from Munsalvaesch' went down
He whom a swan was towing,
On her God's grace bestowing.
At Antwerp he a landing won. 825
She found in him her champion.
He knew his courtly duty.
Men always praised his beauty,
His manliness and handsome face,
In every land and every place,
Wherever news of him was told.
Courteous, pleasing to behold,
Faithful, quietly generous,
He shunned all deeds iniquitous. 10
She welcomed him with greeting kind.
Now hark to how he spoke his mind;
Rich and poor could hear it,
Beside this spot or near it:
"Duchess," thus to her he spoke,
"If I stay here to rule your folk,
I gain no more than I possessed.[43]
Now listen well to my request.
Never ask who I may be,
Then I may keep you company. 20
But if you e'er accost me,
Your love will then have lost me.
If you are not forewarned by that,
God will bid me—He knows what."
She pledged her woman's word for this,
But later, love made her remiss.
She would abide by his behest
And ne'er evade what he'd request:

Should God grant understanding,
She'd follow His commanding.
   That night the maid her love did grant   826
To him, now ruler of Brabant.
The wedding feast was richly planned
And many a baron from his hand
Received a fief, as was his right.
As judge he acted well, this knight.
Right oft he practised chivalry:
His power retained the victory.
Together, offspring fair they gained.
In Brabant many have remained   10
Still o'er their troubles grieving:
They tell of his coming, leaving—
When questioning drove him away—
And how extended was his stay.
With sadness was his spirit fraught:
His friend the swan now came and brought
A little skiff of dainty kind.
As gifts to her he left behind
A sword, a horn, a finger-ring.
Now Loherangrin went journeying.   20
To speak the truth, whate'er befall:
He was the son of Parzival.
By sea and land he followed the trail
Which took him back to serve the Grail.
How was't that she, this goodly wife,
Lost her loved one's devoted life?
"Ask not!" was his commanding,
As he met her first on landing.
Here I should let Sir Erec[44] speak:
He knew with words his wife to tweak.
If master Cristjan, born at Troys,   827
Impaired this tale with some alloy,
Kyot then may justly rail,
For he has told the authentic tale.
The Provençal, before he's done,
Relates how Herzeloydë's son
Acquired the Grail by God's command,
Lost to King Anfortas' hand.

From Provence into Germany
The story came, told properly,   10
Complete unto its very end.
No more I say, nor more intend—
Wolfram von Eschenbach by name—
Than was my master Kyot's aim.
His offspring, *his* deriving,
To tell you I've been striving—
I mean that Parzival, whom I
Have traced to a destiny so high.
The man whose life is ended[45]
So God be not offended   20
Or lose that soul because of sin,
Yet who the while knows how to win
The world's good-will with dignity,
A useful toil his proves to be.
Good women, if they have good sense,
Now give me much more deference
(If any me as worthy hold)
Since to its end this tale I've told.
If for a woman's sake 'twas done,
Sweet words from her I will have won.

Notes

BOOK ONE

1— 1. The first couplet sounds the keynote. By "indecision" (*zwîvel*) Wolfram means inability to make up one's mind: despair of God and vacillation between good and evil, or white and black, or heaven and hell, i.e. inconstancy, disloyalty toward God and men. In effect it is a mortal sin. *Cf.* Hartman's *Gregorius*, 166 ff. and 2698; also below, 119, 25-28; Helen Adolf in *Journal of Engl. and Germanic Philology* XLIX, 285 ff. (but "unbelief" seems to us inappropriate), and the article referred to in note 12 below.
2. White and black, or honor and dishonor.
3. They may still go to heaven or to hell, depending upon themselves.
4. Winged because of the simile of the magpie and the elusiveness of the lesson itself.
5. The mirror and the blind man's dream vision are thought of as offering mere reflections, hence illusions. Medieval mirrors distorted.
6. "Whoever would find fault with me (pluck my palm) where I am not vulnerable"—proverbial—"is false and dangerous but achieves little."
7. "I have good reason for alarm over such tactics."

2— 8. "My treatment of the subject should teach men to elude, escape, and reprimand falsehood and disloyalty. It should help them pursue, turn toward, and praise honesty and loyalty." Is Wolfram alluding to the technique of jousting? *triuwe* (2, 1), faith, loyalty, devotion, divine love kindling love, is one of Wolfram's basic concepts.
9. Like the cow whose tail is too short to ward off the stings of a wasp, so the faithless man lacks the requisite loyalty. Nigel Wireker's *Brunellus* (late twelfth century) has a similar anecdote.

3—10. Mysterious powers were assigned to precious stones. *Cf.* 792, 1 ff.
11. Mere external appearance is meant.
12. After this puzzling introduction (influenced by the Scholastic system of rhetoric), which does not in details bear concretely upon Wolfram's work but which praises fidelity and other virtues in general, in keeping with the ethics of chivalry and Grail knighthood, Wolfram turns to his subject. This introduction has been discussed by scores of critics with divergent results. See esp. Helen Adolf (*Neophilologus* XXII, 110 ff., 171 ff.), who compares it with the elaborate portal of a medieval cathedral, in compressed form expressing the artist's ideals.

4—13. The hero is not born until the end of Book II.
57—14. *I.e.* Belakanë. Her name is explained by some as derived from

Bilquis, the Arabic name of the Queen of Sheba. We suggest a new theory, viz. that it may come from Bliocadran, Perceval's father in the so-called Bliocadran Prolog to Crestien, found in MSS L and P. *Cf.* also Berengaria, wife of Richard the Lion Heart.

15. Feirefiz may be Old French *vaire fiz*, piebald son; or, as suggested by the Russian scholar Veselovskij as early as 1904, the name may mean "true son." Perhaps both explanations are valid. Anshevine is the adjective from Anshouwe, or Anjou. But Golther (*Parzival und der Gral*, p. 181) mentions a line in Lower Austria! *Cf.* Note 20 to Introduction, above. Occasionally we also use the form *Anshevîn* (to rhyme with "queen," etc.).

16. Because of the many spears he would use and shatter.

58—17. In Zazamanc, connected by some with Ethiopia (Casa Mansa?), Wolfram may be thinking of Mauretania. The names Zazamanc and Azagouc were later incorporated into the *Nibelungenlied*.

18. Fridebrand is a Scotch retainer of Isenhart who, after pillaging Belakanë's land, had gone home with Isenhart's belongings. He was now returning these treasures to Belakanë with apologies.

19. *I.e.* Fridebrand.

20. *I.e.* Gahmuret. The name was probably suggested by Crestien, who mentions a king, Ban de Gomoret. But it occurs also in the Old French poem *Atre perilleus* and in *Diu Crone* of Heinrich von dem Türlin.

BOOK TWO

1. Toledo is meant.

59— 2. *I.e.* Gahmuret.

3. Wâleïs is Valois (Crestien's Galois). But originally it referred to Wales.

4. The capital city, perhaps Camp Valois. On the tournament *cf.* Panzer (Note 19 to Introduction, above).

5. An example of Wolfram's sly humor.

60— 6. Shields hung outside, spears inside along the wall.

7. Waleis and Norgals (North Wales).

62— 8. Notice the direct discourse, characteristic of Wolfram's vivid mode of narration.

93— 9. Leoplane is Old French *lée pleine*, far-reaching plain. Wolfram often makes proper names out of French common nouns, possibly because he misunderstood them, or, intrigued by the foreign sounds purposely varied them.

94—10. Amphlisë is meant.

96—11. April as a month of shimmering green would indicate a southern (Provençal) source.

98—12. Obeying the judgment, he has given his word to Herzeloydë and must reject Amphlisë, much as he loves her. But he will always be ready to defend her.

345

      13. The conventional yearning of chivalry is meant.
      14. These envoys from Anjou had not yet talked to Gahmuret; he had heard of the death of Galoës from Kaylet. The inverted shield was a sign of mourning.
      15. This was a prince from Anjou.
      16. *I.e.* Gahmuret.
      17. Distinguishing trophies and insignia of Gahmuret.
99—18. The anchor is a symbol of love.
      19. *Minne* is love, often personified.
100—20. Cohabitation preceded the ceremony.
110—21. The reference is to line 19 below.
      22. Modern, but not medieval, sensibilities are taxed by this.
111—23. Ninivê involves a geographical confusion of the Near East and Egypt.
113—24. Old French for "good son, dear son, blessed son." On the relationship of Books I-II to what follows *cf.* Ernst Cucuel, *Die Eingangsbücher des Parzival und das Gesamtwerk*, Frankfurt, 1937; but his theory has been contested.

BOOK THREE

117— 1. Soltane is a proper name formed from Crestien's *la gaste foriest soutainne*, the wild, lonely woods.
118— 2. The singing of the birds had a peculiar charm for the poets of the Middle Ages, especially the minnesingers.
119— 3. The difference between God and the devil.
120— 4. To emit shrill sounds so as to lure game.
121— 5. Wolfram himself was a Bavarian! Crestien, perhaps influenced by English tradition, speaks disparagingly about the French.
      6. Probably formed of two Celtic place names, Carnac and Karnant.
      7. Old French for "the count Ulterlac." But Ulterlac, or Ulterlec, is merely a personification of the French *ultre lac*, beyond the lake.
123— 8. Knights wore ringed armor. The plated variety came later with the use of firearms.
124— 9. Karnahkarnanz is meant.
125—10. Meljahkanz (names in Mel- are not uncommon) is notorious as a kidnapper of women, among them Guinevere. Originally he was a spirit of death who snatched women.
128—11. Literally: "Alas, that we do not have her family down to the eleventh generation."
129—12. An enchanted forest in Brittany in which most of the adventures of the Round Table occur.
      13. Such tents were often very ornate and needed protective covering. The Sultan of Babylon is said to have given the German emperor Frederick II a tent then valued at what would be the equivalent of several hundred thousands of dollars today.

14. In Crestien he is simply *li orguelleus de la lande*, the proud man of the land.

130—15. In Crestien she has no name. Jeschutë is explained as Wolfram's misunderstanding or playful variation of the words: *el lit tote sole gisoit une dameisele* (Crestien's *Perceval*, Hilka ed., 1932, 1I. 670 f.). C. Pschmadt (*Zeitschrift für deutsches Altertum* LV, 63 ff.) would evolve her from a hind enchanted into a sleeping fairy.

16. He is carrying out his mother's advice (127, 26).

142—17. Generosity was thought to exist only among those of noble birth.

143—18. Hartman was the most popular of the German writers of Arthurian romances. His works were known to Wolfram.

19. Enite is the heroine of Hartman's *Erec*. She was the daughter of poor but noble folk and appeared at court in inferior garb.

144—20. Curvenal was the mentor of Tristan. Eilhart von Oberge had dealt with him in *Tristrant* (about 1180). Gottfried's *Tristan* had not yet been written.

145—21. At Herzeloydë's court in Book II.

22. King Arthur's father.

23. Perhaps Cumberland is meant, the capital being Karidoel, i.e. Carlisle. Crestien however has *la foriest de Kinkerloi*, or *Guingueron*. *leadened* in l. 28 refers to its frequent use: Joos-Whitesell, *Courtly Reader*, Madison, 1951, p. 89.

146—24. *I.e.* to Arthur's court.

25. A symbolic manner of reclaiming possessions was to seize some part of them; here he seizes the goblet (and spills the wine) to signify his claim to Brittany.

26. Another symbolic act to assert a claim was to invert a lighted bundle of straws as though setting fire (and laying claim) to a still untilled field. Ither spurns this because it would soil his hands. See Singer, *Wolfram und der Gral. Neue Parzival-Studien*, Bern, 1939, p. 34.

147—27. This may be young Iwein, the hero of one of Hartman's romances. Crestien has Yones.

150—28. Keyë is the usually grumpy steward of King Arthur; originally he was a mythical figure. By Crestien he is called Keus and Kex.

29. "Let Parzival whip the top" (i.e., Ither).

30. Proverbial.

151—31. Cunnewarë is the sister of Orilus, the husband of Jeschutë. Cf. the name Gunvara in Saxo Grammaticus.

32. She laughed involuntarily because she sensed in Parzivâl the future paragon of chivalry. This is a traditional (fairy tale) motif.

33. The steward could punish those who he thought had violated the rules of etiquette—even ladies and knights.

34. *I.e.*, a door-hinge. Unlike a door, he needed no hinge to pull her braids.

35. In swearing an oath the deponent was touched by the judge with his staff.

152—36. The name Antanor (cf. the friend of Aeneas in Vergil) seems to have resulted from another misunderstanding or variation on Wolfram's part. Crestien says merely: *an son retor trova un sot* (line 1054).
154—37. Ither was a kinsman of Arthur.
     38. *Cf.* 128, 4, above.
     39. So as not to kill his inexperienced foe.
155—40. This is one of Parzival's sins. For reasons of possessiveness he has killed a friendly man who proves to be his kinsman. See 499, 11 f.
163—41. It was customary to keep tame trained birds. The bell attached to the leg would make retrieval easier.
165—42. An allusion to his boorish table manners.
166—43. These tables were either fastened to a wall and raised when the meal was over, or they were mere table tops which were removed.
167—44. It was nothing unusual for girls to attend men in the bath.
     45. Sly but daring humor on Wolfram's part.
168—46. It was customary for a host to supply his guest with clothing.
169—47. Another reference to 127, 21 ff.
171—48. "Do not embarrass a poor guest by display of wealth, and *vice versa.*"
     49. This later proves Parzival's undoing.
173—50. A reference to Parzival's manner and appearance when he arrived.
     51. See note 6, Book II.
174—52. The skilful jouster aimed at the space within the four rivets.

BOOK FOUR

180— 1. The kingdom of Condwiramur.
     2. Belrapeire is French *bel repaire*, beautiful sojourn, probably a traditional name.
181— 3. A sign of readiness for battle.
     4. They were spiritless and weak from hunger.
     5. In Crestien Clamidê is Clamadeu, meaning "call God."
183— 6. The word is *sarjants* (French *serjanz*, fighters on foot).
184— 7. Wertheim is in Lower Franconia at the confluence of the Tauber and Main rivers. The title "mylord" (*min hêrre*—mine host) does not necessarily imply that Wolfram owed the duke (Poppo) allegiance.
     8. They got no grease from food into their wine because they had neither greasy food to eat nor wine to drink!
     9. Queen Condwiramur had rejected his proposal of marriage, and he was wreaking vengeance by pillaging and starving her people.
    10. Because there was none.
    11. A sly local allusion. The town of Trüdingen (*i.e.*, Wassertrüdingen) still exists. It is not far from Eschenbach (near Ansbach) in Bavaria, from which Wolfram hailed. The town was still famed

348

in fairly recent times for the fritters or doughnuts that Wolfram celebrates.

185—12. Ironical. He has all the "comforts" of poverty.

186—13. They were brothers of Tampenteirë and are referred to also in *Titurel* (stanzas 14 and 23). Crestien simply has: *uns miens oncles qui est prieus* (1. 1911). Other manuscript readings for *prieus* are: *priors, priols, prious*. Some would explain the name Kyot or Kiot, not in Crestien, as Wolfram's misreading or variative play on this word. But see the Introduction, especially the theory of Scholte, discussed there. Katelangen looks like Catelonia. Kyot would be a northern French form; the Provençal form is Guizot.

187—14. Wolfram writes Condwir amurs. We usually omit the s; but cf. l. 21 below. The name is usually explained as a corruption of the French *coin de voire amors*, stamp of ideal or true love. Would not the derivation *conduire amour* be simpler?

15. For Jeschutë cf. 130, 2, for Cunnewarë 135, 15, and for Enît 143, 29.

16. Eilhart, an earlier poet, uses this form. The two Isaldes are Isalde of Ireland and she of the white hand.

190—17. See note 13 above.

18. See 186, 26 f. They are immune as members of the clergy.

192—19. *I.e.* what is to follow.

20. The physical and perhaps also spiritual demands of love.

193—21. *I.e.* later, after Parzival awakens (194, 4).

194—22. Crestien has the form *Anguinguerons*. Another reading: *Aguingaron*.

195—23. Already mentioned in 177, 29 as a son of Gurnemanz.

199—24. Parzival's horse had fallen in the encounter and then fled back to town.

200—25. *amis* is Old French for lover or spouse.

201—26. They could fry and broil food again. *Cf.* 184, 18.

27. *Cf.* 184, 4 f. above.

28. *Cf.* 100, 15.

202—29. The headdress indicating married status. Cf. modern German *unter der Haube*. Unmarried women wore their hair unbound.

30. The word is *Liebe*, affection, inclination, friendliness; not *Minne*. On cohabitation the third night *cf.* Singer, *Wolfram und der Gral. Neue Parzival-Studien*, p. 37.

203—31. Cf. 127, 30 and 173, 1. The "new love" 4 ll. below is marital love.

BOOK FIVE

227— 1. The bohourt was a knightly game in which two companies, usually unarmed, charged each other. Such a game would ruin the sod.

2. A procession of knights bearing banners.

3. A village, now Klein-Amberg, near Wolfram's native Eschenbach, where tournaments were held in his day. One of the poet's not infrequent personal allusions.

228— 4. 167, 19. He beamed like sunlight.
5. Usually the cloak was closed by a brooch. It seems to have been especially modish to use a cord instead. Buttons were practically unknown.
6. Repanse de Schoyë (thought or spreader of joy?) is the sister of King Anfortas. Later she marries Feirefiz and becomes the mother of Priest John. It was customary to offer a guest new clothes, cut and made expressly for him.

229— 7. Manuscript G omits this incident.
8. Probably not a court jester but merely a pert retainer. According to Professor Weigand he is under a great strain, having just seen the King's wound treated with a hot spear. Later in Book IX this treatment is described.
9. The wondrous sights that Parzival beholds from this point on will be explained to him by Trevrizent in Book IX. Does the procession reflect the rites of the Templars?

230—10. I.e., Anfortas, the Fisher-King and king of the Grail castle. Frimutel was the son of Tyturel; his children, beside Anfortas, were Trevrizent, Schoysianë, Herzeloydë, and Repanse de Schoyë.
11. Crestien says nothing about aloe. Snelleman (*cf.* note 19 to our Introduction), p. 154 f., proves that it was a precious wood from the East.
12. Wolfram's home? If so, he is jesting again about his own poverty. Or it may be the castle of Count von Durne in the Odenwald, to whom he possibly gave some of his work. *Cf.* its identity in meaning with the Grail castle (251, 2). *Cf.* our note 12 to Introduction.
13. I.e. the inhabitants of the Grail castle.

231—14. In the best sables black and white contrast sharply. Even his meanest one was precious.
15. I.e. the source of their grief, the lance. It was a knight's lance (*glaevin*), not a foot soldier's (*lanze*).

232—16. I.e. they were marriageable.
17. Maidens wore their hair loose and flowing, often decked with a garland of flowers or ribbons.
18. Her name is Clarischanze. In Crestien's *Erec* a place, Danebroc, is mentioned. Is the countess of Pembroke meant?

233—19. Now twelve maidens in all have appeared.
20. By *hyacinth* is probably meant the modern sapphire. The garnet-hyacinth was a bluish stone with a reddish glint. The French writer Marbode and Arnoldus Saxo of Lübeck, *De Lapidibus* (about 1220), mention a similar gem.
21. *I.e.* the top made of the garnet-hyacinth.

234—22. *Cf.* note 17, Book I.
23. This name occurs also in Hartman's *Erec*, 1, 2074.
24. In Crestien (l. 3287) not knives but carving dishes: *Tailleor*.

235—25. The six just mentioned.
26. A green pillow of Arabian silk. Not from *aqua marina*, but from

	Arabic *azzamradi*, emerald one. See C. F. Seybold in *Zeitschr. f. deut. Wortforschung* VIII, 151.
27.	Crestien, 3220 f.: *Un graal antre ses deus mains une dameisele tenoit.* Old French *graal, greals* (Latin *gradalis?*) means "vessel" of almost any kind.
236—28.	One is reminded of the censer in the Roman Catholic service. There are also strong reminders of the Greek Catholic mass.
29.	Crestien says nothing of this.
237—30.	Not for drinking, but for washing, which was done at table before and after the meal.
31.	Clerics who could write.
238—32.	Another example of Wolfram's sly, tongue-in-cheek humor. One is reminded throughout the incident of the monstrance and of transubstantiation of the Roman Church, as well as of the liturgy of the Greek Church.
33.	*I.e.*, they show their skepticism and consequent ire in a perverse manner.
239—34.	The words are môraz (mulberry wine), siropel (a red-colored wine).
35.	"Perhaps I can find out as much about the inhabitants here as I did at Gurnemanz's without questioning."
240—36.	Because by failing to ask the pitying question he had to forego the possession of the Grail kingdom for a long time.
37.	"Unnamed" because no one dares utter it. It is also incurable, except by Parzival's question.
38.	This was the Grail king Tyturel, father of Frimutel.
241—39.	In Book IX, although Sigunë does give some hints in 251, 1 ff.
40.	Wolfram's simile of the bow and arrow, compared with a straightforward, undigressive tale, is involved.
242—41.	The logic is: Here in this large gathering (there are some 1200 persons present) no joy could be found, although in far smaller groups much joy can often be seen.
245—42.	Related in 103, 25 ff. Just before Gahmuret's death Herzeloydë dreamed that lightning had struck her and that she gave birth to a dragon.
246—43.	Parzival's unswerving conjugal fidelity is a unique characteristic of Wolfram's work.
249—44.	In Crestien she is sitting under an oak. But the Vienna manuscript of Wolfram's *Parzival* pictures her in the linden. In fairy tales women are frequently found thus. *Cf.* also Gottfried's *Tristan*, Book XXIII.
45.	It was Sigunë, whom he had met in 138, 11 ff., with her dead lover Schionatulander. Now he fails to recognize her.
250—46.	The knights of the Grail defended the precincts against intruders.
47.	"You are not a knight of the Grail."
251—48.	From Old French *Mont salvage* (*sauvage*), Latin *Mons silvaticus*, not *Mons Salvationis*. It is the Wild Mountain.

49. Since *Salvaesche* is an adjective, the *de* should be omitted. It is the Waste Land (*cf.* T. S. Eliot's poem).
50. The name is also spelled Titurel; Hartman in *Erec* also mentions him, and Wolfram deals with him in his *Titurel*. In an old French lai he appears as an elf or one of the neutral angels flitting in midair.
51. See note 10 above. Schoysianë, however, died before Frimutel. Sigunë does not know that Herzeloydë has also died. She refers in 251, 12 to Anfortas, Repanse de Schoyë, and Herzeloydë.
52. Perhaps from Tref-recevant (*tref=trève*), peace-receiving.
53. He cannot stand, sit, or lie in comfort because of the festering wound in his lower abdomen. See 479, 12.
54. Recognizing Parzival as her cousin, she now calls him by the familiar *du* (thou), but in 255,2 she changes again to *ir* (you) as a sign of rebuke.

253—55. The reference is to Hartman's *Iwein*. Lunetë is the servant of the queen Laudinë; Iwein had killed the latter's husband in battle. When Iwein returns, Lunetë advises Laudinë to spare him, so that she can marry him later. The "she" in l. 12 refers to Lunetë.
56. "If there is anything that could make me happy it would be the curing of Anfortas."
57. Crestien has Trebucet. He is the famous smith of French romance.
58. Crestien has *lac*, or lake, not spring.

254—59. Swords were usually consecrated, often with a magic formula. But in 434,25 ff. it is mended without the charm.

255—60. She was not mentioned before but is referred to in 806,14 as being *von Gruonlant. Cf.* Spanish Garcilaso.
61. Indicative of falseness or faithlessness.
62. Wolfram has *three* negatives!

BOOK SIX

280— 1. Crestien, 4003: Carlion. We also find Cariduel and Carduel, probably influenced by Carlisle in Cumberland. It is a town in Brittany in this case, and the usual headquarters of Arthur.
2. "He" refers to Parzival, but in l. 17 it refers to King Arthur.

282— 3. This incident may well have traditional provenience. It bears characteristics of an Irish folk tale.

283— 4. *bea curs=beax cors*=beautiful body. See Book IV, note 14.

290— 5. It was contrary to chivalrous etiquette to raise the spear or to assume a fighting pose in the presence of ladies.
6. He intended to use a whole forest of spears. *Cf.* 57, 23.

291— 7. See note 30, Book IV. *Liebe* gives *Minne* its true power, according to Wolfram and most of his contemporaries, who agree in assigning spiritual attributes to *Minne*, perhaps under the influence of Bernard de Clairvaux. The passage seems influenced by the *Roman de Troie*.

292— 8. This is one of several complaints which Wolfram makes about his own ill luck and unhappiness in love.
   9. A reference to a work of Heinrich von Veldeke, the first German courtly romancer (late twelfth century). Wolfram may be thinking either of his *Enit* or, more likely, of a lost poem (on the loves of King Solomon?).
   10. André Chapelaine (Capellanus) in *De Amore* (about 1184) devotes a chapter to this subject.
293—11. He, the brother of Condwiramur, is also mentioned in *Titurel* 28, line 1, but how he died of love is not known. Later one of Parzival's sons is named for him.
294—12. "Any ass, beaten as viciously as I shall beat you now, would regret its laziness."
   12a. Cf. *Modern Language Review* XXXV, 529 f. for meaning.
295—13. Cunnewarë in Book III, Parzival in VI (294, 11).
296—14. It is true that wherever French romances were known, Keyë was considered a calumniator and a malicious disturber of the peace. But Wolfram admires him for his valor, loyalty, and observance of the rules of chivalry.
297—15. Landgrave Herman of Thuringia (1190-1217), who resided in the Wartburg, was a patron of the arts. In his castle the contest of the minstrels, in which Wolfram and Walther von der Vogelweide are said to have participated, and which Richard Wagner introduced in *Tannhäuser*, is supposed to have taken place early in the thirteenth century. Walther also comments upon the hubbub at Herman's court.
   16. No such song of Walther has been preserved.
   17. Reisbach in Lower Bavaria, close to Landshut, is not far from Wolfram's home. Nothing more is known of Heinrich, probably marshal at the Bavarian court.
298—18. King Lot, a Norwegian, the father of Gawan, married Sangivë, a sister of King Arthur.
   19. "He" refers to Parzival.
299—20. He is a typical "mother's son," viz. a coward.
300—21. I.e., not *countless*, but father and mother, who were *not counted* among the *sippe*.
301—22. The adventures of Gâwân referred to in lines 10-20 are not mentioned in any other known documents and may be the subject of a lost French poem. Similar incidents are told about him, however.
   23. reine (in Old French also *roine*) =queen. Nothing is known of this queen.
   24. The commentators call it a veil or cloak, a gift of the knight's lady (?). The word is *failen*, from *faile*.
302—25. His dream of Condwiramur was so vivid that he imagined her actually present.
303—26. It would be a disgrace for Gawan if his offer were rejected.

304—27. A whole forest of splinters. An exaggeration, to denote Parzival's agitation.
305—28. Orilus.
306—29. The cord closed the robe around the wearer's neck.
308—30. His guilt in flogging Cunnewarë.
31. He had sought Parzival.
309—32. Even though the Table itself had been left behind, its prerogatives and customs were observed as though it were present.
33. Perhaps Agra in India is meant. Other guesses are Artakoana (Afghanistan) and Accaron (Ptolemais).
311—34. An example of Wolfram's pregnant style. "If you look at him with a proper critical eye, you will say that many a woman has seen herself in a hazier mirror than his beaming lips"—or "that many a woman has seen less beauty in looking at herself in the mirror than he possesses."
35. Because it grips everyone. His beauty, moreover, would tend to prompt fidelity and steadiness on the part of any woman, even a fickle one.
312—36. The name Cundry (Wolfram writes Cundrie) is probably derived from Old French *conree*, the adorned one. In another work of one of Crestien's continuators, Gerbert, *Le roman de la Violette*, she is mentioned as Gondree. A sister of Gawan bears the same appellation and embodies a more pleasant connotation of the name. For such contrasts and parallelisms in Wolfram see the Introduction.
313—37. *I.e.*, handsome people.
314—38. Her name was Ekuba, and she was a heathen queen. She is mentioned several times later. Perhaps her name was suggested by way of Solinus (*Collectanea*, third century A.D.), who mentions Hecuba.
315—39. *I.e.*, as Ither was.
316—40. The bait, which serves to entice the fish, is a symbol of deceptiveness.
41. Perhaps the Persian city of Tebriz is meant, or the *insula Taprobane* (*i.e.*, Ceylon) mentioned by Solinus. It is the capital of the heathen queen Secundillë but is later located near the Caucasus. Wolfram's thought is: If you had asked the question at Munsalvaesche, you would have won greater wealth and fame than the famous heathen city could offer you.
317—42. The queen's name was Secundillë.
43. Gall here probably stands for deceit.
318—44. Here Arthur and his court first learn who Parzival is.
45. They are Itonjë, Cundrie, Arnivë, and Sangivë. Crestien mentions only one maiden and 500 squires with ladies.
46. Old French Chastel de la Mervoille, wonderful castle, usually interpreted as the realm of the dead. Crestien calls it Chastel Orguelleus. Book XIII tells more about it.

332—47. Clamidê is meant. He would marry Cunnewarë because he was deprived of Condwiramur by Parzival.

BOOK SEVEN

338— 1. I.e., his hero.
 2. In this passage Wolfram is engaged in one of his polemical arguments. He is censuring those poets and authors of biographical romances who tell false or misleading tales and who, in order to build up the character of their hero, slight other important characters of their story. He also laments bitterly that the public often applauds these practices and turns away from the conscientious writers like himself. The argument serves to introduce the new phase of the subject, which features Gawan but which by no means disturbs the unity of the work.

352— 3. I.e., Obie.
 4. I.e., Obilôt.

353— 5. In Crestien she strikes her sister in wrath.

358— 6. Obie calls Meljanz her champion because he is fighting to win her, who has spurned him. Her sister's Obilôt's "champion," she ironically implies, is Gawan. Obilot is not yet in her teens.
 7. Because Gawan is standing idly by.

366— 8. It is noteworthy that Wolfram's characterization of both Obie and her sister Obilot is much more kindly and human than is Crestien's. Throughout, Wolfram strives to correct, improve upon, and complete Crestien. Wolfram himself may have had a daughter.

368— 9. Her name is Clauditte. As not unusual in Wolfram, there are two persons by the same name in his work. The other Clauditte is loved by Feirefiz (771, 17).
 10. Wolfram writes: *snalten vingerlîn.*

369—11. "We must help each other mutually."
 12. Because she imagines herself in love with him, she identifies herself with him and hopes he will forgive her if she confesses that love to him.
 13. His reputation will have to stand trial before his good manners if he turns her down. She is amusingly precocious.

370—14. He is under a cloud and should refrain from amorous adventure until he has cleared himself at Schanpfanzun. Note his mock-serious way of answering the child.
 15. *Cf.* note 6 above.
 16. *Cf.* 332, 10.
 17. Gawan alludes to her identification of herself and him (369, 16).

371—18. I.e., to the bitter end. The "host" is used in the sense of the body; *cf.* next line.

372—19. "When you two young girls become mature for love, there will not be enough trees in the forest to supply spears for the knights you inspire."

374—20. Lyppaut (in Crestien Tiebaut) had dreamed of Gawan even before having spoken to him. In one fragmentary MS (Erfurt Gd) the name is Tibâvt—perhaps the only correct reading.

BOOK EIGHT

403— 1. The implication is that Wolfram is more expert in women's beauty than in architecture.

404— 2. The Heitstein castle was in Bavaria, near Chamm. Probably it is Margravess Elizabeth, wife of Berthold of Vohburg (ob. 1204), sister of Ludwig I of Wittelsbach. *Cf.* F. Wilhelm in *Münchener Museum* IV.

414— 3. We follow the reading of MS G: *verdaget*.

4. *I.e.*, from evil to good.

415— 5. These words are spoken to Vergulaht, whose name is usually explained as one of Wolfram's gravest misunderstandings or boldest variations of Crestien, who in l. 6029 writes: *Li sire qui herbergié l'ot*. The syllables *bergié l'ot* would then become Vergulaht!

6. *I.e.* "even if I am only your illegitimate relative."

416— 7. The Burgunjoys are the Burgundians.

8. Galicia is the ancient kingdom in northern Spain. Punturtoys refers to those who acknowledge Brandelidelin as king. He was referred to in 67, 16 f. Brandelidelin=Brandis des Isles.

9. This is the first time Wolfram mentions Kyot as an alleged source. It is true that from this point on Wolfram deviates more markedly from Crestien. *L'aschantiure* is a magician; for Old French *enchanteor* (see Bartsch-Marti ed. I, xliv). The MS reading is *La schantiure* (French *chanteor*), the singer (feminine). Maxeiner in a Marburg dissertation (1897) first proposed our reading. The name is identical with that of Condwiramur's uncle; on its significance see Introduction.

10. *I.e.* in Arabic.

420—11. Hildebrand's nephew, famous in the *Nibelungenlied*. 'Shall I like Wolfhart die fighting for someone else?'

12. Rumolt was the master cook of the Burgundian king Gunther in the *Nibelungenlied* who advised his lord to spurn the invitation of Etzel and Kriemhild. In a supplementary strophe of MS C, Rumolt counsels Gunther to stay at home and mind his cooking. But in the other MSS Rumolt offers to do the cooking.

421—13. "Even if you hadn't advised it, I'd still go to battle."

14. Segramors, a valiant, eager fighter, will be remembered from Book VI.

15. The faithless and cowardly counselor of King Ermenrich who for revenge shrewdly advises the destruction of the king's family.

BOOK NINE

433— 1. *I.e.*, at Arthur's court. Instead of Wolfram's poetical introductory passage (forty lines) Crestien merely says that here the story of Gawan is interrupted and that of Parzival begins again. Insofar as Crestien deals with the phase of the story as found in Book IX, he is very brief, limiting it to 302 lines.

434— 2. According to Crestien the sword, given to Anfortas by a niece, is one of three made by the smith and will break only in a situation known alone to the latter. According to Wolfram's 254,15, a charm was needed to mend it.

3. *Cf.* 253, 30 ff. According to Crestien, Parzival wandered about for five years and during that time sent sixty knights as prisoners to Arthur.

446— 4. In Crestien he meets three knights and some ten ladies, but not their daughters.

447— 5. It was Easter week. The day was Good Friday.

6. The hours, or prayers, of the Roman Catholic Church, to be repeated at stated times.

7. Parzival is referring to Cundry's imprecations in Book VI.

448— 8. The old man and his retinue had just come from the hermit.

449— 9. The entire incident (to 450, 30) is missing in Crestien. If they, who have only a cloak over their bare bodies, should be concerned about Parzival, who is fully clad, it shows their true kindness of heart, in keeping with the Easter season. The daughters object to exposing Parzival to the ordeal of visiting the hermit.

10. Always during Eastertime.

450—11. "May your good manners and decorum be their own reward."

451—12. Parzival had ridden in a different direction from the one pointed out to him as leading to the hermit Trevrizent. Now, changing his mind, he returns to the spot where he had previously conversed with the pilgrim-knight and his family. He knows the way to Trevrizent but wants God to guide the horse.

452—13. The Wild Spring. Sigunë's hermitage, too, is built upon a spring (435, 8): Often a sign of fairy origin.

14. Related in 268, 25 f.

15. Monday is counted the first day of the week, according to Biblical tradition.

453—16. In this passage Wolfram justifies his silence on the subject in 241, 1 ff.

17. Otherwise he could not have understood the mysteries of the Grail.

18. This is probably not a writer's name (although it is true that Jewish-Arabian scholars transmitted Arabic knowledge to the West), but seemingly the title of an unidentified Arabic book: *Felek thani* (second zone, *i.e.* 20-27 degrees latitude), a cosmography using astronomical parallels for geographic purposes, according to the method of the Alexandrine scholars. In such a volume Wolfram may have learned of the *Kaaba*, the Mohammedan sanctuary, which together with the Abyssinian *Tabot* could have suggested properties of the Grail, and also of features of Arabic astronomy and astrology which he introduces later. The author of

such a work has been identified as a certain Thebit, or Thabit, who claimed ancestry from Solomon.

454—19. A reference to the worship of the golden calf.

20. Up to recently all writers on *Parzival* and the Grail have assumed that Wolfram's Grail was brought down from the stars by the neutral angels. However, Professor Hermann Weigand of Yale University has called our attention to Friedrich Ranke's contention (*Trivium* IV, [1946], 1) that Wolfram nowhere says so clearly. The present passage is ambiguous and may mean that the angels had left it behind. In a later passage (471, 15 ff.) Wolfram states expressly that the angels have to come down to earth and serve the stone. As for the old interpretation of *lapsit exillis* (469, 7), now no longer held, see Note 41 below. If Ranke is right, his claim would throw new light upon Wolfram's unique interpretation of the Grail. As for 454, 26, this may have been thus stated in some source used by Wolfram, but later (798, 11 ff.) he retracted it as too unorthodox.

455—21. The progenitor of the House of Anjou and of the family of King Arthur. The name has been associated with MacAdam (son of Adam).

456—22. Love of God, such as is fitting during Easter.

457—23. The name does not occur in Crestien.

458—24. Parzival feels that this is beneath the dignity of the hermit. In the next line the latter speaks.

459—25. On Good Friday the altar is still uncovered in Roman Catholic churches. *Cf.* our note 17 to Introduction, above.

26. *Cf.* 268, 28.

460—27. Related in 271, 10 ff.

28. The jousts with Segramors and Keyë (287, 9 ff.).

29. Related in 271, 12 ff.

30. The medieval psalter contained a calendar.

462—31. Wolfram reverts to the praise of loyalty (*triuwe*), one of the keynotes of his introduction to Book I. Here it is God's love for man. *Cf.* I John 4,8 (Vulgate): Deus Charitas est.

463—32. Astaroth (Astarte, a Phoenician divinity), Baal-Schemen (lord of heaven: Syrian), Belet (the Baal of the Chaldeans), and Rhadamanthus (the Greek judge of the Lower World—here the devil) may be from Talmudic tradition.

33. A crux. If we follow Martin and Singer we read: A human, clad in flesh, was wrought (*i.e.* as Lucifer's successor).

34. Abel violated the purity of Earth, his dame or ancestress (according to 464, 11), by committing the first murder.

464—35. Adam and Eve, given life by God, were born of the Virgin Earth. The whole passage seems suggested by the German *Lucidarius*, ed. F. Heidlauf, *Deutsche Texte des Mittelalters*, Berlin, 1915, p. 12. It is not in the earlier Latin version, the *Elucidarium* of Honorius.

465—36. Plato, and to a lesser extent the sibyls of the ancient Greeks, especially the Erythrean sibyl Herophile, were early regarded as forerunners of Christ, due chiefly to certain Neoplatonists.

37. A reference to Christ's harrowing of hell.

466—38. They praise good and bad.

468—39. "Fidelity to your marriage vows will soon release you from hell if you should be consigned to it." In Wolfram's respect for the bond of marriage he is far ahead of his age.

40. Trevrizent does not know that Parzival has already seen the Grail.

469—41. The name is apparently a corruption. For *exillis* manuscript G has *erillis*, and on this basis the scholar San Marte (Schulz) reads *lapis herilis*, stone of the Lord. Other explanations are still more far-fetched. *lapsit* used to be called a confusion of *lapis*, stone, and *lapsit* (*sic*), it fell, and the explanation was: *lapis* (or *lapsit*, i.e., *lapsus est*) *ex caelis* (the stone, or it fell, from the heavens). The explanation accepted by Burdach in *Der Gral* (1938): *lapis elixir*, conforms to the conception of the Grail as a philosopher's stone.

42. This "message"—a wafer—, the symbol of Christ's body, gives the Grail its power.

470—43. Refers to the brotherhood in 470, 19.

44. Such tales are also told of a monastery on Mt. Sinai and of King Arthur's Round Table.

471—45. The angels who took no part in the struggle between God and Lucifer and who were expelled for their lukewarmness. *Cf.* Revelation 3, 15-16.. But see 798, 6 ff. below.

46. The indifference of the angels did not affect the purity of the Grail which they guarded. According to Mohammedan legend, a disobedient angel was also brought to earth and petrified in the *Kaaba*.

47. Though God had a right to punish them further, He has forgiven them. But Trevrizent retracts this later (798, 6ff.), saying that his present position was merely meant to appease Parzival's disturbed mind (this in spite of his remark in 476, 24 that he is not a deceiver!). *Cf.* also 454, 24 ff. In Dante these angels hover between heaven and hell. On this passage Professor Weigand has written to us as follows: "It seems incongruous and paradoxical that the neutral angels, disgraced and thrust out of Heaven, should have been assigned to the service of the most precious object on earth. Ranke, in *Trivium* (IV, 1), emphasized it was to teach them humility. That is one half the answer which I accept. I think, however, Wolfram might have added: this is to show that the most precious things of earth rank incomparably below the meanest objects of the heavenly sphere. Does not *Lucidarius* tell us (pp. 75 and 76): friendship in heaven is so great that the friendship of David and Jonathan is hostility in comparison; wealth in heaven is a concept that turns Alexander's riches into poverty; the honor of Joseph takes on the appearance of disgrace in heavenly terms?

359

This inference could doubtless be corroborated on the basis of medieval sermons. I wish Wolfram had taken the trouble to pose and answer the question. There are other matters of a similar nature on which unfortunately we cannot consult with Wolfram."

472—48. *I.e.*, the present knights of the Grail.
49. Is the name to be related to Old French *Enfertez* (sick man) or to Latin *Infirmitas*?
473—50. Parzival.
51. The lake in which Anfortas fished when he was still well.
52. Lybbeals=*li beals*, the handsome one.
53. His desecration consisted in taking the dead man's horse. Laeheline (Llewellyn? *Cf.* 128,4) gave it to his brother Orilus, who in turn presented it to Gawan. It is Gringuljete (in Crestien, 6209, *le gringalet*), which Gawan rode in Book VIII.
474—54. Trevrizent thinks Parzival is Laeheline because he is riding a Grail steed. It had been taken from the Grail knight earlier in Book IX.
55. The turtle dove, symbol of fidelity, the sign of the Grail.
475—56. After his first fight. *Cf.* 155, 19 ff.
57. The theme that earth's reward is sorrow often recurs in medieval German literature. *Cf.* especially Konrad von Würzburg's *Der Welt Lohn*. Once the relationship is established, Trevrizent says *du* (thou) to his nephew, but Parzival continues using *ir* (you) to his uncle (476,19).
58. Ither, Gahmuret's nephew, was Parzival's cousin.
476—59. "You robbed all women of their idol."
60. A reference to Herzeloydë's premonitory dream in 104,11 ff. *Cf.* note 42 to Book V, above.
477—61. *I.e.*, Signunë.
62. His rejection of worldly pleasures after her death is also referred to in *Titurel* 22, 4, and in *Parzival* 186,26.
63. In a legend of St. Albans a similar tale is told of the saint's casket, whose weight is lightened by the innocence of the bearers. In Ovid, *Fasti* IV, 247 ff., a comparable story is related of a vessel bearing the Magna Mater Idaea.
478—64. Spiritual love, love of God.
65. Her name was Orgelusë de Logrois, Gawan later weds her.
479—66. Some town in the Near East is meant.
480—67. The lance was made of Spanish cane, or reed.
481—68. Two things kept Anfortas from dying: 1. the sight of the Grail, 2. the fact that, with Trevrizent's retirement, he had no eligible successor as king.
69. These are names of various poisonous snakes, partly derived ultimately from the Greek: $\dot{\alpha}\sigma\pi\acute{\iota}\varsigma$ (English, asp), $\dot{\epsilon}\chi\acute{\iota}\delta\nu\iota o\nu$ (viper), $\dot{\alpha}\kappa o\nu\tau\acute{\iota}\alpha\varsigma$ (a darting snake). *lisis* may be a corruption of *basiliscus* or connected with $\dot{\epsilon}\lambda\acute{\iota}\sigma\sigma\epsilon\iota\nu$, to twist, squirm. *jecis* may be from $\ddot{\epsilon}\chi\iota\varsigma$ (adder) or connected with Latin *jaculus*, javelin. *meatris* seems to be from the Latin *meatrix*, the walker.

This is the passage which Gottfried von Strassburg probably had in mind when he ridiculed Wolfram as an apothecary (*Tristan*, 7939 ff.).

70. The four rivers branching from the river of Eden (in Genesis 2, 10-14 Pison or Phison, Gihon or Gehon or Oxus, Hiddekel or Tygris, and Euphrates). The Grail folk tapped them as closely to Paradise as possible, thinking the waters would then be more potent. The same idea in Philostorgios (fifth century), *Historia Ecclesiastica* X. *Cf.* also *Lucidarius*, p. 9.

71. A reference to the visit of Aeneas to the Lower World, suggested probably by Heinrich von Veldeke's *Enit*.

482—72. The flaming, smoking river of the Lower World. *Cf.* Vergil's *Aeneid* VI, 651.

73. This story of the pelican is often told in medieval natural histories. *Cf.* Isidorus, *Etymologiae* XII, 7, 26.

74. *I.e.*, "we hoped such a spirit of sacrificial love would help Anfortas and us." All these desperate attempts to find mysterious and miraculous cures remind one of primitive practices.

75. A transliteration of Greek μονοκέρως, Latin *unicornu*. This tale of the unicorn is also found in Celtic legends and other medieval sources, such as Solinus and Isidorus; the beast could be captured only by being lured to a maiden's lap. We also find the unicorn as a symbol of the Godhead or of purity and as possessing great healing powers.

76. Wolfram's notion of the presence of a carbuncle under the horn of the unicorn has, to our knowledge, never been traced or explained. Perhaps part of the clue is to be found in the German *Lucidarius* (p. 13), which we think Wolfram surely used (see notes 35, 47, and 70 to this Book, note 8 to Book X, note 24 to Book XII, and note 3 to Book XVI). There we read: "ein tier heizet Monocerroz . . . daz hat nuwen ein horn; daz ist wol vier elen lanc, unde ist schone als ein karfunkelstein." Wolfram's idea, that there is a carbuncle under the horn, may then be a misunderstanding on his part, or a mere lapse. But Professor Weigand reminds us that in the Aeneid IV, 515 f., Vergil refers to the hippomanes, a potent poison and love philtre which, according to Pliny, *Historia Naturalis VIII*, 42 (Teubner ed., II, p. 135), takes the form of a black carbuncle growing in the forehead of a foal still in its mother's womb and bitten off and eaten by the mother after the birth of the foal. *Cf. Publi Vergili Maronis Aeneidos liber quartus*, ed. by Arthur S. Pease, Harvard University Press, Cambridge, 1935, pp. 426 ff., for further copious references. It seems reasonable to assume that this may be the ultimate source for the medieval legend.

483—77. From the Greek δρακόντιον adderwort or snakeweed.

78. The ether here includes the stars.

79. The sign of the zodiac is meant.

484—80. Aloes wood.

485—81. *I.e.* about 3 P.M., as though he had taken monastic orders.
487—82. It was the custom to wash after a meal. Fingers touching the eyes after a fish meal were supposed to harm the eyes, probably because the fingers had salty broth and fish bones on them. Of course they had no fish to eat; the statement illustrates Wolfram's sly humor.
83. "If I, as a hunting bird, were given such meager fare, I would fly elsewhere."
84. *Cf.* 184, 22 ff.
85. He is kind to Trevrizent and will be so later to Parzival.
489—86. To alleviate the pain which the cold caused the wound, the poison-heated lance was inserted in it, one pain killing the other. This explains the red (bloody) lance (490,2), which reminds one of the legend of Telephus in Ovid (*Trist.* V,2,15) and of the lance of Longinus.
490—87. Trebuchet and his knives were mentioned 234, 18 and 261, 1.
88. The part of Anfortas' body near the wound is so cold that it forms a cake of ice around the lance, which is flaming hot with poison—so hot that it ignites the ice!
491—89. These lines are practically identical with 251, 17 f. In Crestien they occur when Parzival, coming from the Grail, meets Sigunë.
90. *Cf.* 483,15 and 490,7. Crestien does not name the lake.
91. His catch would scarcely supply his castle's needs.
92. *Cf.* Crestien, 6420: mes ne cuidiez pas que il et luz ne lamproies ne saumon.
93. These and the following incidents are reminiscences of Parzival from Book V.
493—94. First Anfortas felt a chill, or frost, in his wound, then later the real physical frost and snow came.
95. Nor did the snow come as soon as the chill came to the wound.
96. They checked it by placing the spear, hot with poison, upon the chilled wound.
97. Schwietering (*Parzivals Schuld*, 1944, pp. 25 ff.) calls this "Leidenstreue," or mystic piety of passion. The piety of their suffering gave new meaning to their faith.
98. In Book V Wolfram mentioned twenty-four plus Repanse de Schoyë.
494—99. Their gains consist of their privilege of dedicating their children to the Grail, but they must also make sacrifices.
100. The Grail knight, then responsible for the welfare of this protectorate, must be well treated by his subjects.
101. He was Herzeloydë's first husband, who left her, however, a virgin. *Cf. Titurel* 26, 27. The name indicates chastity.
102. *I.e.* from the Grail.
495—103. He did not care for the sham battles fought in tournaments; he craved only serious encounters.
496—104. Some very distant place, mentioned only here: Mt. Gargano in

Apulia, or some point touched by King Richard on his flight? From here to 499,10 Crestien has nothing that corresponds.

105. Actually the name of a Celtic fairy, Fata Morgana (born of the sea), a sister of King Arthur, but in Wolfram a country. He calls the fairy Terdelaschoyë=land of joy. Is the confusion humorously intentional?

106. A fabled mountain. agre=Latin *acer*, sharp, pointed. Is it Agrimonte near Salerno?

502—107. The host in the Holy Sacrament.

108. Trevrizent relieves Parzival of his sins (if indeed he has the power) at the last possible moment, to give him more time to repent.

BOOK TEN

515— 1. The headdress bands were ordinarily worn down the cheeks and under the chin.

516— 2. *I.e.* "if I were in Gawan's place."

517— 3. Old French for "evil creature." Not in Crestien.

4. "bold" is used ironically, as "fair" is in l. 19.

5. *Cf.* 313, 17.

6. *I.e.* the Ganges.

7. A designation for India. Palibothri on the map of Pomponius Mela.

518— 8. The following excursus is not in Crestien, but in the German *Lucidarius*, p. 12. *Cf.* S. Singer, *Neue Parzival-Studien*, p. 43.

9. Ancient legends about deformed human beings were incorporated in medieval theology through St. Augustine by speculations as to their ancestry.

519—10. Solinus (also Pliny) mention a very tall Arabian woman by this name who died in Rome at the time of Augustus. *Cf.* Introduction above, Note 17.

11. *courtoys*=courtly. The passage is ironical.

520—12. *I.e.*, Malcreatiure, a result of the disobedience of his ancestress in eating certain herbs, and of the influence of unpropitious stars.

13. *Cf.* 256, 17 ff.

531—14. Knights were exempt from tolls. She implies sarcastically that he will be mistaken for a merchant.

532—15. They were considered two distinct gods in the Middle Ages.

16. Wolfram means that he is not susceptible to impulsive *Minne* which flares up sporadically.

533—17. He pictures the stress and woe of love as a knight.

18. "Does love (often pictured as a child) blame her youth when she plays pranks upon people? I should rather blame love's pranks upon her youth than say that they are the result of old age."

534—19. In Crestien he rides despite the inferiority of his horse.

BOOK ELEVEN

565— 1. The Lechfeld, a sandy plain near Augsburg, where large hosts often assembled. The comparison contains sly humor because of course the Lechfeld was much larger than the courtyard of the castle.
2. The roof was probably made of glazed tiles.
578— 3. French for thanks to God.
4. Arnivë is meant.
5. *I.e.* the shade of the screen.

BOOK TWELVE

583— 1. The reference is to the liberation of Queen Guinevere by Lancelot. She had been captured by Meljacanz, called Maleaganz in Crestien's *Chevalier de la Charrete* (Lancelot), Wolfram's possible source.
2. The Arthurian hero of a poem by Pleier (a late thirteenth-century Austrian poet), based in turn upon a lost French source which both Wolfram and Hartman von Aue seem to have known.
3. Old French *Le gué perilleus*, the perilous ford. Also referred to in 600, 12 and 602, 6. It is a ford over which Gawan must leap at Orgelusë's bidding.
4. Schoydelacord=*joie de la cort*, joy of the court. A garden already referred to in 178, 21; the allusion is to an incident in Hartman's *Erec*. *Cf.* also Wolfram's *Titurel* 41, 4.
584— 5. A reference to an adventure of Iwein in Hartman's poem of the same name. In the forest of Briziljan a costly vessel hung beside a well, and next to the well was a miraculous stone. When the water from the well was poured from the vessel onto the stone, a terrible storm ensued, whereupon the lord of the well appeared to demand vengeance. Iwein conquers him and weds his widow Laudinë.
6. *I.e.*, Gawan's heart.
585— 7. Gawan's ancestor, also referred to in 56, 17 ff. Gawan's father Lot was a Norwegian.
8. *Minnë's* power, as exemplified in Ither's winsomeness, could awe or impress the one who heard about him. Those who saw him face to face were even more impressed.
9. Ilinot was a son of King Arthur (and therefore a relative of Gawan and Parzival) who died young. The references here, and in this book generally, are not found in Crestien.
586—10. In Hartman Ganedec, in Crestien Quenedic.
11. *I.e.*, in his own homeland.
12. Where, we do not know.
13. In Book V.
14. Galoës, the brother of Gahmuret, had died serving Annore.
15. This is related in Book XIV.

16. In Crestien Guiromelanz.
17. Surdamur (*sor d'amur*, sister of love) was a sister of Gawan, married to the Greek emperor Alexander. Her son was Cligés, the hero of one of Crestien's romances.
589—18. This staircase is discussed in a Latin dissertation of C. Lucae (1862) in the light of French architecture of the thirteenth century. This early study furnishes presumptive evidence that Wolfram must have had some source besides Crestien.
19. One of the characters in Heinrich von Veldeke's *Enit*, whose costly bier is described by him, lines 9413 ff.
20. Similarly Merlin transported the stone pillars of Stonehenge from Ireland to Salisbury, according to Geoffrey of Monmouth VIII, 10 ff.
21. The description reminds one of Veldeke's description of Camilla's crypt, lines 9470 ff.
590—22. Similar feats are ascribed to Vergil in medieval legends. The pillar is thought of as a sort of crystal.
612—23. "Accept my confession of your surpassing beauty."
613—24. Cidegast exceeded all rivals just as Saturn is the mightiest and highest planet. *Cf. Lucidarius* (Heidlauf ed.), p. 22.
25. *Cf.* 482, 24, where the unicorn also becomes a symbol of trusting faith, seeking purity in the lap of a virgin. Often, however, it is thus captured and killed.
615—26. As related early in Book X.

BOOK THIRTEEN

638— 1. *I.e.*, Orgelusë.
2. Gawan.
639— 3. Another reference to the famous court of the landgraves of Thuringia, a cultural center, here introduced rather whimsically. *Cf.* 297, 16 ff. Lachmann thinks Wolfram is referring to Walther von der Vogelweide.
4. If dancing is referred to, each knight was dancing with two ladies, one at each side, à la Polonaise.
640— 5. Florand is the Turkoite, the Duke of Gowerzin is Lischoys.
641— 6. Because the night-drink signalized the conclusion of the feast and of the love-making for the knights who had not yet won their ladies.
7. To light the way for the knights.
656— 8. Arnivë is speaking to Gawan about Clinschor.
9. Terra di Lavoro, the province of Naples. Richard I had tried to prevent its conquest. Naples (the French form Napels is used) is the locale of many magic feats ascribed to Vergil in the Middle Ages. *Cf.* Comparetti, *Vergil in the Middle Ages*.
10. Crestien mentions not Clinschor but only a wise astrologer. Wolfram shows no further similarities to him in these latter sections, but he does resemble the first continuation of Crestien. In the prose

365

novel of the tale there is a magician, Eliaures (Cliaures?). Clinschor may be connected with Old French *clencheor* and may mean "one who locks"—the deity of death. Caps in the next line is Capua.

657—11. The love affair of Clinschor is also traceable to adventures of the medieval sorcerer Vergil; his castration reminds us of Celtic tales about Chronos or Saturn.

12. *I.e.*, Kalata-Belota near Sciacca in southern Italy. The widow of King Tancred of Sicily had fled there.

13. Because he took vengeance on innocent victims whom he enchanted.

14. Honorius, *Imago Mundi* I,14, following Pliny, speaks of a *country* Persida, the home of magic. From there the three Magi visit Jesus. But Wolfram seems to follow the *Lucidarius* (p. 14), where Persida is a *burc*.

658—15. A mile equivalent to at least three of our miles. *Cf.* 681,16.

16. French for "good spirits and evil."

BOOK FOURTEEN

679— 1. *I.e.*, Gawan's opponent Parzival.

2. Probably from Gahmuret.

3. Gawan thinks his opponent is Gramoflanz because he wears a wreath from the latter's enchanted tree. This he regrets because he will, on pain of disgrace, have to fight him on the spot and not in the prearranged manner in the presence of the ladies and other witnesses.

4. Parzival was riding the steed of the Grail knight who had been unhorsed in 445,15.

681— 5. Is this the Severn? Then the Poynzaclins in line 8 would be the Wye.

6. *I.e.*, the bells on the bridles of their horses tinkled.

7. *I.e.*, the space occupied by his encampment.

682— 8. Punt=French *pont*, bridge. Some seaport in England.

9. Brandelidelin was king of Punturteis.

683—10. These were liegemen; those mentioned before were volunteers.

11. *palmât* is a kind of silk mentioned several times by Wolfram.

12. This seems very much like the viper of 481,8, which is later also found on the helmet of Feirefiz.

684—13. *I.e.*, Orgeluse.

685—14. Gawan had rescued Itonje from enchantment.

15. Not because Gawan is an inferior competitor but because Gramoflanz is used to fighting two opponents at one time—a motif not uncommon in French (Celtic?) romances.

16. *I.e.*, Itonje.

686—17. She had come as messenger from Itonje to Gramoflanz and was supporting his arms, to rest them.

18. Gawan was Itonjë's brother.
19. It is the same ring that Gawan had been given for his sister by Gramoflanz.
20. "If a sister of mine should cause me as much trouble and embarrassment as Itonje caused Gawan on account of Gramoflanz, I should rather have no sister at all."

687—21. Parzival's father and uncle.
22. The king of Centriun, according to 770,12 who was defeated by Feirefiz.
23. Ipopotiticon (i.e. Hippopodes, according to Solinus) is also mentioned in 770, 13; Acraton in 309, 18, and 399, 17.
24. *I.e.*, The Agathyrsi (Solinus 82, 12).

688—25. *I.e.*, Parzival.
689—26. His escutcheon, misfortune, under which he has lived and fought so often, is again in evidence.
27. Both trace ancestry to Mazadan.
28. *I.e.*, also yourself.

690—29. I.e., the armies of Arthur and Gramoflanz.
694—30. *I.e.*, Gawan's and Parzival's.
31. *I.e.*, Arthur's host.
695—32. Related to Parzival through Utepandragûn (Ut, the serpent head), the father of Arthur.
33. The reference is to Cundry's curse, 314, 23 ff.
696—34. Orgelusë was repelled by this friendly treatment by one who had spurned her in Book XII.
697—35. An example of Wolfram's offhand, humorous manner of dealing with details.
699—36. By Cundry.
37. So as to give all those assembled a chance to participate.
701—38. *Cf.* 679, 14.
39. Gawan's brother is Beakurs, his kinsman Gaherjet.
703—40. *I.e.*, Parzival.
41. We interpret *banier* here as a bundle.
704—42. *I.e.*, between Gawan and Gramoflanz.
706—43. *I.e.*, the armies of Arthur and Gramoflanz.
44. Itonjë was Gramoflanz's lady-love. As a sister of Gawan, she was related to Parzival, and the latter is here referred to. He, too, fought a bitter fight.
46. Because as a relative he should have enjoyed Gramoflanz's friendship.
46. *I.e.*, man from Valois—Parzival.
47. These knights are retainers of Gramoflanz.
707—48. *I.e.*, the five onlookers.
732—49. *bêâ flûrs* is Wolfram's Old French for "beautiful flower." *Cf.* Book VI, note 4.

BOOK FIFTEEN

734— 1. Until she, too, found the Grail.
735— 2. For Agremuntin see 496, 10.
      3. Salamanders were much discussed in the Middle Ages. The products which they were supposed to produce remind one sometimes of crocodile's skin and sometimes of asbestos. Sometimes as here they seem to perform the function of silk worms.
736— 4. For ecidemon see 481,8, and 683,20.
738— 5. I.e., they had the same heart's blood.
      6. A widespread belief in the Middle Ages derived from the *Physiologus*, also in Isidorus, *Origines* 12, 1.
      7. A reference to the fighting fame of their father Gahmuret. For a source for the fraternal duel *cf.* Panzer, Note 19 to Introduction.
739— 8. Thasmê was one of the countries subject to Feirefiz. Tshesme in Smyrna is meant (?).
      9. Thabronit was the conquered country of Feirefiz's heathen love, Secundillë. The thought of her gave him new courage. The *insula Taprobane* mentioned by Solinus (*i.e.* Ceylon) is meant. But later Wolfram locates it in the Caucasus!
741—10. *I.e.*, chrysoprase.
     11. *I.e.*, in the Near East. This distinction is also found in Isidorus, Jerome, and other writers.
743—12. These lines are used as a basis for the hypothesis that Wolfram had children of his own.
744—13. Parzival had won the sword from Ither.
     14. *I.e.*, Feirefiz.
     15. A jest. The heathen, forced to his knee, looked as though he were praying!
745—16. In French (Celtic) romance it is customary only for the vanquished to mention his name.
747—17. *Cf.* 328, 16.
748—18. It was customary for medieval poets to ascribe the Greek and Roman gods to the Saracens. Especially Juno, Jupiter, and Apollo are mentioned. The Romans themselves often used the names of their own gods to describe barbarian deities.
749—19. Parzival has been using the more formal *ir* instead of the familiar *du* in addressing Feirefiz. He continues doing so until he is king of the Grail. But Feirefiz has been addressing Parzival *du;* does he lack occidental refinement?
750—20. Gahmuret had acquired these lands from Belakânë, his former wife.
751—21. Gahmuret, a paragon of all qualities that would endear him to women—woman's reward.
     22. This is related in Book II.
752—23. Wolfram means that there are more than family ties between father and son; he refers to identity of blood, a thought which he has expressed before (300, 16). Similarly the *Sachsenspiegel*, I, 3.

778—24. The insignia of the Grail castle.
779—25. She, Cundry, hopes that they will not hold against her what she said to Parzival in Book VI.
26. A kiss was a usual symbol of forgiveness. But Cundry feels so guilty that she is willing to forego this.
780—27. I.e., Arthur and Feirefiz.
28. *I.e.*, the turtle doves.
29. And which she still wore.
781—30. Secundille had presented Cundry and her brother Malcreatiure to Anfortas.
782—31. *I.e.*, in Arabic, which was considered a heathen tongue in thirteenth-century Western Europe.
32. Under the impress of the Middle Ages, which believed that the relative position of the planets influenced the fate of man, astrology was born of the astronomy of the ancients. The seven planets (in the order named), given in forms garbled from the Arabic, are supposed to correspond to Saturn, Jupiter, Mars, the Sun, Venus, Mercury, and the Moon. *Cf.* C. F. Seybold in *Zeitschrift für deutsche Wortforschung* VIII, 147 ff. The reading *azofir* in l. 10 is Seybold's conjecture. On ll. 14 ff. *cf.* Note 17 to our Introduction.
783—33. Spoken again to Cundry. He means recompense for the wrong she had done him in Book VI.
34. In failing to show Anfortas pity.
784—35. In her service Anfortas had been wounded.
785—36. I.e., Feirefiz's niece Itonjë.
37. "No note or letter ever brought such a response in the form of precious gifts."
786—38. By leaving them.
39. The camp consisted of four wings, those of Arthur, Gawan, Orgeluse, and Gramoflanz.

BOOK SIXTEEN

787— 1. Their love and loyalty forbade them to comply with his wish that they kill him.
788— 2. *I.e.*, Parzival, whose possible joy had been dissipated when on his first visit he failed to ask the symbolic question.
789— 3. This may be a reference to the epicycles of the Ptolemaic system. Wolfram's astrology is well supported by *Lucidarius*, p. 22.
792— 4. *I.e.*, Parzival, who had been relieved of cares.
5. *I.e.*, between Joflanz and Munsalvaesche.
795— 6. Because he will be dead. He is being kept alive because he sees the Grail; missing its sight for a week, he will die.
7. The question which Parzival is supposed to ask will lose its efficacy if Anfortas himself prompts it.
8. In Crestien the questions are: Why does the lance bleed?, and whom does one serve with the Grail? But that an ethical import is

implied by Crestien, too, is maintained unconvincingly by Burdach in *Der Gral*, Stuttgart, 1938, p. 436.

9. According to the legend of Pope Sylvester (*ob.* 335) he, in an argument with Jews, watches them kill a steer by whispering to it the name of their God. Then Sylvester revives the steer by calling upon Christ. Wolfram's source may be the *Kaiserchronik* (about 1150).

796—10. Medieval French and German writers frequently praise the beauty of Absalon.

11. Middle High German *raste*, rest, a measure of distance.

797—12. *Cf.* 288,23.

13. *Cf.* 282,20 ff.

14. Trevrizent speaks.

15. "word" λόγος, as in the Gospel of St. John.

798—16. Herzeloydë was, of course, Trevrizent's sister.

17. The explanation for this curious passage is perhaps that Wolfram had been criticized for the heretical views he had expressed in 471, 15 ff., and that he is now trying to justify himself.

799—18. In Book IX. Now Trevrizent respectfully addresses Parzival, the new king, with *ir* (you), while Parzival (798,3) calls him *du* (thou).

19. Where Arthur was camping when Parzival came to him.

20. *I.e.*, mounted knights holding the shields.

21. *I.e.*, a ring or circle of tents.

800—22. *I.e.*, in Munsalvaeschë.

23. The tent in which Condwiramur's wardrobe was stored.

802—24. He had remained true to his wife despite many temptations.

806—25. *Cf.* note 60 to Book V. Groenlandsfylki is meant.

26. Lunel is in southern France. She may be the daughter of Iwan in 234,12.

27. *Cf.* note 18 to Book V.

807—28. Repansë was the daughter of Frimutel, who was also the father of Herzeloydë.

29. Condwiramur is meant.

30. Here Wolfram attempts to explain why the Grail had been shown to Parzival on his first visit in Book IX. It was done not because the occasion itself merited it but because the knights had hoped he would be their savior.

31. *I.e.*, she donned her *gebende*, or headdress. While travelling, women hooded their heads.

808—32. The land of the Seres, or China. For Thasmê (line 8) see note 8 to Book XV.

33. *I.e.*, Condwiramur.

809—34. *I.e.*, in Book V.

35. See note 34 to Book V.

810—36. This is the *Achmardi*. See note 26 to Book V.

37. Repanse de Schoyë.

38. "When I see Repanse I wonder if I have ever known real love before." "I am repelled by what I used to think was love."
39. "In confiding this to you so soon I discard my good breeding; I have not yet done anything for you."

811—40. One of her rich lands.
41. Repanse.

822—42. (*In prose summary*): The chronicler Otto von Freising reports from hearsay that the *rex et sacerdos* John, a Nestorian in the Far East and a descendant of one of the three Magi, defeated the three Samiardi in a fierce battle. Is John perhaps Kuchan el Avar, a Chinese potentate, who defeated the Sultan Sandjar in 1141 and raised Christian hopes of securing unexpected aid against the Turks? If an Ethiopian origin of the Priest John legend, as espoused *e.g.* by Helen Adolf in *PMLA* LXII,2, 306 ff., is accepted, the concept of priest would be derived from the fact that all Abyssinian kings were deacons; the name John would then derive from the title *Zan*, meaning "Majesty." The confusion of Ethiopia with India is traditional. A so-called letter of Priest John of 1165 is probably a hoax. But see Snelleman, *op. cit.* p. 181, and Hagen in *Zeitschrift für deutsche Philologie* XXXVIII, 209.

825—43. *I.e.*, he gives up the Grail kingdom to be ruler of Brabant. Wolfram included the (purely Teutonic?) Lohengrin tale or myth on a not very convincing pretext. Other noble families also claimed to be involved in the story, and other towns besides Antwerp (Nimwegen, Cleve, Mainz) are named as Lohengrin's landing place. Late in the thirteenth century, the tale was told independently of Wolfram by Konrad von Würzburg; in a poem, *Lohengrin*, by a Bavarian knight; and again in the fifteenth century (*Lorengel*). The name seems suggested by the Old French romance *Garin le Loherain* (*i.e.* of Lorraine). But in France the chevalier au cygne is called Helias and usually champions a maligned mother. The author of the *Sone de Nausai* and Gerbert, one of the continuators of Crestien, were also familiar with the legend and like Wolfram linked it with the story of Parzival and the Grail.

826—44. In Hartman's *Erec* the hero forbids Enit to speak and punishes her when she does so, even though she speaks to warn him of impending danger.

827—45. Here Wolfram again states the keynote of his work—more specifically than he had at the beginning.

www.ingramcontent.com/pod-product-compliance
Lightning Source LLC
Chambersburg PA
CBHW021759220426
43662CB00006B/118